Studies in African Hi

Sékou Touré's Guinea

An Experiment in Nation Building

Studies in African History
General Editor: A. H. M. Kirk-Greene
St Antony's College Oxford

1 Senegal: A Study in French Assimilation
Michael Crowder
(*Out of print*)

2 Kingdoms of The Yoruba
Robert S. Smith

3 Swahili: The Rise of a National Language
Wilfred Whiteley

4 The Military in African Politics
W. F. Gutteridge
(Out of print)

5 The Nigerian Army 1956–1966
N. J. Miners

6 Ghana Under Military Rule 1966–1969
Robert Pinkney

7 Ancient Ghana and Mali
Nehemia Levtzion

8 Botswana: A Short Political History
Anthony Sillery

9 Kingdoms of the Sudan
R. S. O'Fahey and J. L. Spaulding

10 The Kingdom of Toro in Uganda
Kenneth Ingham

11 Military Regimes in Africa
W. F. Gutteridge

'Ladipo Adamolekun

Sékou Touré's Guinea

An Experiment in Nation Building

Methuen & Co Ltd

*First published in 1976 by
Methuen & Co Ltd
11 New Fetter Lane London EC4P 4EE
©1976 'Ladipo Adamolekun
Typeset in Great Britain by
Preface Ltd, Salisbury, Wilts
and printed Offset Litho in Great Britain by
Cox & Wyman Ltd, Fakenham, Norfolk*

ISBN 0 416 77840 2 hardback
ISBN 0 416 77850 X paperback

*This title is available in both hardback and
paperback editions. The paperback edition is
sold subject to the condition that it shall not,
by way of trade or otherwise, be lent, re-sold,
hired out, or otherwise circulated without the
publisher's prior consent in any form of binding
or cover other than that in which it is published
and without a similar condition including this
condition being imposed on the subsequent purchaser.*

Distributed in the USA by
HARPER AND ROW PUBLISHERS, INC.,
BARNES & NOBLE IMPORT DIVISION

for 'Kemi

If you are a labourer, say to yourself that you are the equal of Mr Sékou Touré; if you are a farmer, say to yourself that you are the equal of Mr Sékou Touré, above any minister, above any public servant...
Sékou Touré, 1958.

We shall not hesitate to sacrifice, if it is necessary, the individual for the benefit of the community.
Sékou Touré, 1958.

Guinea is for us a growing entity and we do not know into what it will develop... if it happens that a state can really be established there... We shall establish our relations with Guinea in the light of what happens... We shall do that without acrimony, but without having, I should say, the certainty that what is today could continue tomorrow.
Charles de Gaulle,
President of France and
of the Franco-African
Community, 1959.

Contents

	Acknowledgements	viii
	Abbreviations	ix
	Glossary	xi
	Tables	xiii
	Map: Natural Regions, Communications, Main Towns and Major Mineral Resources	xiv
1	Introduction	1
2	The Political Institutional Framework for Nation Building	16
3	Economic and Social Development:	41
	A. The Strategy for Development	
4	Economic and Social Development:	74
	B. Assessment of Performance	
5	The Quest for a National Identity	116
6	Balance Sheet of the Guinean Experiment and the Prospects for the Future	153
7	Conclusion: Some Theoretical Reflections on the Guinean Experiment in Nation Building	176
	Notes	193
	Appendices	
	A Prelude to the Ballot Box Revolution of September 1958	213
	B. The Constitution of the Republic of Guinea	215
	C. Extracts from the Statutes of the Democratic Party of Guinea	223
	Sources and Select Bibliography	237
	Index	245

Acknowledgements

I am indebted to a long list of people and institutions for the production of this book. First, I should like to thank the following institutions that made my two study visits to Guinea possible: the Institute of Administration, University of Ife, for granting me study leave and for financing the short study visit of 1968; the Rockefeller Foundation whose generous grant enabled me to spend four months in Guinea in 1970–71; the Nigerian Embassy in Conakry for its assistance and support (His Excellency, Mr Ayo Afolabi who was the Ambassador during my second visit deserves special thanks for his kindness and hospitality); and, finally, the Guinean government for its co-operation.

Second, I have benefited from the criticisms and suggestions of several colleagues including Dr William Ajibola, Department of Political Science, University of Ibadan, Dr 'Jide Osuntokun also of the University of Ibadan, Dr O. Aluko of the Institute of Administration, University of Ife, and Dr Paul Beckett of the Ahmadu Bello University, Zaria. I owe a special debt of gratitude to my friend and companion, Dr 'Kole Omotoso, whose encouragement has hastened the production of the book. Mr A. H. M. Kirk-Greene of St. Antony's College, Oxford, who is also the general editor of 'Studies in African History' series, encouraged the idea of this book from the beginning and his editorial suggestions have been useful. I am also indebted to Mr J. O. Oyelowo, a senior typist at the Institute of Administration, University of Ife, who patiently typed the drafts and the final version of the book.

Finally, I should like to thank my wife, 'Kemi, who warmly welcomed 'Guinea' to our household as a 'second wife' during the preparation of this book.

Abbreviations

BPN	Bureau Politique National (National Political Bureau)
CAP	Coopérative Agricole de Production (Co-operative of Agricultural Production)
CC	Comité Central (Central Committee)
CER	Centre d'Éducation Révolutionnaire (Centre of Revolutionary Education)
CMR	Centre de Modernisation Rurale (Centre of Rural Modernization)
CNPA	Centre National de Production Agricole (National Centre of Agricultural Production)
CNR	Conseil National de la Révolution (National Council of the Revolution)
CNTG	Confédération Nationale des Travailleurs Guinéens (National Confederation of Guinean Workers)
COPAC	Coopérative de Production Agricole et de Consommation (Agricultural Production and Consumer Co-operative)
CUP	Comité d'Unité de Production (Party Committee of Production)
ESA	École Supérieure d'Administration (Advanced School of Administration)
FIDES	Fonds d'Investissement pour le Développement Économique et Social de la France d'Outre-Mer (Investment Fund for the Economic and Social Development of Overseas France)
FWA	French West Africa

x *Abbreviations*

IPC	Institut Polytechnique Gamal Abdel Nasser de Conakry (Gamel Abdel Nasser Polytechnic of Conakry)
JORG	Journal Officiel de la République de Guinée (Official Journal of the Republic of Guinea)
JRDA	Jeunesse de la Révolution Démocratique Africaine (Youth of the African Democratic Revolution)
OCA	Office de Commercialisation Agricole (Office of Agricultural Commercialization)
PDG	Parti Démocratique de Guinée (Democratic Party of Guinea)
PRL	Pouvoir Révolutionnaire Local (Local Revolutionary Authority)
RDA	Rassemblement Démocratique Africain (Democratic African Assembly)

Glossary

arrondissement   an administrative unit below the district composed of about twenty local revolutionary authorities (the smallest administrative units)

balafon   a traditional musical instrument

canton   an arbitrary geographical area composed of a group of villages which served as an administrative unit below the district until December 1957.

cercle   title used until 1957 to designate an administrative district

circonscription   title used to designate an administrative district between December 1957 and January 1959

commandant de cercle   administrative officer in charge of a district

cora   a traditional musical instrument

émigré   a political or voluntary exile

Fula   a Guinean national language

Kisie   a Guinean national language

Kpele   a Guinean national language

Loma   a Guinean national language

Mandika   a Guinean national language

marabout   an islamic religious leader or priest

métropole   mother country (France)

Oneyann a Guinean national language

Soso a Guinean national language; some linguists call it *Susu*

syli local (Soso) name for an elephant; it is now used as the basic denomination of Guinean currency (since 1973)

tam-tam a traditional musical instrument

toum a traditional musical instrument

Wammey a Guinean national language

Tables

1 Some Indicators of Economic and Social Development in Guinea, Ivory Coast and Senegal, 1956. 43
2 The Progress of Educational Development in Guinea since Independence. 99
3 'Ethnic Arithmetic' in the Distribution of Key Political and Administrative Posts in Guinea, 1958–1967. 131

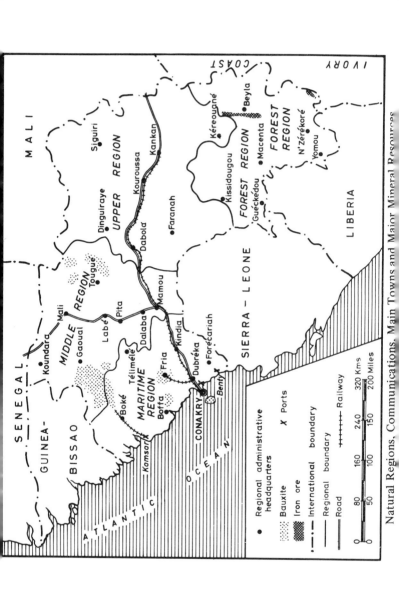

Natural Regions, Communications, Main Towns and Major Mineral Resources

1. Introduction

In September 1958, the world was startled by the news that a small West African French territory called Guinea had rejected the Franco–African Community proposed by the French government[1] and had opted for independence with the following defiant sentence: 'We, for our part, have a first and indispensable need, that of our dignity. Now, there is no dignity without freedom ... We prefer freedom in poverty to riches in slavery.' The French government took the Guinean decision as an act of 'secession', stopped all technical, economic and financial aid with immediate effect, and withdrew all French administrative personnel from Guinea; the new state was left to fend for itself. In November 1970, another startling item of news emerged from Guinea: the country's sovereignty was threatened by a Portuguese-led invasion from the sea. Apart from the extensive news coverage generated by these two sensational events, very little academic attention has been paid in the English-speaking world to the developments in Guinea since the country became independent in 1958. The primary aim of this book is to attempt a systematic and comprehensive analysis of the post-independence developments in Guinea.

There are several reasons why a comprehensive study of Guinea is necessary. First, Guinea is the only African state, and one of the rare post-colonial states in the world, that has pursued a policy of dissociation with the former colonizing power. How has Guinea survived this abrupt break and what remains of the colonial legacy in present-day Guinea? Second,

1

the ruling regime in Guinea is one of the few in Africa with a clearly defined and consistent political philosophy: the doctrine of party supremacy. What is the influence of this doctrine on the different aspects of Guinea government and politics? Third, Guinea has been continuously under the same regime and ruled by the same Head of State, President Sékou Touré, since 1958. What are the effects of this continuity of regime and leadership? Finally, since 1967, the Guinea regime has opted for the construction of a socialist state, not on the basis of an 'African' or 'Guinean' socialism as is the case in a number of African states, but on the basis of scientific socialism. What steps have already been taken in the direction of transforming Guinea into a socialist state and what are the regime's chances of success? This study seeks to throw some light on these important questions and other related matters.

The existing studies of post-independence Guinea can be divided into two broad categories: sectoral studies and general studies. By 'sectoral' studies we mean studies that are focused on one or more aspects of post-independence developments and by 'general' studies we mean studies that attempt to examine all aspects of post-independence developments. The greater part of the existing studies of Guinea belong to the first category.

The most common theme in the sectoral studies is the nature of Guinea's single party, the Democratic Party of Guinea (*Parti démocratique de Guinée*, PDG). Broadly, the PDG is characterized as a party possessing an ideology which draws heavily on a Marxist–Leninist doctrine of political organization and the role of the party in the state but derives its definition of the goals of government and society from the objective conditions of the country's realities. Some analysts refer to this ideology as 'one-party ideology'; others call it 'socialism'.[2] Two of the studies that are focused on the PDG deserve to be mentioned. One is I. Wallerstein's analysis of PDG ideology in 'The Political Ideology of the PDG,' *Présence africaine*, XL, 1 (1962) and the other is B. Charles' succinct account of the organization and functioning of the PDG in 'Un Parti politique africain: le Parti démocratique de Guinée', *Revue française de sciences politiques*, XII, 2 (June 1962).

Other themes examined in the sectoral studies include the economy, the administrative system, education, religion, the emancipation of women, the mobilization of youth, the élites of the regime, foreign policy, and the role of President Sékou Touré. Of these studies, special mention should be made of C. Rivière's *Mutations sociales en Guinée* which is a collection of sectoral studies on four themes: ethnic integration, the emancipation of women, the mobilization of youth and religion. Each subject is examined critically and in some detail. Besides Rivière's collection of studies, many of the others are articles in journals, a few are contributions to books and there are a number of unpublished dissertations and theses. The majority of these studies are in French with only a few in English.

Although almost every important area of activity in post-independence Guinea is examined by one study or another, very few general readers can have access to the different sources. The problem of reading both French and English or the problem of locating the scattered sources (especially those that exist only inside Guinea) or a combination of both are enough obstacles in the path of a general reader who may be keen on learning about post-independence Guinea.

The obvious advantage of general studies over sectoral studies is that the problem of scattered sources associated with the latter does not arise in the case of the former. The most important general study on Guinea to date is Jean Suret-Canale's *La République de Guinée*. This is a descriptive account which is particularly good on the problems and achievements of socio-economic development programmes. But the references to both domestic and external political policies are inadequate and this makes the book fall short of being a comprehensive study. B. Ameillon's *La Guinée, bilan d'une indépendance*, examines almost every area of activity up to 1963. This means that it is already out of date. And in the areas where Ameillon covers the same ground as Suret-Canale, the latter provides more detailed information. A. Diawara's *Guinée, la marche du peuple*, is a participant–observer's account of post-independence developments in Guinea. Although it deals with virtually every aspect of development up to 1967, it is rather sketchy and superficial. Finally, Guy de Lusignan in his *French-Speaking Africa Since Independence* has a section on Guinea in which he attempts a general survey of post-independence developments in the country. This is the only general study of Guinea available in English. Its merit is that it faithfully records most of the important events in the different fields of activity but it is not analytical.

Only a few of the studies reviewed above have a theoretical underpinning or a conceptual framework. The single theoretical theme in these studies consists of relating the post-independence developments in Guinea to Marxist–Leninist principles and practices. The analysts who adopt this approach consider it appropriate for the following reasons. First, Sékou Touré who led the PDG to power and has since remained the President of the Republic was impregnated with orthodox Marxist ideology during his trade union days under colonial rule. For this reason, it is assumed that his actions will be influenced by Marxist ideas. Second, some of the policies pursued by the Touré-led PDG government in the years immediately after independence appeared to have been influenced by Marxist–Leninist ideology: the role of national direction and guidance assigned to the single party; the state control of some vital sectors of the national economy; and the creation of a national currency. Third, the external relations of Guinea were more intimate with Eastern bloc countries than with the Western bloc countries. Fourth, the government relied on the services of many self-professed socialist teachers and technicians from Africa and Europe who had come to fill the gap created by the abrupt departure of French personnel in 1958.

Although these reasons are, on the whole, accurate, they do not add up to a formal governmental commitment to Marxist-Leninist ideology. The policy statements of President Touré, which were the nearest thing to a statement of government policy, specifically denied a commitment to socialist ideology during the first years of Guinean independence.

> We are told that we must necessarily choose between capitalism and socialism, but I regret and — let it be said between ourselves — we are practically unable, all of us, to define what capitalism is, what socialism is... *There is no question of knowing what system we shall permanently adopt; the question is to know perfectly our concrete realities and, within the framework of a revolutionary action, to find the best means to allow us to achieve our economic, social, moral and intellectual objectives.*[3]

In these circumstances, those analysts who have attempted to examine the developments in Guinea in the years immediately after independence against the background of socialist principles and practices were, in fact, bound to come up with a predictable answer: that Guinea was not developing along socialist lines. The most representative of the studies in this category is B. Ameillon's *La Guinée, bilan d'une indépendance*.

In contrast, C. Rivière, in his *Mutations sociales en Guinée* uses an empirical, conceptual framework based on the claim of Guinean leaders that their aim is to transform Guinea from a traditional and colonized society into a 'modern' and 'progressive' society. In analysing the different aspects of social life he selected for study, Rivière relates what has actually happened to the stated objectives of the regime's leadership. The result is a thorough and thoughtful analysis which throws considerable light on the evolution of social life in post-independence Guinea.

The approach adopted for the present study is similar to Rivière's but it is more comprehensive. While Rivière limited himself to the events in the social sphere, we are concerned with all the various aspects of post-independence development To this end, we shall use an empirical, conceptual framework based on the concept of nation building which Guinean leaders, like the leaders of many other new states, use to describe their overall post-independence objective.

The Guinean Approach to Nation Building

According to President Touré,[4] when French Guinea became an independent Republic in 1958, it became a state in the sense of a member of the international state system. However, the new Guinean state was only a 'juridically constituted state without historical entity'.[5] This fact, according to Touré, distinguishes the Guinean state from the older states of Europe and the explanation for this difference is that 'contrary to what happened in the old established monarchies, in Guinea, it was not the organization of a nation which created the state but a nation which has to be built on to the framework of a state'.[6] Touré's idea of what nation building involves is as follows: 'The nation which we shall construct will be made up of the whole of our populations to which we shall give a collective personality, a personality which is defined in the economic, political, social and cultural sense.'[7] As spelt out elsewhere in his writing, this notion of nation building involves the pursuit of three major objectives: the establishment of a political, institutional framework for nation building, the promotion of socio-economic development and the search for a national identity.[8] How has Guinea sought to cope with these important tasks?

There are three major factors in the Guinean approach: a mobilization-oriented single party, an inflexible party ideology which serves as the national ideology and a flexible charismatic leader. We shall examine each of these factors in turn in relation to the basic questions that have to be tackled in the process of nation building. The importance attached to party organization in Guinea derives from the doctrine of party supremacy that was adopted at independence. According to this doctrine, the only and ruling party, the Democratic Party of Guinea (PDG), is the supreme authority in Guinea: 'The party assumes the directing role in the life of the nation: the political, judicial, administrative, economic and technical powers are in the hands of the Democratic Party of Guinea.'[9] In practical terms, this means that the party is regarded as the legitimate authority of the state. One way in which the authority of the party is demonstrated is that its structures determine those of the state.

> In order that the power of the party should not exist only in the domain of theory, the *Guinean state structures have been copied from, and harmoniously adapted to, the structures of the PDG* (*sic*), and this concretely confers on the village committee, the steering committee of the section, the federation bureau and the National Political Bureau, the power to stimulate and control respectively the administrative authorities of the village, of the arrondissement, of the region and of the nation.[10]

The significance of organizing the party structure to cover the entire territory of the state is that the arrangement enables the party organization to be used as an instrument for achieving territorial integration. Since the party is the supreme authority of the state, its presence throughout the territorial area of the state means the presence of the effective central authority.

Another important element in the role of the party is the doctrine of the mass line. There are two parts to this doctrine;

first, the party has a mass membership and second, there is emphasis on mass participation in the political process. With regard to the membership of the PDG, President Touré claims that 'the PDG is the entire people of Guinea'. In practice, membership of the PDG is automatic for every adult Guinean as he pays the party dues as an integral part of his state tax. The Guinean leadership is silent on the implied compulsion in this automatic membership[11] but is quick to point out that mass membership of the party helps to bring the entire population together within the same party structures thereby obviating in part the problem of an elite-mass gap. For example, a PDG base committee (the smallest unit in the party structure) in the capital, Conakry, groups together civil servants, teachers, traders, skilled and unskilled workers and farmers.

In order to ensure that there is a high degree of mass participation in the political process — the second part of the doctrine of the mass line — the party structure operates according to the principle of 'democratic centralism'. This principle requires the party structure to have a clearly defined line of communication from the base to the summit. The lowest levels of the party structure are subordinate to the higher levels but the high levels have to take account of the opinions expressed by the lower levels before arriving at decisions that become binding for the whole party. To the extent that national decisions are effectively taken within the party structure then to that extent will a fairly high degree of mass participation be possible.

To sum up, the party organization is considered as the supreme instrument for establishing an effective central authority for the state and it is used for both the bridging of the élite-mass gap and the involvement of the mass of the population in the political process. In other words, the party is the dominant feature of the Guinean political, institutional framework.

Introduction 9

The second major factor in the Guinean approach to nation building is the existence of an inflexible party ideology. The term 'ideology' is used here to refer to the political, economic and social orientations whose achievement is expected to engage the attention and energy of the entire Guinean population. The chief exponent of the Guinean ideology is President Touré who, since 1958, has held the posts of Secretary-General of the PDG and of President of the Republic. We have already mentioned the major orientations in the political sphere: the doctrine of party supremacy and the doctrine of the mass line. Two terms have been used to sum up the socio-economic programme: a 'non-capitalist way' and a 'socialist approach'. The first term was in use from 1958 until 1967 when the latter term was introduced.[12] In reality, both terms have been used to describe the same economic policy namely one which attaches great importance to state control of the economy. In his report to the sixth Congress of the party in 1962, President Touré explained the country's economic policy as follows:

> Our way is a non-capitalist way. It will remain so because this way is the only one which safeguards the interests of the community while freeing every individual from the injustice which characterizes all relations of exploitation of man by man.[13]

In this economic policy special attention is paid to the broad field of rural development where the objective of the regime is to establish co-operatives with a view to improving the quality of agricultural production and the social structure of the masses. In 1969, the term 'socialist communities' was introduced as a synonym for co-operatives and special emphasis was placed on the role of education and the literacy campaign in achieving this transformation of rural Guinea.

All these actions in the social and economic fields are expected to contribute to the task of nation building.

Although this contribution is considered important it is nevertheless formally regarded as subsidiary to what the political action of the PDG is expected to contribute. This position, in fact, represents the application of the doctrine of party supremacy to the economic field: the supremacy of politics over economics. President Touré explained the point in 1960 as follows:

> The economic action which we wish to carry out cannot separate us from the political orientation which is ours for the economic domain constitutes one of the aspects of our political problem. *We shall therefore have the economy of our politics and not the politics of our economy (sic).*[14]

The inflexible application of the doctrine of party supremacy also extends to the question of creating a national identity which is primarily regarded as the task of the party. For President Touré, the real issue involved is the transformation of the Guinean man and in his opinion 'the transformation of man can only be achieved radically and effectively within a political organization; it is the party which can achieve this revolution, in a satisfactory manner, by educating the people and organizing its creative action.'[15] The structure of the party within which the entire population is organized is considered as a major instrument for inculcating into all Guineans the sense of a common national identity. In this connection mention should be made of three other organizations which constitute an integral part of the party structure. These are the youth, women's and workers' organizations. The youth organization, the Youth of the African Democratic Revolution (*la Jeunesse de la révolution démocratique africaine*, JRDA) is the single national organization for Guinean youth and is organized at exactly the same levels as the party with its own executive bodies. Both the women's and workers' organizations are organized along the same lines except that the latter is not represented at the village level. Instead, the workers within each of the country's public enterprises and the ministerial departments constitute a party committee of production (*comité d'unite de production*, CUP). The idea behind these unitary national organizations is that the effective mobilization of the population within them will enhance their sense of national belonging. The extent of the mobilization that is possible within this organizational arrangement is illustrated by the fact that there were about 300,000 elected officials for the different organizations in 1970, about one official for every fourteen Guineans.

The third major factor in the Guinean approach to nation building is the availability of a flexible and charismatic leader in the person of President Sékou Touré. Touré was a foundation member of the PDG and in 1952 he became its Secretary-General. In this capacity he played a critical role in transforming the party into a mass party and he led the party campaign that culminated in the country's accession to independent status in 1958. Since 1958 he has combined the leadership of the party with the post of President of the Republic and Head of Government. Partly because of his long involvement with the PDG and partly because he personally believes that the party is superior to the state, President Touré has consistently emphasized that the party is the legitimate authority in Guinea. The most effective way in which he has done this is that he presents his personal political, economic and social ideas in the name of the party and not in his own personal name; it is these ideas that are collectively referred to as PDG ideology. The volumes of Touré's writings which contain his ideas are officially described as 'The Works of the PDG'.

There is also another important aspect to President Touré's position in the Guinean political system, his charisma. By the time he was emerging as the leading Guinean nationalist in the mid-1950s, he had become a charismatic leader in the Weberian sense of the term: many Guineans saw him as a personality endowed with specifically exceptional powers.[16] Although the concentration of powers in the hands of Touré at independence provided the occasion for him to use his charisma as the source of legitimate authority for the state, he did not do this; instead, he put his charismatic qualities at the disposal of the party. Thus, for example, instead of constituting his ideas into 'Touréism', he calls them PDG ideology.

Perhaps the most interesting aspect of his contribution to the task of nation building in Guinea is the flexibility that characterized his concrete actions. On the face of it, this contrasts markedly with the inflexibility of the party ideology of which he is said to be the chief exponent. How can a flexible leader be the author and operator of an inflexible ideology? In reality, the contradiction identified here is not as serious as one might imagine. According to Professor Smelser, Touré's method is capable of achieving political stability: 'one key to political stability seems to be ... the practice of *flexible* politics behind the façade of an *inflexible* commitment to a national mission.' (italics added)[17] Professor Smelser also claims that a leader can use an inflexible ideology to achieve three ends: to enhance his own claim to legitimacy; to procure otherwise unobtainable sacrifices from the populace which may be committed to modernization in the abstract, but which resists making concrete breaks with traditional ways; and to repress protests.[18]

For our purpose, the significant point made by Smelser is that a leader can achieve some concrete results by practising flexible politics behind the façade of an inflexible ideology. In the Guinean context, Touré has used this method to good effect with regard to each of the three crucial subjects subsumed under the concept of nation building. First, Touré has rejected the idea of modifying the Western-style constitution adopted by the country shortly after independence to take account of the doctrine of party supremacy.[19] According to this constitution,[20] state powers are shared between an executive (the President of the republic and the government), a parliament and a judiciary. The president of the republic appoints the members of his government and is responsible before parliament for the government's policies. The president and parliament alone may initiate laws whose constitutionality is controlled by the judiciary. The judiciary is an independent authority with responsibility to act as the 'guardian of individual liberty'. The adoption of these conventional constitutional arrangements implies an acceptance of the doctrine of the separation of powers as the method for establishing the legitimate authority for the state. This, of course, contrasts with the doctrine of party supremacy according to which the party is the legitimate authority of the state. As will be shown later in the study, the preservation of this contradiction enables Touré to operate the doctrine of party supremacy which he favours with some flexibility.

In the economic sphere, the party ideology emphasizes state control of the economy and a commitment to transforming the rural areas into co-operatives and socialist communities. In his capacity as both the leader of government and of the party, President Touré has ensured the adoption of an investment code which guarantees favourable conditions to prospective foreign private investors. This means that some flexibility is allowed in the interpretation of the policy of a state-controlled economy.

Finally, with regard to the problem of creating a national identity, the emphasis placed in the party ideology on the role of the party as the major instrument for achieving this objective is balanced by a highly flexible strategy prescribed by President Touré.

> The best form of struggle against ethnic exclusiveness should not consist of a pure and simple denial of ethnic groups which actually exist, or even of some kind of repression. The best form of struggle against ethnic exclusiveness should consist of a consciousness about the conditions for the survival and full growth of each ethnic

group through a greater development, strengthening and full growth of the whole national community. No ethnic group will survive if the nation perishes under the dissolvent action of ethnic particularisms.[21]

There are three major elements in this strategy. First, it rejects the idea of denying the existence of ethnic groups which implies the abandonment of policies that would not take account of ethnic diversity. Second, emphasis is placed on the development of the different ethnic groups within the framework of the national community. According to President Touré it is for this reason that 'the party has emphasized since independence, the need to observe a strict equality between the ethnic communities ... [and] the development of the national culture by the rebirth of our written languages...'[22] Third, the Guinean strategy seeks to create national loyalty by making the different ethnic groups accept a common destiny for the future. All this adds up to a very pragmatic and flexible approach.

The problem of ethnic diversity is central to the quest for creating a national identity in Guinea because it overshadows the other aspects of the problem such as religious, linguistic and regional differences. With regard to religion, about eighty-five per cent of the population are Muslims; the rest are Christians and adherents of traditional forms of worship. A consistent secular policy pursued by the party especially in the field of education helps to reduce the areas of conflict. The linguistic and regional differences are closely connected with the ethnic problem and they are tackled through the same strategy.

To sum up, there are two major features in the Guinea approach to nation building. First, the concept of nation building is interpreted to focus essentially on the nature of the political institutional framework, the programme for socio-economic development, and the quest for a national identity.

Second, there are three major factors that are considered to be of critical importance in pursuing the task of nation building: a mobilization-oriented single party, an inflexible party ideology, and a flexible and charismatic leader.

As the sub-title of this book suggests, *An Experiment in Nation Building*, we consider the Guinean approach to nation building as an experiment. The remaining chapters of this study will be devoted to a systematic and analytical study of the experiment. Although attention will be paid to chronological evolution, it is the thematic method that is adopted. The chapters are based on the subjects that are considered critical to the nation building effort: the nature of the political, institutional framework, socio-economic development and the quest for national identity. On each subject, we shall examine the contribution made by the three factors that constitute the Guinean approach and present an account of the existing position. One chapter will be devoted to an overview of the Guinean experiment in nation building; it will be concerned with an assessment of its achievements, problems and future prospects. Finally, in a concluding chapter, we shall attempt to relate the Guinean experiment to the existing literature on the concept of nation building.

2. The Political Institutional Framework for Nation Building

As mentioned in the preceding chapter, the political, institutional framework for nation building in Guinea is expected to ensure the achievement of three major objectives: establishing a central authority throughout the territorial area of the state, bringing the government close to the governed and bridging the élite-mass gap. The purpose of this chapter is to describe the institutions that have been created to perform these functions, examine their functioning and assess their effectiveness.

Establishing a Central Authority

According to the doctrine of party supremacy, the PDG is expected to assume the major responsibility for these tasks. With regard to the establishment of a central authority throughout the territorial area of the state emphasis is placed on the party's organizational structure. This structure is pyramidal with a large number of committees at the base and a single national Central Committee at the apex. The base committees are known as local revolutionary authorities (*pouvoirs révolutionnaires locaux*, PRL). Every village in rural areas and every quarter in the towns and cities constitutes a PRL; there are 6000 of the former and 2000 of the latter making a total of 8000 PRLs. Each PRL has a thirteen-member executive which is elected every two years by the party members.[1] The PRLs are grouped within 210 sections to constitute the next level of the party structure. Each section has a thirteen-member executive (called the steering committee) elected every two years by the executive members of its constituent PRLs. The next level above the section is the federation of which there are thirty. Each federation has a thirteen-member executive (called the federal bureau) elected every three years by the members of the constituent steering committees.

The level above the federation is the summit of the party structure and it consists of four bodies: the Congress, the National Council of the Revolution (*Conseil national de la révolution,* CNR), the Central Committee, and the National Political Bureau (*Bureau politique national,* BPN). The Congress is the supreme institution of the party and has responsibility for laying down the broad outlines of national policies. It is summoned at least once in every five years[2] and the members are about 700 representing the federations. In between the sessions of the Congress, the CNR whose members are also delegates from the federations (about 150) acts as the supreme party institution. It is summoned in ordinary session twice a year. The Central Committee is the national ruling body of the party and its twenty-five members are elected by the party Congress for a five-year term. It meets monthly. The BPN is the executive of the Central Committee and is composed of seven members including the Secretary General of the party who proposes the names of the six other members. [The party Congress conducts a separate election for the post of Secretary General whose term of office is also for five years.] The BPN meets fortnightly.[3]

Attention has already been drawn to the fact that every Guinean is a member of the PDG.[4] This means that the party structure involves every citizen of the state. Because the functioning of the party structure is based on the principle of 'democratic centralism' (*supra*), great importance is attached to the maintenance of a line of communication from the base to the summit. In particular, the periodic meetings, conferences and congresses held by the different levels of the party structure serve as the occasion for emphasizing that the nation-wide party organization represents one central authority. Special mention should be made of the weekly meetings of the PRLs which serve as a very effective forum for communicating developments in both the national and international political scenes to the masses. Since all events are interpreted as directed by the national party leadership (these interpretations are spread through the party-controlled radio and press), the existence of a central authority for the whole state is thereby constantly brought to the knowledge of the masses.

Besides the party structure described above, there are two other institutions which contribute to the establishment of the central authority in Guinea. The first is the state administrative machinery and the second is the youth, workers' and women's organizations. The former is referred to as the 'instrument' of the party and the latter as the 'parallel institutions' of the party. As will be shown below, these institutions are made to conform to the doctrine of party supremacy.

At independence, Guinea inherited an administrative machinery which was used to maintain the authority of the French colonial power. In 1957, the French colonial administration in Guinea was centred around a number of French administrators called *commandants de cercle*. The whole of Guinea was divided into twenty *cercles* (a *cercle* was an administrative area unit roughly equivalent to 'district' in anglophone administrative terminology) and at the head of each *cercle* was a commandant who was generally responsible for the effective administration of the area. He was assisted in this task by African chiefs who were selected to head the *cantons* and villages within the area. While the villages were natural settlement units, the *cantons* were often arbitrary geographical areas created for administrative convenience; a *canton* consisted of a group of villages. The village and *canton* chiefs were entirely subordinate to the commandants who in

Political Institutional Framework for Nation Building 19

turn were the hierarchical subordinates of the Governor of French Guinea, the local representative of the imperial power, whose headquarters was located in Conakry. It was in this way that French authority was maintained throughout Guinea.

As a result of a reform of French colonial administration in West Africa embarked upon in 1956 — commonly referred to as the *loi-cadre* reform[5] — a local executive was established in Guinea in May 1957. This local executive was given powers to run the administration of the territory. The PDG formed this local executive by virtue of its overwhelming majority in the Territorial Assembly that elected its members. Sékou Touré was appointed Vice-President of the Council of Government.[6] Having won control of the territorial administration, the PDG proceeded to reform the existing administrative machinery. Two major changes were made. First, 'traditional chieftaincy' was abolished; the village and *canton* chiefs ceased to play a role in the administration. Second, 4200 elected village councils and ninety-five administrative posts (*postes administratifs*) were created to replace the former villages and *cantons*. The village councils were headed by elected village chiefs while the administrative posts were placed under civil servants. These changes notwithstanding, the administrative machinery continued to serve as the instrument for maintaining the central authority throughout the territory.

With the adoption of the doctrine of party supremacy after independence the state administrative machinery was assigned the role of serving as an instrument of the party. In order to make this idea a reality, 'the Guinean State structures have been modelled on, and harmoniously adapted to, the structures of the PDG'.[7] What this means in practice is that there exists an interlocking relationship between the party structure and the state administrative machinery with a considerable degree of overlapping in the personnel that operates both structures. The party and administrative structures are set out in the diagram on the next page.

Starting from the base, the PRL is at the same time the

20 *Sékou Touré's Guinea*

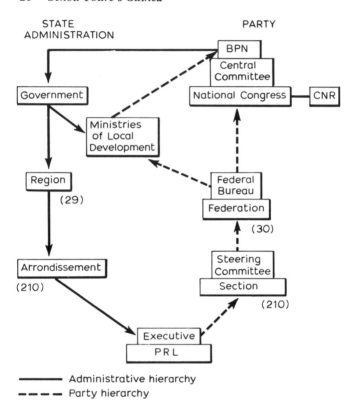

Notes: The region of Conakry, the national capital, is divided into two federations; hence, 30 federations for the 29 regions.

Party and Administrative Structures in Guinea

basic unit of the administration and of the party. In the years immediately after independence, the village councils created by the *loi-cadre* government existed side by side with the party base committees. By 1962, the party leadership admitted that conflicts were developing between the elected village councils and the party officials in the village base committees. These conflicts were described as 'dangerously compromising the unitary character of the State one of whose pre-occupations is to cause to disappear any idea of a functional partition or barrier between the different organs of the administration and those of the party.'[8] As a way out, the party's base committees were substituted for the existing 4200 villages and the party's base committee executives replaced the village councils. In 1967, the party's base committees which numbered about 7000 were baptized as local revolutionary authorities (PRLs); the number is currently estimated at about 8000.

Above the PRLs are the arrondissements, the new name given in 1963 to the administrative posts created by the *loi-cadre* government. These arrondissements numbered about sixty-three and they were used as the lowest units within which the work of the central government was organized. In 1964, it was decided to emphasize the role of arrondissements as units for maintaining effective central government authority in rural areas. To achieve this objective, it was decided to make the area and number of arrondissements correspond to those of the party section. As a result, the number of arrondissements rose from 63 in 1963 to 175 in 1965 and to 210 in 1970. More significantly, the commandants of arrondissements are by right members of the steering committee of the party section and this arrangement is intended to emphasize the fact that both the party structure and the administrative machinery represent the same central authority. An additional factor in favour of using both the party and administrative structures to assert the central authority is the fact that the majority of the members of almost every steering committee are civil servants;[9] inevitably both the civil servants who operate within the party structure and those who operate within the state administrative machinery are bound to see themselves as the representatives of the same central authority.

The *cercles* which constituted the pivot of the colonial administrative system were preserved by the *loi-cadre* government which increased their number from twenty to twenty-five and renamed them *circonscriptions*. The name was changed again in 1959 to regions and their number increased to twenty-nine. Although the administrative officer at the head of the region — called the regional governor — has continued to be regarded as a key figure in the maintainance of the central authority within the region, his role has been integrated with that of the party executive within the region. In 1963, a party institution called a federation was created at the level of each region. Each party federation has an elected executive called the federal bureau of which the regional governor is by right a member. As at the arrondissement level, the majority of the members of federal bureaux are civil servants who combine party functions with their normal civil service duties.[10] This arrangement also helps to ensure that the party and administrative structures at the regional level are used to maintain the central government authority.

In 1964 the administrative regions within the same natural regions of which there are four were constituted into a ministerial delegation, and each was placed under a national party leader who was expected to provide both administrative and political leadership for the administrative and party institutions within his area. Except for the period 1967 to 1972, the head of a ministerial delegation has always been a member of the national executive of the party. In 1972, the title of ministerial delegation was changed to that of ministry for local development but without any real change in the emphasis placed on the role of the ministers in charge;[11] they continue to be regarded as the local representatives of the central authority in their respective areas.

The summit of these administrative levels consists of the administrative services of the State which are organized within ministries placed under political heads. The outstanding

Political Institutional Framework for Nation Building 23

characteristic of the Guinean governmental structure is the fact that since independence the leading positions have always been reserved for the members of the party's national executive. In 1967, the party's eighth Congress decided to constitute the party executive, the BPN into the cabinet[12] of the government. The entire work of government is shared between the seven-member cabinet with each member in charge of a *domaine*. In 1972, the seven *domaines* were as follows: the Presidency, the *domaine* of the Prime Minister, the *domaines* of Social Affairs, Economy and Finance, Trade, Education and Culture, and Interior and Security.[13] The President of the Republic who is also the Secretary General of the party appoints a number of ministers who assist the ministers of *domaine*.[14] This style of organizing governmental work constitutes a logical summit to the administrative machinery described above. There is an intimate liaison between the administrative and party institutions both in regard to structure and to the personnel who operate them. This arrangement is intended to serve as a means of using both institutions to establish the central authority throughout the territorial area of the state. Given the nation-wide grass-root institutions over which the national institutional arrangements are superimposed, it will be fair to conclude that there exists a well-developed institutional framework for maintaining the central government authority in Guinea.

As a means of strengthening the institutional arrangements described above, the youth, women's and workers' organizations which are officially called the 'parallel institutions' of the party have been developed. The youth organization called the Youth of the African Democratic Revolution (*la Jeunesse de la révolution démocratique africaine,* JRDA) is the single national organization for Guinean youth and is organized at exactly the same levels as the party with its own executive bodies; its national leaders are represented within the party Congress, the CNR, and the Central Committee, and its first regional and local leaders are members of the federal bureau, the steering committee and the PRL executive. Both the women's and workers' organizations — known respectively as the Women's Wing of the PDG and the National Confederation of Guinean Workers (*Conféderation nationale des travaillers guinéens,* CNTG) — are organized along the same lines as the youth organization except that the CNTG is not represented within the PRLs. Instead, the workers within every administrative service and within each of the country's public enterprises (about seventy of them in 1971) constitute a party committee of production (*comité d'unité de production,* CUP). Like the PRL, each CUP has a thirteen member executive elected annually.

Bridging the Élite-Mass Gap

In addition to serving as the framework for asserting the central authority throughout Guinea, the institutions described above are also used to pursue the objectives of bridging the élite-mass gap and of ensuring public participation in the political process. We have already mentioned the PDG doctrine of the mass line and its practical application in the sense that every adult Guinean is an automatic member of the party by virtue of the fact that he pays the party dues as an integral part of his state tax.[15] One positive result of this mass membership of the party is that at a PRL meeting in Conakry, for example, one can find side by side a civil servant, a teacher, a trader, a skilled worker, an unskilled worker and a farmer. This was, in fact, the professional diversity within the PRL whose meetings the writer attended in January and February 1971. The base committees of the youth and women's organizations also have this kind of mixed composition. Similarly, the national congresses of the party and of the youth and women's organization are attended by delegates drawn from all walks of life. For example, the breakdown by profession for the 682 delegates to the party's ninth Congress

Political Institutional Framework for Nation Building 25

held in April 1972 was as follows: 170 farmers and plantation owners, 9 craftsmen, 25 housewives, 36 workers, 186 teachers, 73 medical workers, 2 military representatives, 148 officers in the general administration and 33 commercial employees.[16]

In some sense, then, it can be said that some concrete actions have been taken in Guinea to bridge the élite-mass gap. There are, however, two important problems in the Guinean approach. First, the idea of automatic membership of the party implies some compulsion and does constitute a serious constraint on individual choice. Before the idea of automatic membership of the PDG was introduced in 1962, it was claimed that 1,650,000 Guineans voluntarily bought PDG membership cards. This figure represented about 50% of the entire population and almost the whole of the adult population.[17] But there is no evidence to show that the same proportion of Guineans would have continued to buy the party's membership cards if every adult citizen were not required to pay his membership dues with his state tax. The point being made here is that the bringing together of Guinean citizens within the PDG structure (including its 'parallel institutions') has involved some compulsion and this raises some doubt as to its effectiveness.[18]

The second problem relates to the position of the party officials who constitute the 'élite' of the mass party. In other words, in attempting to use a mass party organization to solve the problem of élite-mass gap, the same problem is created within the party organization. The party élite referred to here consists of the elected party officials at the different levels of the party organization. In 1971, their number was estimated at about 300,000. The élitist character of these officials is underlined by the fact that while every Guinean is a member of the PDG some are excluded from becoming party officials.

> All the people are members of the party but it is only the dynamic part, the part faithful to the people, that directs the party. The trader can be a member of the party, the

industrialist can be a member of the party but neither can direct the party.[19]

Practical observation in Guinea shows that the party officials effectively constitute an élite group if one compares their standard of living and their social status with those of the ordinary members of the party. The higher one climbs on the élitist ladder, the wider the gap between the officials and the ordinary citizens.[20] In effect, the fourteen per cent Guineans who hold party posts constitute an élitist group within the mass party.

From the above, it cannot be said that there is no élite-mass gap in Guinea. But it is correct to say that the élite-mass gap that is commonly found in African states (marked by an urban-rural dichotomy and professional 'segregation') does not exist in Guinea; instead, Guinea is faced with the problem of bridging a gap between the party élite and its mass members. The extent to which either gap can hinder the peaceful evolution of the political community concerned will depend on how far apart are the élites and the masses. In the absence of a sociological survey (such an idea is taboo in present-day Guinea) one can only rely on personal observation. On the basis of what the writer saw in Guinea in 1971, it could be said that the élites there are closer to the masses than is the case in many other African countries but the gap that exists between the two groups is still considerable. More significantly, it was not quite clear whether efforts were being made to bridge the existing gap or whether the gap was being allowed to become wider.

Involving the Masses in the Political Process

The third purpose of the Guinea political, institutional framework is to facilitate the involvement of the mass of the citizens in the political process. Two aspects of PDG ideology deal with this subject. The first is the party's conception of the

Political Institutional Framework for Nation Building 27

state as an institution that will eventually wither away. According to President Touré, this means that:

> The state will cease to be an entity separated from the political and social reality of the people. The withering away of the state, at our level, is the incarnation of the entire organic structures of the state, of the entire attributes of the state, by the organized people, which corresponds, in a word, to the existence of the power of the people allowing them at every level of their organization to solve the problems posed at that level, the state no longer being an apparatus separate from the people. In the withering away of the state, it is the people who seize the power of state to exercise it at all levels.[21]

The administrative machinery which constitutes the most important state apparatus is destined to wither away too:

> We consider our administration as an element of transition, for a time which history will fix, between an inferior state of social and political organization and a superior state which the nation will reach thanks to the progress which she will fully achieve in all domains.[22]

In order to prepare for this eventual withering away of the administration, a policy of associating the people with the work of the administration has been adopted with a view to progressively leaving administrative work in the hands of elected representatives of the people.[23]

The second aspect of PDG ideology that is related to the effort aimed at ensuring public participation in the political process is the doctrine of 'democratic centralism'. As already mentioned in Chapter I, this doctrine requires the lowest levels of the party structure to be subordinate to the higher levels but the higher levels are to take account of the opinions expressed by the lower levels before arriving at decisions that become binding for the whole party. Since the party is said to exercise the legitimate authority in Guinea, the faithful observance of the doctrine of democratic centralism would mean that the nation-wide party structure is involved in the exercise of state power.

In practice, the degree of public participation that exists in the Guinean political process has been achieved through a pragmatic interpretation of the ideological principles summarized above. Although the party is proclaimed the repository of state power, the effective exercise of power is carried out through the state administrative apparatus rather than through the party structure. As mentioned in Chapter I, Guinea adopted a Western-style constitution at independence and according to this constitution, state powers are shared between an executive (the president of the republic and the government), a parliament and a judiciary. And as if to translate this constitutional arrangement into practice, institutions were established through which these powers were to be exercised; the government at the national level with representations within the natural regions (Ministries for Rural Development), the administrative regions, arrondissements and local revolutionary authorities (PRLs); a national legislature called National Assembly and elected representative institutions at the regional, arrondissement and PRL levels; and judicial courts throughout the territorial area of the state.

While the above constitutional arrangement still has a theoretical existence in Guinea, in practice, the doctrine of the separation of powers on which it is based is totally rejected. And President Touré gives the reason for rejecting the separation of powers as follows:

> In reality, the separation of powers has no other result than to dispossess the people of its prerogatives by making superior to its interests, either those of the state, of the army, of justice or, in parliamentary democracy, of the parliament. By opposing to the power of the sovereign

Political Institutional Framework for Nation Building 29

people the power of the state apparatus, the sovereignty of which it is the legitimate and unique depository is purely and simply confiscated. Conscious of the fact that democracy cannot preserve its progressive content unless it is effectively exercised and placed under the control of the people, *we have given up the faked forms* (that is, the principle of the separation of powers) *which falsify it in order to preserve for it, without any sharing, its popular nature* .. (sic),[24]

The unitary 'popular' power referred to above is claimed for the party but in practice it is not exercised wholly within the party structure except at the PRL level. Above the PRL level, the party institutions are involved in the exercise of state powers by virtue of the intimate liaison that exists between them and the formal constitutional institutions that are supposed to share in the exercise of state power.

At the PRL level, the elected party executive has responsibility for the collection of taxes, the maintainance of law and order, the administration of justice and the keeping of birth, marriage and death records. Every PRL executive is also expected to mobilize the citizens within its area for locally initiated projects aimed at promoting social and economic development. For this purpose, the PRLs have been encouraged (since 1968) to create brigades for their major activities such as production, trade, public works, health, education and the defence of the revolution (current name for the maintainance of law and order). The brigades are led by the executive members who recruit ordinary PRL members to the ranks.

A good illustration of the work of PRLs is in the field of judicial administration. The president of every PRL executive and four other members constitute a popular tribunal of first degree with jurisdiction over disputes concerned with birth, marriage, death, divorce, public fights, minor thefts, succession problems and land disputes. In all these areas, the popular tribunal of the PRL is expected to achieve a settlement through conciliation. Failure at this level means that the matter will go before the popular tribunal of second degree at the party section. Another important illustration of the work of PRLs is the fact that since 1969, each PRL has a budget consisting of a fraction of the regional tax collected within its area. Although the budget needs the approval of higher administrative bodies, it is the general assembly of the PRL which votes it while the PRL executive is responsible for its implementation.

If all the 8000 PRLs in Guinea were functioning properly, this would mean that the 104,000 PRL executive members and many other citizens effectively exercise state power within their areas. President Touré has summed up this ideal situation as follows:

> The PRL constitutes in each base committee in the rural zone the government of the village, allowing progressively this village collectivity, through the exercise, on the local plane, of all the attributes of national sovereignty, to resolve correctly all the problems conditioning the harmonious development of the village in all domains ... political, economic, social and cultural ... By creating the PRL, the party is applying the historical solution valid at least for Guinea, of the withering away of the state within the revolution, a withering away which is in reality the reinforcement of the state of the revolution by the concrete, direct total and coherent exercise of the body of state power by the people at the level of each cell which constitutes it.[25]

In reality, the ideal state described by President Touré does not exist. Not all the 8000 PRLs function normally; at the end of 1970 there were many PRLs which performed only a small fraction of the functions assigned to them.[26] There is also evidence to show that the freedom of the PRLs to administer their own affairs is sometimes circumscribed by intervention from above. For example, when in 1969 the majority of PRLs voted to use their budgets to build schools and dispensaries, the president of the republic issued a *communiqué* to all of them stating that the budgets should be used to build stores for stocking agricultural products.[27] Furthermore, some of the PRLs' functions are performed unsatisfactorily because of lack of guidance and assistance from the higher authorities who are expected to supervise them.[28] However, notwithstanding these limitations, the very existence of numerous PRLs and the activities that many of them carry out show that there is a genuine commitment in Guinea to involving the masses in the political process.

At the arrondissement level, the party's executive, the steering committee, is also the constitutional representative institution with the different title of arrondissement council. The membership of the two bodies is identical. As at the PRL level, the elected party officials of the arrondissement are involved in judicial administration. The president of the steering committee and four of its members constitute the popular tribunal of second degree which hears appeals from the popular tribunal of first degree. This tribunal is also expected to achieve settlement through conciliation. Appeals go from it to the popular tribunal of third degree at the federation level of the party structure. Unlike the situation within the PRLs, the administrative services within arrondissements are entrusted to paid civil servants. The elected party officials are expected to be involved in the work of the administration in two ways. First, they vote the arrondissement budget which is to be used for financing local projects These projects include the construction of minor roads, wells and local markets. Second, they are expected to control and supervise the action of the administrative officials. In practice, all this amounts to a very limited involvement in the administrative process. In particular, the idea that the elected party officials should control the actions of the administration has not proved effective and cases of abuse of authority by civil servants are frequent:

> If political pre-eminence had been honestly asserted, we would not have witnessed the abuses of authority by certain dishonest and incompetent civil servants . . . . It is our (party) sections which are responsible for these deeds because they have not been able to impose on these unworthy civil servants the principles of the party.[29]

Part of the explanation for the inability of the steering committees to supervise the work of the administrators is the fact that personnel overlap between both institutions (*supra*). In all, then, the involvement of elected citizens in the exercise of state power at the arrondissement level is very limited.

The situation at the regional level is similar to that at the arrondissement level. The constitutional representative institution of the region called regional assembly is in practice composed of the members of the party's federal bureau[30] and the leading youth, women's and workers' leaders within the region. The major function of the regional assembly is the voting of the regional budget. In practice, the control which these assemblies is supposed to exercise is rarely carried out. While several regional budgets were not approved by the government between 1959 and 1970 there was no single case where the regional assembly either amended or rejected the budgets presented by the governor. The other activities at the regional level involve only the party federal bureau members who constitute a sort of executive for the regional assembly. The federal bureaux serve as the popular tribunals of third degree to which appeals come from the second degree tribunals at the section level. Like the other popular tribunals, they are expected to settle conflicts by conciliation and if they fail, a case is expected to go before the regional justice of the

Political Institutional Framework for Nation Building 33

peace who will handle it according to the common law. And like the steering committees, too, the federal bureaux are expected to control the work of regional administrative officials. For more or less the same reasons, this control has not been effective.

To improve the situation, it was announced in January 1971 that every federal bureau would henceforth share equal responsibility with the governor for the operation of all central government activities within the region. As a corollary to this new measure, it was stated that praise and punishment would be equally shared. Both the bureau and the regional administrative officials should report their activities at quarterly intervals to the federal conference.[31] This new arrangement, according to the presidential circular that set it out, is to ensure more popular control of administrative action:

> the people themselves, through the quarterly conferences will play the essential role of controller and judge of the morality and regularity of the use made of public property, the use made of the property of the entire regional collectivity.[32]

It is not known whether or not this new arrangement is functioning properly. The situation prior to the 1971 innovation was that very little popular involvement in the exercise of state power took place at regional level.

At national level, the emphasis is on involving elected citizens in the decision-making process. Although a National Assembly has been preserved, it does not exercise the legislative powers provided for in the constitution: 'The National Assembly alone votes the law. The domain of law is unlimited.'[33] Instead, it is used as a chamber of codification: 'Guinean deputies are first and foremost responsible militants to whom the people have entrusted the care to put in legal forms their political decisions.'[34] In recognition of the limited role of the National Assembly, its members — party leaders (including the thirty federal secretaries) nominated by party institutions and elected without any campaign or opposition in every election — only receive sitting allowances.

National decisions are taken within the party Congress, the CNR, the Central Committee and the BPN. As already mentioned, the members of these institutions represent the grass-root organizations of the party. But it is important to mention that the BPN occupies a dominant position in the decision-making process. For example, its reports to the meetings of these institutions, especially those submitted to the Congress, usually contain the decisions that are eventually adopted.[35] However, the existence of these institutions contribute to popular participation in two important ways. First, the adoption of major policies by about 700 delegates at every party Congress has the advantage of associating a large number of citizens with these policies. The fact that these delegates usually report back to the lower party institutions which they represent helps to familiarize a large proportion of the population with these policies. Among the major policies adopted by the party Congress since independence is the option for a planned economy in 1959 and the option for a socialist society in 1967. Second, the proceedings within the CNR and the Central Committee are not always like those of the Congress where the decisions contained in BPN reports are simply adopted by the delegates. Although the BPN still plays a dominant role, real debate takes place within both institutions before decisions are arrived at. The debates are sometimes conducted around the reports and recommendations submitted by the grass-root leaders who are members of these bodies. Most of the decisions concerning educational, economic and administrative reforms since independence were taken during the meetings of the CNR and the Central Committee.

The implementation of these decisions is the responsibility of the state administrative machinery — ministerial departments and public enterprises. The party leaders who dominate the government which is expected to lead, supervise and control these institutions merely carry out functions that are performed by the political executives in other countries. (Only the methods of election may be significantly different.) Where some degree of popular participation has been attempted in the execution of decisions in Guinea there is an attempt to achieve worker-participation through the setting up of committees of production (CUPs) within the administrative services and the public enterprises. For example, the CUP within a public enterprise is expected to 'participate in the preparation and watch over the implementation of the production plan, the budget and programme of activity of the enterprise.'[36] In 1971, it was admitted that the CUPs had consistently failed in their task, both within the public enterprises and within the other state administrative services.[37]

And like the lower party institutions, the CNR and the Central Committee are also involved in judicial administration. The permanent revolutionary committee of the Central Committee created in 1965 has investigated all the alleged plots against the regime, a role formally assigned to the *juge d'instruction* (investigating magistrate) in the judicial system. In May 1969, the CNR was constituted into a revolutionary tribunal to judge people accused of plotting to overthrow the government. In 1971, a similar function was assigned to the National Assembly (which is in practice a party institution) in connection with the trial of those allegedly involved in the abortive invasion of November 1970.

However, it should be mentioned that in spite of the systematic involvement of elected citizens in the administration of justice, the bulk of the work connected with judicial administration is still in the hands of professionally qualified officers in the Ministry of Justice (*Domaine* of Interior and Security). With regard to the popular tribunals, the initial reason for their creation was the limited personnel resources available for administering the common law system established in the country after independence. In 1958, the country had only nine magistrates and this number rose to only seventeen in 1967. The entire staff available for the administration of justice in 1967 was sixty-two. It was because of the congestion that resulted from this acute judicial manpower shortage that the government decided from 1962 onwards to entrust to the party institutions at the PRL, arrondissement and regional levels the responsibility of settling a number of civil cases by conciliation. It is this pragmatic reaction to a manpower problem that was later baptized as 'popular justice' and it is now held up as an outstanding illustration of the party's commitment to involving the masses in the political process.

Although the involvement of the national party institutions in the criminal trials of those alleged to have plotted against the regime is also described as an aspect of 'popular justice' (and the lower party institutions were involved in the 1971 'trials') this latter aspect has very little in common with the former. In the criminal trials, the accused persons are never present (except through recorded tape statements relayed during the trials and over the radio) and considering the severity of the sentences commonly passed — death sentences, imprisonment for life and hard labour — the whole exercise looks more like a travesty of justice or a 'judicial comedy' as the International Court of Justice has put it,[38] than a genuine case of involving citizens in judicial administration. However, disapproval of this style of 'popular justice' should not be allowed to conceal the former aspect where elected citizens are usefully involved in resolving judicial conflicts through conciliation.

To sum up, the above account shows that there is a genuine commitment in Guinea to the idea of involving the masses in the political process. A functioning, institutional framework has been created for this purpose and some concrete results have been achieved. However, there exists a considerable gap between what the party ideology claims and what really happens in practice. Perhaps the most striking point that emerges in this section is the fact that effective mass participation in the political process diminishes as one moves from the pyramidal base of the party structure to its apex. Thus, while the ordinary citizens led by their elected members are virtually responsible for administering their own affairs within the functioning PRLs, at the national level, the elected party leaders merely occupy a position analogous to that of a political executive in most other countries; the real task of administration is left to professional civil servants. The lesson here appears to be that as the work of government becomes more complex the chances of a meaningful involvement of ordinary citizens in the governmental process diminishes.

Another interesting feature of the Guinean approach connected to the point made above is the fact that the party structure does not occupy as dominant a position as the party ideology suggests. The state administrative structure which handles the complex work of government is, by definition, bound to be very important. A critical factor determining the importance of the administrative machinery is the fact that its personnel are career civil servants enjoying permanency of tenure, fixed salary, recruitment by qualifications or through competitive examinations and regular promotions. The additional recruitment requirement that Guinean civil servants should be party militants has not radically altered the career nature of the civil service.[39] This contrasts markedly with the party personnel who are part-time volunteers (most of them career civil servants) except the thirty federal secretaries. Given this serious imbalance in the personnel strength of the party and state administrative structures, the elected party officials are greatly handicapped in the extent to which they can exercise state powers. President Touré is certainly aware of this state of affairs but he also realizes that unlike Eastern European countries he has no reservoir of qualified personnel from which to staff the party structure. In the circumstances, he insists on proclaiming that the full exercise of state powers is carried out by elected party leaders in order to present the appearance of conformity to the party ideology. However, behind this facade of an inflexible attachment to the party ideology he allows the better-staffed state administrative machinery to exercise more powers than those permitted by the party ideology.

It should also be mentioned that some Guinean citizens are systematically excluded from effective participation in the political process. These are the traders, the industrialists and others who are disqualified from contesting for party posts (*supra*). Since it is the elected party officials who are mostly involved in the political process, those citizens who cannot compete for these posts are denied an important opportunity for political participation.

Conclusion

Referring to the political institutional framework examined above, President Touré has boasted before his countrymen that 'we have structures which enable us to assert that the Guinean people are among the best organized peoples in the world.'[40] In this chapter, we have been concerned with the suitability of these structures for achieving the threefold objectives of establishing a central authority throughout the territorial area of the state, bridging the élite-mass gap and involving the masses in the political process. In the absence of empirical studies of similar structures throughout the world, we shall not embark on a global comparison as President Touré has done; instead, we shall limit these concluding remarks to an overall assessment of the effectiveness of the existing political structures in Guinea.

Political Institutional Framework for Nation Building 39

There are three major elements in the Guinean political institutional arrangements: the ideological underpinning, the organizational structures and the practical operation of the structures. All three aspects are interrelated. It is fair to say that the doctrines that underlie the political institutions in Guinea are clearly set out: the doctrine of party supremacy, the doctrine of the mass line, the doctrine of the withering away of the state and the principle of 'democratic centralism'. While these doctrines are broadly related to the objectives pursued by the party, the analysis presented in this chapter shows that there are some important contradictions within them. For example, while the doctrine of the mass line emphasizes the mass membership of the party, the members do not enjoy the same rights within the party.

With regard to the political structures that have been created, the emphasis on the party organization appears justified as a means of establishing a central authority for the state and of reducing the intensity of the élite-mass gap. Although the party organization also makes a significant contribution to the commitment to involve the masses of the population in the political process it has achieved far less than has been claimed for it in this sphere. According to the party ideology, the state administrative machine is only an instrument of the party and is not considered as a significant factor by itself. The evidence provided in this chapter suggests that the state administrative machine has a more critical role to play in the nation building process in Guinea than the party ideology admits. It contributes positively to the objective of establishing a central authority for the state, but its dominant position in the execution of national policies still has to be reconciled with the objective of achieving mass participation in this activity.

Finally, the operation of the existing institutional arrangements is due on the one hand to the interrelationship between the institutions and the ideology that underlie them and on the other hand to the personnel who operate these institutions. Attention has been drawn in different parts of the chapter to a number of operational problems arising from these two points. Here we would like to comment briefly on the role of President Touré in the fashioning of Guinea's political institutions. He is the leading articulator of the party ideology; as the secretary general of the party he occupies the central position in the party structure; and as the president of the republic he dominates the state administrative machine. This means that he has to uphold the party ideology, to ensure that the party organization effectively dominates the institutional framework, and to preside over an efficient and effective state administrative machine. In handling the conflicts and contradictions that arise from his different roles, President Touré has consistently followed the Smelser principle of practising flexible politics behind a facade of ideological inflexibility. Thus, he excludes serious contenders for political power from party posts but maintains that the party has a mass membership. Similarly he presides over the state administrative machine whose career personnel with their training and expertise dominate the complex work of the government and still asserts that it is the party organization that dominates the entire political process.

In all, notwithstanding the criticisms that have been made in this chapter about the Guinean political institutional framework, it appears reasonable to say that it is a fairly satisfactory framework for pursuing the task of nation building. However, a final verdict cannot be passed until we have considered the effects of these institutions on the two other major subjects subsumed in the concept of nation building: the promotion of social and economic development and the quest for a national identity.

3. Economic and Social Development

A. The Strategy for Development

In this and the following chapter, we shall examine the place of economic and social development in the process of nation building in Guinea. After examining the developmental strategy adopted by the Guinean regime in some detail, we shall describe and assess the developmental activities that have been carried out since independence. But first, let us examine briefly the state of the country's economic and social development prior to independence.

Level of Economic and Social Development in 1958

When Guinea became a French colony during the last decade of the nineteenth century, the major economic products of the country were rubber, palm produce, groundnuts, hides and skin and gum. A few other products were subsequently added to this list (for example, banana and coffee in the 1920s) but it was not until after the Second World War that the French colonial administration embarked upon a programme of planned development in Guinea.

This development plan which Guinea shared with other French colonies was established by a French law of April 1946. To finance the plan, a special fund called the Investment Fund for the Economic and Social Development of Overseas France (*Fonds d'investissement pour le développement économique et social de la France d'Outre-mer*, FIDES) was created. From the available information on the activities of FIDES, about $78 million was invested in Guinea out of which $34,360,000 went to Conakry (the capital) for housing, public health, municipal repairs and improvement of air and seaport facilities.[1] The following table gives some idea of the level of economic and social development in Guinea towards the end of the FIDES plans. Guinea's position is compared to that of Senegal and the Ivory Coast which together with Guinea and five other countries — Dahomey, Mali, Mauritania, Niger and the Upper Volta — were constituted into a single administrative unit called French West Africa around 1900.

Considering the fact that the French colonial administration was aware that Guinea possessed important agricultural, mineral and energy resources, the record of FIDES shows clearly that very little was done to develop these resources. Indeed, in October 1949, the colonial governor in Guinea, Mr. Roland Pré, declared that 'it can be said that the territory of Guinea is certainly the most richly gifted [in natural resources] of all the territories of French West Africa.'[2] The following brief account of the activities carried out in the major sectors will show the wide gap that existed between Guinean development potentials and what had been realized after more than sixty years of colonial rule.

In 1957, two agricultural export crops, coffee and banana, were responsible for about eighty per cent of the total exports of Guinea. But neither of these crops was given adequate attention by the colonial administration. Banana cultivation was dominated by French and Syro-Lebanese planters with Guineans cast in the role of cheap labourers. As for coffee, its future was seriously compromised by a mistake of the agricultural services of the colonial administration which, between 1950 and 1958, encouraged a variety that was susceptible to a destructive disease called tracheomycosis.[3] The less important agricultural crops (palm produce, groundnuts and pineapple) and livestock were equally neglected.

Table 1: Some Indicators of Economic and Social Development in Guinea, Ivory Coast and Senegal, 1956

Countries	Exports, % of total FWA	Imports % of total FWA	Public Investment per capita, 1947–56 (cfa francs)	Rate of school attendance % of school age	No. of non-agriculture wage earners
Guinea	8.5	10	5,000	10	44,500
Ivory Coast	43.8	30	7,000	28	75,000
Senegal	35.0	52	10,000	24	83,000

Note: All three countries had roughly the same number of inhabitants.
Source: Adapted from E. Berg, 'The Economic Basis of Political Choice in French West Africa', *American Political Science Review*, LIV, 2 (June 1960), p. 400.

Perhaps the most eloquent testimony of the colonial administration's failure to promote agricultural development is the fact that Guinea was importing about 10,000 tons of rice between 1955 and 1958 in spite of repeated claims by successive colonial governors (from 1949 onwards) that Guinea could become 'the rice granary of French West Africa'.[4]

In the industrial sector, it was the same story of unrealized potentials. With the discovery of gold in Guinea around 1900, there was a 'gold fever' in French capitalist circles and by 1906 more than 338 permits for gold search had been issued.[5] Subsequently, attention was turned to diamond, iron ore and bauxite. Although the mining of these minerals started in the 1920s, no significant results were achieved until the 1950s. By 1958, Guinea was exporting some quantity of gold, diamond, iron ore and bauxite. Of these, the most promising was bauxite but it was precisely the mining rights over the most important known deposit of this mineral at Fria that the colonial administration sold to an international consortium consisting of France, the United States, the United Kingdom, Switzerland and West Germany with extraordinarily generous conditions.

Besides the industrial units connected with the mining activities, there were only a few privately-owned industrial units concerned with the manufacture of such products as beer, soft drinks, soap, canned fruits and furniture. Most of them were small-scale industries employing between five and fifty workers. All this means that very little industrial development had taken place in Guinea before 1958.

One major determinant of the rate of both agricultural and industrial development in any country is the state of the existing infrastructure, especially transport. Despite the fact that nearly one half of the total FIDES investment in Guinea was devoted to the provision of transport infrastructure, the transport facilities available in 1958 were grossly inadequate: a port was developed in Conakry and there was a small subsidiary port at Benty for handling the export of bananas; there was a railway line from Conakry to Kankan (about 673 kilometres) with some of its locomotives using diesel oil; a few hundred kilometres of all-season roads had been constructed; and there was an airport in Conakry. A good commentary on the services provided by these facilities is the fact that the railways did not function throughout 1958 becuse the rails were in a very bad state. It is also important to mention that only about 187 kilometres of the existing roads (Conakry—Kindia and Coyah—Forecariah) were tarred.

Finally, the colonial administration's record in the social sector was equally poor. For a population of about 2,800,000 in 1958, there was only one big hospital (located in Conakry), one second-rate hospital and ninety-nine dispensaries managed by fifty-eight doctors. As shown in Table I above, only about ten per cent of the school-going population were in school in 1956. More significantly, it should be pointed out that this percentage was achieved as result of nationalist agitation for increased educational facilities in the 1950s. In 1935, there were only 6558 pupils in schools and by 1947 the number had risen to just a little over 11,000. Out of the latter figure only 540 were in secondary schools. The result of all this was that at independence, Guinea had only about a dozen graduates in all fields.[6]

In all, then, the French colonial administration did very little to promote economic and social development in Guinea. This is not surprising since the greater part of colonial rule (1900—1945) was devoted to the consolidation of French authority over the colony while the resources made available under the FIDES programme were grossly inadequate. Perhaps the crucial point to mention here is the fact that the promotion of economic and social development in Guinea was of little importance to the colonial administration's central task of maintaining French rule in Guinea. To achieve this objective, the colonial power relied on its military power during the period of conquest and afterwards it created an administrative machine whose major task was to keep the population obedient to French authority. The limited achievements recorded in the economic and social fields were in reality conceived of and realized more on the basis of French capitalist interests (the greatest supporters of colonial rule in the metropolitan country)[7] than in the interest of the Guineans. The transport infrastructure helped the French capitalists to transport their goods while the small African educated élite was useful at the lower levels of the colonial administration.

The Post-Independence Strategy for Development

In addition to their dissatisfaction with the low level of economic and social development which the French colonial administration had carried out in Guinea by 1958, Guinean nationalist leaders were also dissatisfied with the manner in which the little that was done was carried out. In a speech before the French-dominated Chamber of Commerce of Conakry on 1 September 1958 Sékou Touré who was then the president of the local executive established in 1957 (*supra*) expressed this dissatisfaction as follows:

> ... with FIDES, it is not my government which will be able to tell you, Mr. Martin [the French President of the Chamber], 'you will undertake for me under the following conditions, the following assignment.' It is they in Paris, who decide the programmes, it is they who arrange the contracts. And we are unwilling, because FIDES effectively allows us to realize some economic progress, to engulf ourselves for that reason in its negative aspects.[8]

The point being made by Touré here is that the Guineans ought to have been allowed to participate in determining the contents of FIDES programmes. If this had happened, perhaps the interest of Guineans would have been taken into consideration. A good example of an economic decision which took no account of Guinean interest was the agreement signed in 1958 between the French colonial administration and the Fria consortium. The consortium was granted rights for seventy-five years over a bauxite deposit of about 150 million tons and a privileged fiscal arrangement to last for twenty-nine years covering such subjects as stability in the rates of customs charges, and in the tax on industrial and commercial profits.[9] No leaders of an under-developed country are likely to accept such terms that are sure to deprive the country of a considerable part of the profits accruing from its major industrial unit. We shall see later the serious difficulties encountered by the Guinean leadership when it decided to alter these agreements.

Since independence, one of the fundamental principles of Guinean development policy has been that economic decisions must take account of the interests of the citizens. This principle as well as a number of others which we shall discuss later on are subsumed under a broad developmental strategy which is called the 'non-capitalist way to development'. Since 1967, the expression 'socialist approach' has been used as a synonym of 'non-capitalist way'. Both terms are used to refer to a development policy which attaches great importance to a state-controlled economy and some form of collectivist organization in the rural areas. The major reason advanced by the Guinean leadership for justifying the option for a 'non-capitalist way to development' is that it is 'the only one [way] which safeguards the interests of the community while freeing every individual from the injustice which characterizes all relations of exploitation of man by man'.[10] The critical point here is that developmental activities are to be closely tied to the social relations within the Guinean society. The political will necessary for this linking of economic policy to social relations is provided in the Guinean leadership's assertion that they consider the economic domain as one of the aspects of the political problem. And President Touré has put this as follows: 'We shall therefore have the economy of our politics and not the politics of our economy.'[11] This approach to economic policy is commonly referred to as the supremacy of politics over economics.

As was pointed out in Chapter I, the policy of subordinating economics to politics represents the application of the doctrine of party supremacy to the economic field. On the face of it, this gives the appearance of ideological tidiness and inflexibility. To some extent, the Guinean leadership has tried to guide the evolution of the country's economic and social development in a manner consistent with the party ideology. But some important factors in the national and international politico-economic scenes have led to the emergence of significant inconsistencies. We shall now examine in some detail the theory and practice of the Guinean developmental strategy by focusing on three critical subjects that cover between them the different areas of development activity: the planning process, the respective roles of the public and private sectors and the reorganization of rural life.

The Planning Process

In 1959, the party's fifth Congress took the decision to plan the Guinean economy. In April 1960, a National Conference of the party was summoned to consider and approve the country's first plan, the Three-Year Plan, 1960–1962. Officially, this plan is presented as the work of the party and it is said to illustrate a faithful application of the doctrine of party supremacy in the field of the economy. In reality, the party's role in the preparation of this plan was insignificant. The brains behind the preparation of ths plan was a French team of economic experts led by Professor Bettelheim. It was this team that prepared a questionnaire that was sent to Guinean villages in order to find out the state of agricultural production whose development was to be the plan's priority. It was also the team that fixed the total estimate of investments at thirty-eight billion francs and worked out the proportions for the different sectors including the details of the activities to be carried out within each sector. When the party's National Conferences met in April 1960, it simply adopted the proposals of the French team without any significant changes.

Special mention should be made of the decision to create an independent Guinean currency which an informed observer of the Guinean scene has described as the 'central part' of the Three-Year Plan.[12] The formal decision to create this currency was taken at the Preparatory Economic Conference summoned at the initiative of the party in February 1960. The purpose of this conference which met at Dalaba was to discuss the financing of the plan and it was attended by the French team, a few leading ministers and some senior civil servants. In its submission on the details of the plan's finance, the conference recommended the creation of an independent Guinean monetary zone. The government accepted the recommendation and on 1 March 1960, it announced the creation of the independent Guinean franc.[13] In actual fact, the decision to create an independent currency was forced on the government more by circumstances than by any of the groups present at Dalaba. In spite of the abrupt break with France in 1958, Guinea remained in the franc zone. However, because of the political tension between Conakry and Paris, the French-controlled financial institutions in Conakry continuously created problems for the Guinean Government, especially through the flight of capital out of Conakry. So serious was this problem that the Guinean leadership considered the idea of creating an independent monetary zone in 1959 (see Benot, *op cit.*, p. 4). The significance of the Dalaba Conference's recommendation, in the circumstances, was that it removed any doubts the government might still have had on the subject.

Why was the party's role in the first plan so limited? It was essentially because of the lack of a personnel that was qualified to prepare a plan. At independence there were only about thirty Guineans who occupied senior-level posts in the public sector (there were none in the private sector).[14] Although all these officers were nominal members of the party only a handful of them could be described as party leaders. In any case, the important point to make is that because there were no Guinean planners neither the party nor the state administrative machinery (its 'instrument') played any significant role in the preparation of the first plan. Indeed, by the time the plan was approved in April 1960, no administrative machinery for planning had been established.

The role of the party in the country's second development plan, the Seven-Year Plan, 1964–1970, was radically different from what it was during the first plan. When, in April 1964, the party summoned a meeting of the National Council of the Revolution (CNR) to adopt the second plan, it was presented with a list of economic and social projects which was compiled from proposals put forward by both the party institutions (PRLs, sections and federations) and the central government ministries, all of which were centralized at the Ministry of Economic Development. The plan proposals compiled by the ministry were considered and adopted by the BPN in whose name they were presented to the CNR meeting by the Minister of Economic Development, himself a member of the BPN.[15]

The plan proposals bore no evidence of the use of the

techniques of economic analysis as they consisted essentially of targets to be achieved in the specified areas of social and economic activity. There was no mention of any quantitative goals for the growth of the entire economy or for any of the individual sectors (except for the declaration of the industrial sector as the priority of the plan)[16] nor was there any analysis of the interrelationships among the various sectors. Furthermore, there was no mention of the financing of the plan. At the end of the CNR's three-day meeting the plan was adopted. It was launched in a public speech by the President of the Republic on 1 May 1964.

If in 1960 a plan, qualified to be called a plan by commonly accepted standards, was prepared without the active involvement of the party then in 1964 the party played the dominant role in preparing a plan that was no more than a shopping list of projects. In other words, it has not been easy for the Guinean regime to reconcile a leadership role for the party in preparing a plan with the production of a well-prepared plan.

The explanation for what happened in 1964 was that while the country's personnel position had not improved substantially (five years was too short a time for such a task), the regime's leadership decided not to make use of foreign experts as it had done for the first plan. This decision was taken in the light of certain developments in the domestic political scene that had made the Guinean leaders suspicious of foreign experts. Between 1958 and 1964, they claimed to have discovered two 'plots' aimed at overthrowing the regime in which some foreign countries were involved.[17] While the effective non-participation of foreign experts in the preparation of the 1964 plan can be held up as a demonstration of the doctrine of the supremacy of politics over economics, it is equally true that the fact that no proper plan was prepared contradicted the party's commitment to a planned economy.

In the third plan, the Five-Year Plan, 1973–1977, an

attempt was made to achieve the goal that had hitherto eluded the party, namely, to combine a deep party involvement in plan preparation with the production of a good plan. On the basis of the available evidence, it appears that some measure of success was achieved. The preparation of the plan started in 1971 and it was not completed until 1973. First, there was a series of conferences on the state of the different sectors of economic and social development (they were called economic conferences). These were essentially technical conferences attended by the leading officials concerned with each of these areas of activities. The presence of the party was limited to the participation of the BPN members (the cabinet of the government, *supra*) and the fact that President Touré was the chairman of every conference. These conferences started late in 1971 and did not end until early 1973. In June 1972, a presidential circular was sent to the party institutions and the ministerial departments to submit their plan proposals to the Ministry of Planning and Statistics.[18] In assembling the different proposals, the Ministry of Planning and Statistics carried out the necessary technical analysis and produced a draft plan which took account of the relative importance attached to the different sectors in the presidential circular and of the funds available for financing the plan. The third and final stage was the adoption of the plan by the party's tenth congress held in September 1973. The plan was formally launched on 2 October 1973.

The difference between the third and second plans is obvious from the above accounts of how the two plans were prepared. The fact that very little was achieved from the second plan (*infra*) appears to have convinced the Guinean leadership of the need for a well-prepared plan. At the same time, the intensive efforts that had been devoted to the expansion of educational facilities since independence made it possible to have many more planners by 1971. It is reasonable to suggest that henceforth the Guinean regime should be able to reconcile an active role for the party in the plan preparation with the production of a well-prepared plan.

While the discussion of the execution of the development plans is reserved for the next chapter, it should be mentioned that the Guinean regime has also sought to assign a leading role to the party in plan execution in accordance with the doctrine of party supremacy. During the first plan, the party was as ineffective in plan execution as it was in plan formulation and this was for more or less the same reason: absence of a trained and competent personnel. The result was that the regime had to depend on the services of about 1500 Eastern European experts for the implementation of the plan.[19] Of course, the Guinean leadership kept on claiming that the party was playing the leading role in the implementation of the plan. Because of the political developments between 1958 and 1964 which led the Guinean leadership to consider foreign experts as potential saboteurs (*supra*), the idea of relying on foreign experts for the implementation of the second plan was virtually dropped. Thus, while as many as 1500 foreign experts were involved in executing the first plan, the corresponding number in 1967 was only ninety-nine.[20] In the circumstance, the regime had to rely on the national manpower shared between the party institutions and the state administrative machine. Although the party institutions were formally assigned the leading role in the execution of the plan — the sectoral targets were fixed in the name of the party federations rather than that of the administrative regions — they achieved very little. The bulk of the available national manpower was found in the civil service and it was responsible for the small part of the plan that was successfully implemented.

On the basis of the past experiences, it is not easy to predict what the role of the party would be in the implementation of the third plan. It may be safely assumed that the Guinean leadership will continue to assert that the party plays the leading role in plan implementation. In reality, the party's role may be limited to control and supervision while the state administrative machine is given the full responsibility for plan implementation. As a result of the gigantic programme of educational expansion embarked upon since 1958, the national manpower resources have improved tremendously and this means that the number of foreign experts employed would no longer be of critical importance. The point being made here is that it is possible that for the third plan the Guinean leadership may have assimilated Lenin's warning that 'without the guidance of specialists in the various fields of knowledge, technology and experience, the transition to socialism will be impossible'.[21] A 'non-capitalist way' to development in Guinea is only likely to succeed when the actual implementation of development plans is entrusted to these kinds of specialists.

The Respective Roles of the Public and Private Sectors

In the Guinean strategy for development, the emphasis is on the creation of a large public sector while keeping the private sector to the minimum. Foreign private investment is to be tolerated while indigenous private enterprise is to be positively discouraged. President Touré stated the regime's position as follows in 1960: 'We have never excluded co-operation with capital; we have only rejected capitalism as a form of social organization which does not correspond to our stage of development.[22] The 'capital' referred to above is foreign (both public and private). In practice, there are two distinct and diametrically opposed views towards the Guinean position by the foreign countries that possess surplus capital to invest abroad. On the one hand, there are the Eastern European countries and China who operate a socialist economy and are, like Guinea, opposed to capitalism as a form of social organization. On the other hand, there are the Western European countries, the United States and Canada who operate a capitalist economy and see nothing wrong with capitalism as a form of social organization.

From the above, it is clear that the Guinean leadership would find it easy to co-operate with the capital from Eastern European countries and China (henceforth referred to as the Eastern bloc countries) while co-operation with the Western European countries, the United States and Cananda (henceforth referred to as the Western bloc countries) would present some ideological problems. These problems were further complicated by the contrasting attitude of the Eastern and Western bloc countries to the declaration of Guinean independence in 1958. While the Eastern bloc countries enthusiastically welcomed Guinean independence, the Western bloc countries were cool in their reaction largely in deference to France, their ally, which had considered this independence as an act of 'secession' from the French Community. Thus, while eight Eastern bloc countries had concluded bilateral agreements with the Guinean regime within twelve months of Guinea's independence, the Western bloc countries (excluding France) had merely accorded a verbal recognition of this independence.

Despite the problems mentioned above, the regime has co-operated with capital from both the Eastern and Western bloc countries. There are two explanations for this action. First, the assistance that the Eastern bloc countries provided was inadequate. As we have already seen, Guinea's industrial, agricultural and energy resources were under-developed by 1958. In addition, the country was in dire need of a transport infrastructure as well as an urgent expansion of educational, health and medical facilities. Not only was the totality of the Eastern bloc assistance inadequate for these numerous developmental needs, some of this assistance proved ineffective because they were not suitable for Guinean conditions. The following observation of an American economist who visited Guinea in the early 1960s helps to illustrate this point.

> The first sugar sent from the Soviet Union was too soft; it melted and spoiled in the tropical heat. Later shipments were too hard the sugar refused to melt in coffee . . . . In Conakry thousands of toilet units lay in the sun, unused and unusable in a country with little plumbing. Many Eastern bloc vehicles proved ill-adapted to African conditions, and scarcity of maintainance and spare parts led to a frightening mortality rate for them. Soviet projects were ill-planned, and proceeded very slowly.[23]

Part of the explanation for the mistakes of the Eastern bloc countries was the fact that Guinea was the first country in tropical Africa to which they accorded substantial aid. But there is evidence that some of their projects are still badly planned.[24] Furthermore, the assistance of the Eastern bloc countries was inadequate because they did not show interest in developing certain activities connected with manufacturing and mining.

The second explanation was the decision of the Guinean leadership to pursue a policy of 'positive neutrality' in the country's relations with the Eastern and Western bloc countries. President Touré summed up this policy as follows:

> Guinea wishes to co-operate with all the independent states in the world, on the basis of the recognition of the independence of all peoples, their right to self-determination and the respect of sovereignty. We shall not join either of the blocs, we shall determine our policy in advance and all those who wish, on the basis that we have defined, to co-operate with us, will be our good partners.[25]

With Guinea's admission to membership of the United Nations Organization in December 1958, the Western bloc countries began to change their cool attitude towards the new state and before the end of 1959, some of them had concluded bilateral agreements with the new state. This development was dictated by the Western bloc countries' desire not to allow Guinea to become 'an African bridgehead for world Communism'.[26] This preoccupation is understandable if one remembers that the 'cold war' was still raging high in the late 1950s and there was an intense East-West competition for the allegiance of newly emergent nations.

To woo Guinea successfully, the Western bloc countries came forward with offers of capital investment. Having declared a commitment to the policy of positive neutrality, the Guinean leadership could not reject these offers outright. However, the Eastern bloc countries had gained the upper hand by being the first to offer assistance to Guinea and for the first few years of Guinean independence, the Western contribution to Guinean development was very small indeed. This state of affairs was radically affected by an internal political crisis which culminated in the expulsion of the Russian ambassador to Guinea, Daniel Solod, for alleged involvement in Guinea's internal affairs.[27] Although this conflict with Russia was subsequently patched up, it marked the end of an era. For the Guinean leadership it was a demonstration of the country's commitment to the maintenance of national independence against any interference from an external power. The lesson of the incident for the Western countries was that the Eastern bloc had not become too well-established in Guinea and there was therefore hope for them to invest more as a means of competing more effectively with the Eastern bloc countries.

It was just at about this time, too, that the Guinean dissatisfaction with both the scope and content of Eastern bloc assistance began to be aired publicly. This was accompanied by some official statements aimed at encouraging Western bloc countries to invest more in Guinea. Thus, the editorial of 7 April 1962 of the official party organ, *Horoya*, contained the following: 'It is important to recall that the take-overs and nationalizations carried out so far by the government relate to the sectors of sovereignty, the abandoned sectors and those where our laws were violated.' And in October 1963, President Touré declared that 'State trade was established in Guinea because the Eastern countries who came to our aid after independence would only deal with state-owned institutions.'[28]

At this point one could justifiably wonder whether the Guinean leadership was genuinely committed to the establishment of a state-controlled economy. This doubt is further confirmed by the regime's policy announcement of October 1963 that 'a quasi-total freedom is given to private trade, on the basis of trust and patriotism'. State trading stores and transport enterprises were abolished and it was hoped that the state would 'progressively reduce the activities of the national enterprises to only the strategic products and products of vital necessity for the masses'.[29]

What had happened was that just as the preponderance of Eastern bloc assistance between 1958 and 1961 was accompanied by the establishment of numerous state enterprises, the growth of Western investment after 1961 led to the abolition of some of these enterprises and their replacement with private enterprise, the economic formula with which the Western capitalists are familiar. However, there was no official change in the regime's commitment to the 'non-capitalist way' to development.

The changes that occurred between 1962 and 1963 were short-lived. In November 1964, the Guinean leadership announced that the national private entrepreneurs were exploiting the masses, thereby dangerously undermining the stability of the regime.[30] About a year later, the regime announced the discovery of a 'plot' which was baptized as 'The Traders' Plot'.[31] Finally, there was a diplomatic confrontation between Guinea and the United States – which by now was the leading Western investor in Guinea – when the Guinean government put the American ambassador in Conakry under house arrest because of the American government's refusal to secure the release of a Guinean ministerial delegation detained in Accra, Ghana, during a stop-over of the Pan-American Airways aeroplane on which it was travelling.[32] The result of all these incidents was that the Guinean regime became disenchanted with both foreign and domestic private enterprise and it was not surprising that at the party's eighth Congress held in 1967 the commitment to a 'non-capitalist way' to development was re-affirmed and given the new label of 'socialist approach'.

Since 1967, the Guinean regime has decided to translate the 'non-capitalist way' to development in the following ways. First, the overall state control of the economy is emphasized by the creation and maintenance of a very large public sector, the participation of the state in a number of foreign-financed enterprises and a close state control of other private enterprises (both foreign and national). As an indication of the size of the public sector, there were seventy-one state enterprises at the end of 1970. It is believed that this is the best way to guarantee the interests of the masses as well as national independence. Second, foreign investment by both the Eastern and Western bloc countries is allowed without any apparent preference for either side. Thanks to the reduction in the cold war competition since the late 1960s economic co-existence has replaced the earlier competition for pride of place between the blocs. It may also be that the Guinean conflict with Russia in 1961 and with the United States in 1966 has contributed to the creation of an environment favourable to economic co-existence of the two blocs inside Guinea. Finally, it is important to stress that the Guinean pre-1967 experience had demonstrated that an excessive reliance on either of the two blocs was fraught with dangers including a threat to national independence. The result of this economic co-existence of the two blocs is clearly demonstrated in the substantial investments that both Western and Eastern bloc countries have made in the mining industry in Guinea since 1967.[33]

One interesting feature of these agreements is the fact that they are all very favourable to Guinea; in almost every case, the Guinean share of the profits is larger than her share of the investments. For example, in the mixed enterprise company called the *Compagnie des bauxites de Guinée* which was established in 1968 to exploit the rich bauxite deposits in the Boké region, Guinea owns forty-nine per cent of the investment but is to receive sixty-five per cent of the taxable profits. Also, these same terms were agreed upon between the Fria enterprise and the Guinean government in February 1973 after about fifteen years of tough and protracted negotiations. (The 1968 agreement was reached after five years of negotiations.) There is no doubt that the great attraction of Guinea's high-grade bauxite deposits has played an important role in making these agreements possible. But one should not underestimate the importance of the determination of the Guinean leadership to secure the best terms possible. And in this regard they effectively demonstrate what they mean by economic decisions that take into account the interests of the Guinean population.

With regard to indigenous private enterprise, the Guinean regime believes that its growth would favour the exploitation of man by man and lead to the emergence of antagonistic classes: the 'exploiters' and the 'exploited'.[34] Immediately after independence stringent conditions were introduced for regulating private enterprise with a view to discouraging its growth. Then, between 1962 and 1964, private enterprise was boosted as a result of some changes in official policy (*supra*). When new controls were introduced from late 1964 onwards, it was found that the total disappearance of indigenous private enterprise was impossible. Reluctantly the regime was forced to accept its existence but its members are treated as though they make no contribution to the development process. For example, they are excluded from holding party posts (*supra*).

In 1970, an official publication summed up the entire private sector of the Guinean economy as follows: 41 commercial enterprises, 499 retail traders, and 770 specialized traders (petrol, cinema, bars and so on).[35] An official announcement in February 1972 that the state-run hotels and cinema were to be transferred to indigenous entrepreneurs[36] may mean that the regime is beginning to realize that a well-developed private sector could make some useful contribution to the development effort.

In the socio-cultural sector of development the Guinean regime has maintained a total state monopoly. In 1961, the private educational institutions in the country which were attended by about 13,000 pupils were nationalized and since this date, education has remained an exclusive concern of the state. Similarly, the institutions that provide health facilities are all state-owned. Furthermore, no private initiative is allowed in the fields of sports and cultural expression – theatre, music, folklore and so on. The only exception is cinema whose administrative management was transferred to private entrepreneurs in 1972 while the state maintained effective control over its content.

The Guinean regime considers the educational institutions as the best instruments for inculcating a socialist mentality into young Guineans and this, it is hoped, will turn them into active builders of a society where the exploitation of man by man is unknown. President Touré has summed up this idea as follows: 'We have entrusted to the Guinean school the mission to be the foundation, the root, the growth cells of the new society to which our history invites us, the socialist society.'[37] It is understandable that in such a context, private education has no role to play. Culture is essentially considered as an excellent method of preaching mass commitment to the ideology of the regime and this also means that private initiative cannot be tolerated. In all, state control has been quite effective both in theory and practice in the socio-cultural development. The details of the activities carried out by the state in this sector are discussed in the next chapter.

The Re-organization of Rural Life

The final major area where it is important to examine the theory and practice of the Guinean developmental strategy is its application to the rural areas. The regime's stated objective in this area is to re-organize the rural areas by encouraging the masses to constitute themselves into co-operatives as a means of achieving increased agricultural production (both in quantity and quality) and of establishing a new social structure which would emphasize collective and communal cultivation rather than individual and family production. It is believed that while collective and communal effort is conducive to the establishment of the kind of social relations favoured by the regime, individual and family production could lead to the exploitation of man by man and the emergence of a rural bourgeoisie from among the more successful individual farmers. This development would certainly be diametrically opposed to the regime's objective.[38]

Although the French colonial administration first introduced the idea of co-operatives into Guinea in the 1930s (pseudo-co-operatives called *Sociétés indigènes de prévoyance*, SIP)[39] as a means of improving agricultural production in rural areas, no fully-fledged co-operatives had been created by 1958. More significantly, the post-independence regime's support for the idea of co-operatives was motivated by a desire to establish a special kind of social relations in the rural areas — an objective that was absent from the design of the colonial administration. When the PDG leaders constituted the first local executive in Guinea in 1957, they established a Mutual Society for Rural Development (*Société mutuelle de développement rural*, SMDR) in every *circonscription* (district) as a means of promoting the establishment of co-operatives. It was hoped that the SMDRs would fade away once the co-operatives had been effectively established.

Because of the failure of the SMDRs, the Three-Year Plan provided for the establishment of three new institutions that would be used for re-organizing the rural areas: National Centres of Agricultural Production (*Centres nationaux de production agricole*, CNPA), Centres of Rural Modernization (*Centres de modernisation rurale*, CMR) and Co-operatives of Agricultural Production (*Coopérative agricoles de production*, CAP). A CNPA was conceived of as a state farm and a few of them were to be established as models of highly mechanized farming. A CMR was to be established in each administrative region to serve as 'model enterprises for the training of peasants, the demonstration of new material and the propagation of modern methods'.[40] The CAPs were to be established to involve farmers in the collective use of some new farming materials and, in some cases, to lead to the mechanized cultivation of collective farms.

By 1963, none of the twenty CNPAs envisaged in the plan had been established, the CMRs created were in ruins, and only 291 CAPs were in existence instead of the plan target of 500.[41] Since all land was declared state property shortly after independence (by a decree of 20 October 1959), it was not envisaged that the acquisition of land would be a problem in the establishment of the state farms. While this expectation was on the whole proved true, finance turned out to be a serious obstacle and it was largely for this reason that no single state farm was established throughout the life of the plan.[42] The collapse of the CMRs was partly due to inadequate finance and partly to their mismanagement by the officials put in charge. By 1963, the CMRs had disappeared and some of their property, especially the tractors, were taken over for private use by some of the officials. As one observer has put it:

> Some leaders of CMR used the machines put at their disposal either to increase the exploitation of some big farmers in the region, or to create their own large exploitation where they employed salaried workers.[43]

The disappearance of the CMRs compromised the chances of success of the CAPs as it meant the end of technical assistance and financial support. The result was that there were only 291 co-operatives in 1963 against the 500 in the plan target.

The failure of the CNPAs, the CMRs and the CAPs (the number of the latter continued to decrease after 1963 at a very rapid rate) did not discourage the Guinean leadership in its desire to re-organize rural life. In 1965, a new institution was created, the Agricultural Production and Consumer Co-operatives (*Co-opératives de production agricole et de consommation*, COPAC) at the regional level as the successors of the CMRs whose property they inherited (i.e. the property that had not been confiscated by the officials). Each COPAC was to buy agricultural produce from farmers and sell it to the national export enterprise, Guinexport. In return, it would buy consumer goods from the national enterprises in charge and sell them to the farmers.

In 1966, the function of supplying consumer goods to farmers was 'hived off' from the COPACs and entrusted to newly established General Stores within the regions. In 1970, Popular Stores were created within the arrondissements as the local agents of the General stores. and these Popular Stores were in turn to re-sell to the PRL stores. When it was found that the COPACs were not handling the function of selling rural agricultural produce properly a new institution was created for this purpose called *Office de Commercialisation agricole* (OCA). The functioning of these institutions can be summarized diagramatically as follows:

Structures for Marketing Agricultural Produce and Consumer Goods in Rural Guinea

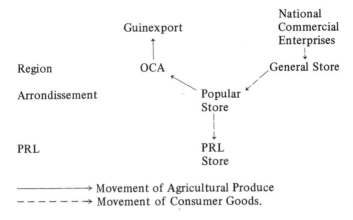

———————→ Movement of Agricultural Produce
— — — — — —→ Movement of Consumer Goods.

The OCAs buy agricultural produce from the farmers (sent through the PRLs and Popular Stores) at prices fixed by the government and re-sell them to the national enterprise responsible for exporting agricultural produce, Guinexport. To meet the needs of the farmers in consumer goods the General Stores buy these products from the national commercial enterprises and re-sell them to the farmers through the Popular Stores and the PRL stores at prices fixed by the government. (Before the creation of the Popular Stores in 1970, consumer goods were sold in rural areas by licensed retail traders who bought from the General Stores.)

Two important features of the above arrangements deserve to be emphasized. First, the government recognizes the need to have an effective institutional framework for marketing both agricultural produce and consumer goods in rural areas. It is admitted that farmers are likely to use some of the proceeds from their agricultural produce to purchase consumer goods and therefore the availability of consumer goods in rural areas at prices within the reach of the farmers is an incentive to increase agricultural production. Second, the government considers that the marketing system needed in rural areas should be operated by the state. This accords with the overall emphasis on state control of the national economy. This marketing system is characterized by a strict price control for both agricultural produce and consumer goods. The obvious intention of the government with regard to price control is to ensure that on the one hand farmers receive adequate pay for their products and on the other hand consumer goods are sold to them at reasonable prices. By entrusting all these arrangements to the state, the government is controlling an area of activity that is left to private enterprise in most African states. And it is common knowledge that the successful traders in the rural areas of Africa form part of the emerging bourgeois class. In other words, the Guinean government's action is aimed at achieving its determination to prevent the emergence of a rural bourgeoisie in the country.

Unfortunately, these institutions have not functioned properly, especially the supply of consumer goods to the farmers. Also, some farmers do not like the prices fixed for some of their products. Because of these reasons and some others which affect the entire Guinean economy (the other reasons will be discussed in the next chapter) there exists a black marketing system parallel to the state marketing system described above. A very important proportion of agricultural produce is sold on this market which in turn provides a large amount of consumer goods sold in the rural areas. Since the black market is run by individuals, these individuals in reality constitute a rural bourgeois class inside Guinea. However, unlike the situation in most other African states, it is a clandestine class, small in number and subject to permanent harassment.

With regard to increased agricultural production, the government decided in 1966 that a civic brigade should be created in each arrondissement to help to promote agricultural production.[44] Each arrondissement's civic brigade was to consist of 100 to 150 members recruited for a period of two years from among the youth of between the ages of seventeen and thirty. This was to add up to a total of nineteen to twenty-eight thousand for the whole country. Each civic brigade was to be self-sufficient in food production while the proceeds from the other products they cultivated were to be used for financing local development projects. By 1970, less than half of the arrondissements had established functioning civic brigades and none of them was self-sufficient in food. As a result of the wave of *coups d'état* in African states after 1966, these brigades were essentially regarded as agents for the 'defence of the revolution', a task that was initially considered of secondary importance. In 1971, the role of the civic brigades in promoting agricultural production was completely abandoned as all the 8000 civic brigade members (a figure much less than the 28,000 maximum expected) were incorporated into the Guinean popular army.[45]

As soon as the Guinean leadership realized that the civic brigades could not contribute much to the promotion of increased agricultural production, it decided that the best approach was to work through the educational institutions in the rural areas. While it was true that inadequate finance and administrative mismanagement contributed much to the failure of the Three-Year Plan's programme for re-organizing the rural areas, the conservative attitude of Guinean farmers was also an important factor in this failure. It was found that the agricultural co-operatives proposed by the government were not the same thing as the traditional communal farming that existed side by side with a strong attachment to individual effort. Having seen the force of these traditional attitudes, the Guinean regime decided that better results would be achieved by concentrating on the training of young farmers who would be familiar with modern agricultural techniques, the use of fertilizers and improved seeds and would be easier to organize into co-operatives.

For this purpose it was decided that each arrondissement should have a college of rural education (*Collège d'enseignement rural*, CER) where post-primary pupils recruited within the arrondissement would receive both general and agricultural education. It was hoped that in future each CER would become a co-operative. In October 1968, the CER system was generalized for all cycles of education (that is, from primary to university level), with the title changed to *Centre d'enseignement révolutionnaire*. (In October 1970 the title was further changed to *Centre d'éducation révolutionnaire*.) This arrangement meant that general education and vocational training were to go *pari passu* at all levels of education. However, only the second cycle CERs which corresponded to the original colleges of rural education were to develop into co-operatives, with the new title of socialist communities.

Once the socialist communities begin to function properly, it is hoped that the modern agricultural practices as well as the new social relations within them will prove superior to the traditional life of the farmers within the PRLs which are located in the same geographical areas. In such circumstances, the PRLs would willingly fuse with the socialist communities (the adult literacy campaign launched with UN assistance in the late 1960s is also expected to help the PRL members to appreciate this superiority) and the whole of rural Guinea will consist of socialist communities capable of producing large quantities of agricultural produce which are also of high quality. The social relations within these communities would be a kind of communal life where the exploitation of man by man would be unknown.[46]

In all, the Guinean government has actually tried to create an institutional framework within which to re-orient rural life in Guinea with regard to agricultural production and the social relations between those engaged in this activity. However, by 1971, the practical steps that had been taken to get these institutions to function properly had met with very limited success. Out of about 240 second cycle CERs to be created, only 165 had been established and of these only twenty-four were functioning as socialist communities.[47] As for the PRLs, only ten to fifty per cent of them had organized local brigades for promoting agricultural production.[48] On the basis of the available information by 1973, it appears that the ultimate objective of transforming rural Guinea into socialist communities will not become a reality within the present decade.[49]

In accordance with the party ideology, the Guinean leadership consistently assigned a leading role to the party structure in ensuring the success of the various programmes described above. Apart from the enthusiastic reception which every level of the party structure gave to the announcement of successive experiments, they did very little to ensure their success. In some cases such as the problem of inadequate finance, they could not offer any solution. Similarly, the party personnel could not provide the trained agricultural extension workers which the state administrative machine needed for promoting increased agricultural production in the rural areas.[50] In the area of control and supervision where the party officials could be expected to seek to increase the level of performance of the state administrative machine no positive result was achieved. Rather than serve as watchdogs over the administration, many party officials actively contributed to the mismanagement of the different programmes by joining some civil servants in embezzling the funds allocated for these programmes.[51]

The result of all this is that as in the management of the non-rural development projects the party structure has made no significant contribution to rural development programmes, and the credit for the little that has so far been achieved belongs to the state administrative machine. However, in the effort to translate into practice the current programme of transforming rural Guinea into socialist communities, the party structure especially the PRLs clearly has a significant role to play. It remains to be seen how well this role will be performed.

The only successful use of the party structure in promoting rural development to date was the idea of 'human investment' which was launched in 1958. This was a kind of self-help programme which relied on the party institutions in the rural areas for mobilizing the masses to participate in the development process. By the end of the Three-Year Plan it was estimated that projects worth about 3 billion GF had been carried out through human investment.[52] The projects included hundreds of schools, dispensaries, markets, mosques, roads and bridges. However, as a result of the emergence of some coercion and numerous administrative and technical difficulties, this programme of mass involvement in the development process was gradually abandoned and it was not invoked during the second plan. In particular, the enthusiasm of the Guinean masses cooled off as it became clear that there were no teachers for the schools, no nurses or medical supplies for the dispensaries and no vehicles for the roads. In 1970, President Touré recalled the contributions made by human investment in the immediate years after independence and called for its rehabilitation: 'Human investment remains one of the dynamic forms of economic development; it must henceforth be rehabilitated.' But he warned that the old abuses and other shortcomings should be avoided.[53] By 1973, there was still no official statement on how human investment was to be revived.

Summary and Conclusion

In the above account, we have examined in some detail the developmental strategy adopted by the Guinean leadership after independence. It was shown that the central plank of this strategy is a commitment to a 'non-capitalist way' to development. The Guinean leadership sees this policy as the best means of safeguarding the interests of the masses and of creating a social relationship where there is no exploitation of man by man. In particular, it is expected to lead to the establishment of some kind of collectivist organization in the rural areas. Finally, the entire operation of the national economy is subject to the political doctrine of party supremacy which in the economic sphere means the supremacy of politics over economics. The faithful application of this doctrine also means that the party structure should be assigned the leading role in ensuring that the party policy in the economic sphere is translated into reality.

The examination of how the Guinean developmental strategy was translated into practice revealed a number of important conflicts and contradictions resulting in a considerable divergence between theory and practice. Thus, for example, the attempt to make the party structure assume the leading role in the preparation and execution of the Seven-Year Plan meant in practice that the state did not really operate a planned economy between 1964 and 1971. Another example of a serious gap between theory and practice is related to the regime's declared policy of discouraging the growth of private enterprise. Because of some developments in the national and international politico-economic scenes, this policy was abandoned between 1962 and 1964 and private enterprise was encouraged to develop.

The only area of activity where practice was always consistent with theory was in the regime's programme to re-organize rural life. Despite the failure of the successive programmes aimed at achieving this objective, the regime remained faithfully attached to it and continued to launch one programme after another. In 1968, the regime finally launched a programme which appears capable of producing the desired results. But while serious difficulties are being encountered in carrying out this new programme – the establishment of socialist communities throughout rural Guinea – the cumulative effects of the long years of failure have led to the emergence of a flourishing black market system which is undermining the new rural programme's chances of success.

In what ways does the analysis of the different elements of the Guinean developmental strategy carried out in this chapter relate to the task of nation building? First, it should be pointed out that the formal commitment to a 'non-capitalist way' to development is presented as a policy position diametrically opposed to the economic policy of the colonial power which was capitalism. Having rejected colonialism, the country also rejected capitalism and both are declared to be bad for the Guinean people; in the place of colonialism the country opted for independence and instead of capitalism, it is the 'non-capitalist way'. In explaining this policy to the masses, the Guinean leadership emphasizes the fact that under a capitalist system the interests of the citizens were not taken into consideration in making economic decisions and there was exploitation of man by man. The new policy, it is claimed, attaches the utmost importance to the interests of the citizens and is against the exploitation of man by man. Considering the sufferings imposed on the masses by the colonial system, it is easy to see that they will react enthusiastically towards this policy and this helps to strengthen their feeling of attachment to the new state.

Realizing the important contribution that the option for a 'non-capitalist way' to development makes in getting the citizens to feel attached to the state, the Guinean leadership has been unwilling to announce a modification even when some economic decisions taken openly contradicted this policy. In other words, the Guinean leadership's attachment to an inflexible ideological position has contributed to the nation building effort.

With regard to the regime's determination to re-organize rural life, it appears that the leaders are genuinely convinced that what they are seeking to achieve is really in the interests of the masses. Thus, they have not been deterred by the early unsuccessful programmes. It is likely that they have successfully communicated this conviction to a sizable proportion of the population who in turn will feel strongly attached to the state under whose umbrella this programme is to be carried out. If this is the case, it is possible that the small group of people who operate the black market system will eventually be neutralized.

Finally, attention must be drawn to the fact that President Touré's role in the economic sphere as the leader of both the party and the state fits into the pattern identified in the previous chapter: as party leader, he is the chief defender of party orthodoxy but as Head of State, he is inclined to practise flexible politics. For example, while he was asserting that the party was playing the leading role during the Three-Year Plan, he was responsible for recruiting both the French experts who prepared the plan and the Eastern bloc experts who dominated its execution. He was also aware of the fact that the state administrative machine played a more significant role than the party structure. Perhaps, most important of all, after experiencing a serious confrontation with the respective leadership of the Western and Eastern bloc countries, President Touré has been the chief negotiator in the economic agreements which allow the representatives of the two blocs to co-exist in Guinea while as party leader he has continued to assert that the regime's approach to development is 'socialist' or 'non-capitalist'. Thus, in the Guinean socialist environment, capitalist America and socialist Russia together with their respective allies have established important industrial and manufacturing enterprises.

4. Economic and Social Development

B. Assessment of Performance

In the last chapter we examined Guinea's post-independence developmental strategy. The purpose of this chapter is to assess the results achieved from translating the strategy into practice. After examining what has actually been achieved in the different sectors of development activity there will be a brief discussion of the way in which the findings of the chapter relate to the nation building effort.

Industrial Development

As was pointed out in the preceding chapter, the level of industrial development in Guinea at independence was very low. The only important industrial unit was the Fria mining complex owned by an international consortium of European and American capitalists. Because of the terms of the agreement signed between France and the Fria society, the Guinean government was not able to integrate this industrial unit within the Three-Year Plan launched in 1960. According to the Egyptian economist, Samir Amin:

> In an economy like that of Guinea, a project like Fria cannot become a pole of development of a great effectiveness as a result of the 'dualism' that is the juxtaposition of two economies, that of the country and that of the great inter-territorial unit, both of them hardly integrated.[1]

In his *La République de Guinée,* Suret-Canale spells out the 'dualism' referred to above as follows:

> An island of an *avant-garde* industry in the midst of the traditional African bush, Fria is a good example of an economic 'enclave'; with its own railway line and port, Fria lives, oriented towards the outside world, depending closely on the mother enterprises of Europe and America, but totally independent of the African context.[2]

The result of all this was that only twelve per cent of the total investment made by Fria between 1960 and 1963 (about 1.2 billion Guinean francs) was of benefit to the Guinean economy.[3] However, Fria performed the important role of being the principal foreign exchange earner during the plan period: it was responsible for between forty and sixty per cent of Guinea's total exports from 1961 onwards.

In all, the Three-Year Plan earmarked 21.3 per cent of the total investments for the industrial sector — 8.3 billion Guinean francs (GF) out of a total of 38.8 billion GF. At the end of the plan period, only 17.7 per cent of the plan investments had been spent on the industrial sector. The major successes recorded were a cigarettes and matches factory, a saw-mill factory, a furniture factory, a canned fruit and meat processing factory, a printing press and a diamond mining enterprise. In the second plan, the Seven-Year Plan, the industrial sector was formally declared the priority area of activity. The list of projects to be established included: the processing of groundnut oil, coconut oil, palm kernel oil and other by-products, oxygen production, bicycle assembly, motor vehicle assembly, radio assembly, petroleum refinery, sugar refinery, cement factory, ceramic factory, paper factory, cotton ginnery, glass factory, cassava flour, pharmaceutical products, aluminium smelter, caustic soda-chlorine, fertilizer, explosives, electric steel mill and salt. The project list also included the establishment of gigantic industrial units based on the country's rich mineral resources; bauxite, iron ore and diamonds.

The number of industrial units that were actually established (including the additional post-plan period of 1971–73) is much smaller than the target proposed in the plan. In manufacturing and general goods, the projects that were successfully established include the following: a textile complex, two oil processing factories, a canned fruit juice factory, a soft drinks and chocolate milk factory, factories for manufacturing dresses and shoes (grouped together with leather production to constitute a complex operated by the military), a tea factory, bicycle assembly, truck assembly, tyre recapping and factories for the production of tiles, particle boards and aluminium roofing.

In the mining section, a number of important industrial units have either been fully established or are in the process of being established. The most important among these is the Boké mining project which was inaugurated in 1973. The authority of this project is the *Compagnie des bauxites de Guinée* jointly owned by Guinea (forty-nine per cent) and a group of Western capitalist interests (fifty-one per cent).[4] It is expected that this project will yield $50 million a year to the Guinean treasury. There are three other bauxite projects, still under construction, in which the Guinean government is associated with Yugoslavia (the Dabola project), Russia (the Kindia Project) and Switzerland (the Tougué project).[5] In addition to these bauxite-based projects, a cement factory is under construction (in partnership with Spain) and a multi-national project called MIFERGUI (*Société des mines de fer de Guinée*) for mining the rich iron ore of Nimba-Simandou mountain ranges is also under construction. (Guinea's partners in this project are Algeria, Nigeria, Zaire, Japan, Spain and Yugoslavia.)

All the projects mentioned above belong to the public and semi-public (that is, mixed economy) sectors. There is also a number of industrial units that are owned entirely by private entrepreneurs. The major difference between the private enterprises and the public ones is that while the majority of the latter were established after independence, most of the former were established prior to independence. They are largely small-scale enterprises employing an average of about fifty workers. Some of these industries are concerned with food processing (baking, canned fruit and juice, beer, soft drinks, syrups and so on) while the others produce such goods as perfumes, raincoats, sandals, metal construction material, soap and nails.

Finally, mention should be made of the Fria mining industry which until February 1973 was a private enterprise and the most important single industrial unit in Guinea. For example, in 1966 it employed 1375 salaried workers compared to 1718 for all the other private enterprises combined and 4069 for the state-controlled enterprises. (These figures refer to all enterprises: industry, mining, agriculture, trade, finance and general services.)[6] In February 1973, the Guinean government entered into partnership with the Fria enterprise on the favourable term of forty-nine per cent ownership for sixty-five per cent of the profits. This amounts to a very significant addition to the number of industrial units under state control.

In what ways have the above developments in the industrial sector affected the overall evolution of the Guinean economy? From the available evidence, it appears that the industrial sector has not made a very significant contribution to the economy. First, the Fria industrial unit which has dominated the scene since independence was not at all integrated with the rest of the economy and as a result there were hardly any positive 'spill over effects' from it to the national economy. Second, the important mining projects enumerated above were embarked upon only in the late 1960s and by 1972 none of them had entered into production. Although the successful execution of these projects holds out great promise, the concrete advantages that they are likely to bring to the economy still remain to be seen.

Third, many of the industrial enterprises in the public and semi-public sectors have been badly planned and very badly managed. For example, some projects were launched without adequate preparation. When the textile complex was completed in 1966 (with British financial assistance), the local production of cotton which was expected to supply one-third of the factory's 10,000 tons per year need amounted to only 60 tons. This unsatisfactory state of affairs occurred because the arrangement made for the cultivation of cotton was unrealistic. Instead of concentrating energy and attention on areas with favourable soil and climatic conditions arbitrary production targets were set for party federations which were expected to produce 1000 tons by 1966 and 4000 tons by 1970. Similarly, the canned fruit and meat processing factory constructed with Russian aid in 1963 has never been able to function at full capacity because no adequate plan had been made for supplying the necessary raw materials. While the factory needed about 2000 tons of tomatoes each year only 285 tons and 308 tons were produced in 1966 and 1967 respectively. Furthermore, the ultra-modern abattoir constructed within the factory for the purpose of producing tinned meat has never been used because no cattle have been supplied.

With regard to the management of these enterprises, the critical problem has been the poor quality of the managers. These enterprises were established when the number of trained personnel in the country was very small. In the circumstances, posts of high responsibility were entrusted to untrained officers who were completely unfamiliar with the management of such enterprises. The following statement of the Minister of State for Justice and Administrative and Financial Control in 1963 sums up the problem: 'In reality, many of our cadres, especially in the state enterprises and in the financial sector are not incompetent elements, but they are not trained for the work which they have been called upon to do. . . .'[7] The cumulative effect of these problems is that a majority of the industrial enterprises operate below full capacity.

In addition to the above problems, some of the industrial enterprises have produced serious negative side effects. The most notorious example in this regard is the Fria industrial unit which has been described as a 'pole of corruption'.[8] The salary of its workers and the social benefits that they enjoy (including eating food imported from France) makes them enjoy a standard of living that is very far above that of the ordinary Guinean. The result of this in the surrounding area is that everybody wishes to work for Fria — leading to the abandonment of farms.

There are, however, a few bright spots. The Chinese-aided cigarettes and matches complex has been very successful, providing substantial annual profits which are in turn ploughed back into the economy. For example, out of a total profit of 2,065,534,597 GF made by all the state enterprises in 1967, the cigarettes and matches factory produced 1,517,403,154 GF. In 1968, too, its profit amounted to 1,627,885,864 GF. Some of the enterprises have successfully trained a number of Guineans on the job thereby preparing the ground for better management in future. In this regard, special mention should be made of the centre of apprenticeship established by the Fria enterprise for training between sixty and ninety Guineans annually in various technical skills. With the great expansion that is currently taking place in bauxite mining, this centre is destined to render invaluable service.

The Commercial Sector

Under colonial rule, the commercial life in Guinea was dominated by a number of foreign firms of which the following were the most important: the *Compagnie française de l'Afrique occidentale* (CFAO), the *Société commerciale de l'ouest africain* (SCOA), Paterson-Zochonis (PZ), Peyrissac, Chavanel and the *Société industrielle et automobile de Guinée* (SIAG). These firms dominated the import-export trade, wholesale trade and some aspects of retail trade. There was a substantial participation by Syro-Lebanese businessmen in retail trade while the indigenous traders were largely involved in petty trading. This was the situation when Guinea became independent in 1958.

Immediately after independence, the Guinean government established a mixed economy enterprise called *Société africaine d'expansion* (with fifty per cent ownership) to handle the country's trade relations with the Eastern bloc countries which had enthusiastically entered into commercial agreements with the new state. In January 1959, the function of the mixed economy enterprise was taken over by a new state enterprise called *Comptoir guinéen du commerce extérieur* (CGCE). It was granted a full monopoly over a number of imports such as rice, sugar and cement and partial monopoly over certain export crops: banana (fifty per cent), palm products (seventy-five per cent) and coffee (thirty per cent). In May 1960 a similar enterprise was created for internal trade – the *Comptoir guinéen du commerce intérieur* (CGCI) with full monopoly over wholesale trade. A regional *comptoir* was established in the headquarters of each administrative region to serve as the subsidiaries of the CGCI. Retail trade was left in private hands.

The immediate result of the state intervention in the trade sector was the rapid elimination of the foreign private trading firms which had hitherto dominated the scene. This state of affairs was brought about by two events that were connected with the circumstances in which Guinea became independent. On the one hand, France was hostile towards the new state and the firms (most of them French-owned) had no confidence in the ability of Guinea to survive as a sovereign state without French assistance. They therefore decided to transfer their capital to France. On the other hand, the Eastern bloc countries which had signed trade agreements with Guinea asked to trade with Guinean-controlled trade institutions. By creating state monopoly trading enterprises, the Guinean government was simply taking the only logical step demanded by the circumstances. These enterprises were used to neutralize the sabotage of the foreign firms and to satisfy the request of the friendly Eastern bloc countries. In addition, it was hoped that the profits accruing to the foreign trade firms would henceforth belong to the state and this could be used to finance some of the projects in the Three-Year Plan.

In September 1961, both the CGCE and CGCI were abolished because they were badly managed and were therefore unable to handle the functions assigned to them. A number of national commercial enterprises were established in their place while the regional *comptoirs* were constituted into regional enterprises placed under the control of the regional administrative officers and political leaders. The regional enterprises were as badly managed as their predecessors and in October 1963 they were also abolished.

Partly in order to limit the sufferings imposed on the masses by the unsatisfactory performance of state-controlled trade, and partly as a reaction to the changes in Guinea's external economic and political relations with the Eastern and Western bloc countries (*supra*), an important dose of private trade was introduced in 1962. By November 1964, private trade was discredited as the sufferings of the masses worsened rather than showed any improvement. Regional enterprises were re-instated with the new title of General Stores. These General Stores were to distribute consumer goods in the rural areas. External trade was brought back under state monopoly and a number of national enterprises were added to the few existing ones to perform this function. The enterprises established for imports covered such items as agricultural material and produce, food products, building material, drugs, electrical goods, ready-made dresses, technical material, cooking utensils, books, stationery, textiles, petroleum, furniture, air, land, sea and rail transport material and pharmaceutical goods. For exports, there is one national enterprise, Guinexport which has regional subsidiaries called *Offices de commercialisations agricoles* (OCA). (See diagram on page 65, Chapter 3.) The current position is that wholesale trade is almost entirely controlled by the General Stores (with the exception of the distribution of petrol and of pharmaceutical goods). The state also participates in retail trade through two general stores called Nafaya and Sabouya and a mixed enterprise (in partnership with Yugoslavia) which sell miscellaneous consumer goods and through some branches of the national enterprises located in the regions.

Since the re-instatement of state control over trade in 1964, the private sector has been reduced to a very limited role. By 1970, there were only 41 private commercial enterprises (each of them limited to operating in only one administrative region), 499 retail traders and 770 specialized traders. But the entire private trade sector has to buy from the national enterprises or from the General Stores in the regions. In January 1972, the most important of these private enterprises which dealt with petrol distribution – Shell, Texaco, Total and Mobil Oil – were taken over by the state and merged with the existing state enterprise which had hitherto co-existed with these private enterprises. The few commercial private enterprises that remain are largely owned by foreigners while the retail and special traders include a sizable number of Guineans. (The Syro-Lebanese who have naturalized as Guineans while preserving their original nationalities are classified as foreigners by this writer.)

How does the post-1964 experience compare with the previous experience when it was found that both the public and private institutional arrangements established for trading did not function properly, and that the masses suffered from the inavailability of consumer goods as well as of some basic necessities while exorbitant prices were demanded for the few products that were available? From the available evidence, it does not appear that any significant improvement has taken place. First, the twin problems of bad planning and bad management that characterized the industrial enterprises have also plagued the commercial enterprises.

The problem of bad management has been essentially due to the manpower shortage in the country. In an attempt to solve this problem, the Guinean government appointed some private traders to occupy high posts in the commercial enterprises hoping that their experience in private trade would prove useful. The experiment failed woefully and President Touré tried to rationalize this failure in 1964 as follows: 'Our directors of enterprises could not adapt to their new duties overnight, they were ignorant of certain commercial rules ... Some of them committed mistakes and, confusing the national interest with their private interests, they have committed malversations and embezzlements.'[9] Instead of decreasing, these malversations and embezzlements have been on the increase. In 1972, President Touré up-dated his observations on the subject as follows:

> We must admit that state trade has been considered by the majority of the state employees as a sector of easy enrichment through theft and malversations. Since 1958, how many billion GF had been embezzled by corrupt elements of our society ... It is unnecessary to recall the successive stages we have passed through, all of them negative: *Comptoir du commerce extérieur, Comptoir guinéen du commerce intérieur, Comptoir régionaux* ...[10]

The direct result of the unsatisfactory functioning of the state trading enterprises is that the objectives that the regime sought to achieve have been defeated. The decision to bring the greater aspect of trading activity — the whole of import, export, and wholesale and a sizable proportion of retail trade — under state control was expected to facilitate price control by the state, and to ensure an efficient marketing system for the export of national agricultural products and for the distribution of basic necessities and some consumer goods throughout the state. Using the power of price control, the regime hoped to ensure that reasonable prices were paid for the agricultural products and that the rural masses responsible for these products could purchase both their basic necessities and some consumer goods at reasonable prices. Finally, it was hoped that the concentration of commercial activities in the hands of the state would help to prevent the emergence of a class of 'exploiters' in the trading sector.

While the major responsibility for the regime's failure to achieve its objectives in the trading sector can be attributed to the failure of the state's trading enterprises, attention should also be drawn to two ecological factors that were opposed to the regime's objectives and consequently to the institutions established for their realization. The first is geographical and the second is sociological. Geographically, Guinea is surrounded by six states whose economic and social policies are fundamentally different from those of Guinea.[11] Prior to colonial rule, these boundaries were unknown and there was free movement of people and goods. With the establishment of colonial rule, the frontier states fell under French (three states), British (one state) and Portuguese (one state) rule. The sixth, Liberia, was established as an independent territory. Despite the restrictions that the colonial powers tried to establish, people and goods still flowed over the frontiers but the movement of goods across frontiers in response to differences in prices became known as smuggling. According to available statistics, the smuggling that existed throughout West Africa in the 1950s was on a very large scale and the colonial powers were unable to suppress it.[12]

In the light of the above, the regime's decision to control

the prices of goods within its area could only have been based on the assumption that the independent government would succeed better than the colonial regime in suppressing smuggling. This optimism did not envisage that the introduction of an independent national currency would lead to the emergence of speculators who would make smuggling more difficult to combat. Indeed, since the introduction of the national currency — not convertible in the six neighbouring countries — some people who manage to accumulate large profits inside Guinea readily pay high prices for agricultural products which they sell outside at reasonably high prices for convertible currency which is then used to smuggle in some consumer goods. Others succeed in 'exporting' large sums of Guinean currency to the surrounding countries where they exchange it at rates that have ranged from three to seven times the official exchange rate and the buyers of this cheap currency return into Guinea to 'invest' it in black market activities.

The sociological factor relates to the existence within Guinea of numerous traditional traders who had been involved in the smuggling in the colonial era described above. This embryonic trading bourgeoisie is dominated by Malinké traders who are commonly referred to as 'dioulas'. The success of the regime's objectives in the trade sector depends in part on either a voluntary self-liquidation by these traders (some of whom know no other profession) or on the regime's ability to crush them. So far, neither of these alternatives has materialized.

It is in the context of these unfavourable factors that the state trading enterprises have been established. When, in 1959, the regime decided to sell some quantity of rice presented as a gift by the People's Republic of China at a very cheap price, most of the rice disappeared within a few weeks, to be sold across the border at the higher prices prevailing there.[13] Subsequent attempts met with the same result, thereby showing that Guinea's borders have remained as permeable as they were under colonial rule.

With the failure of the early trading enterprises, private traders were allowed to flourish between 1962 and 1964. During this period they demonstrated their readiness to exploit the masses and this led to the re-installation of the state's dominant role in trading towards the end of 1964. However, the continued failure of the state's trading enterprises and the fact that the regime has failed to find a solution to the country's permeable borders have combined to produce a favourable environment for the private traders in spite of government harassment. The measure of their success is that they have developed a flourishing parallel marketing system — commonly called the black market — which competes (with some measure of success) with the state's marketing system.

Although the regime remains steadfast in the pursuit of the objectives set for state trade, it openly acknowledges the seriousness of the difficulties that exist. President Touré summed up the situation in 1970 as follows: 'The chief target of counter-revolution today is, it is necessary to say, state trade. It is this vital sector that the enemy wishes to sabotage by all the means of economic and financial embezzlements.'[14] It is true to say that the realization of the Guinean regime's objectives would be to the advantage of the masses but it is also true that in the prevailing circumstances in which the obstacles are still beyond the control of the regime it is the masses who suffer. There are shortages of some basic necessities as well as of consumer goods. As a way out, the masses turn to the black market operated by a trading bourgeoisie whose major concern is profits — thereby becoming the victims of the very exploitation from which the regime is seeking to free them.

Agricultural Development

At independence, Guinea's agricultural resources were largely untapped. As a potential 'rice granary' for the whole of French

West Africa, she was importing about 10,000 tons of rice between 1955 and 1958. Judging by the production targets fixed in the Three-Year Plan, it appeared that the Guinean regime was determined to pay attention to agricultural development. According to the plan, twenty state farms were to be established; ploughing was to become generalized throughout the country; agricultural modernization centres (CMRs) and co-operatives (CAPs) were to be created in rural areas; and the following targets were set for the major export crops: bananas, 160,000 tons, coffee, 16,000 tons, palm produce, 25,000 tons and groundnuts, 32,500 tons. The successes recorded were very limited. Very little progress was made with regard to spreading the use of ploughs by farmers; the CNPAs, CMRs and CAPs were almost a complete failure except that some CAPs were successfully created; and, finally, the actual figures of cash crop production were very much below the target set out in the plan: bananas, 50,000 tons, coffee, 9000 tons, palm produce, 7000 tons and groundnuts, 6000 tons. (All the figures of actual production are for 1963 except in the case of groundnuts which are for 1962.)

Under the Seven-Year-Plan, the achievements of the Guinean regime in the areas mentioned above did not show any significant improvement. With regard to the institutions aimed at constituting the basic production units, the CMRs and the co-operatives, the regime tried one experiment after another until it arrived at the idea of creating socialist communities throughout the rural areas of Guinea. By 1973, only a start had been made in translating this objective into reality. As for the objective of increasing the production of export crops, the following figures speak for themselves. The targets fixed for bananas and coffee by 1970 were 100,000 and 43,000 tons respectively. Actual production for each was 35,000 (1970) and 8000 (1968) respectively.

Two other areas of agricultural activity which were highlighted in both plans — food crops and crops for industrial processing — also show a poor record of performance. The major food crop in Guinea is rice and in recognition of this fact as well as of the fact that Guinean soil and climate are favourable for both extensive and intensive rice cultivation, the Three-Year Plan contained two proposals for rice cultivation. The first was the cultivation of an area of 7000 hectares in Upper Guinea, to produce 20,000 tons of rice per year and the second was the cultivation of 5000 hectares in Maritime Guinea. Both projects failed and in 1962, twenty-three per cent of Guinea's total imports bill was used for rice. Half-way through the second plan the Guinean regime launched an 'operation self-sufficiency' in rice. This programme achieved very little as Guinea imported about sixty thousand tons of rice annually between 1967 and 1971[15] in addition to a substantial quantity supplied under the American PL 480 programme. (This programme enabled the Guinean government to purchase American rice with local currency and was considered as part of American aid to Guinea.) We have already seen that the production of crops for industrial processing was not very successful — the cases of cotton and tomatoes.

Several factors were responsible for tne failure of the Guinean regime to promote agricultural production. Inadequate finance was a major constraint. While the first plan envisaged that 26.4 per cent of total investments would be spent on agriculture only 11.4 per cent (less than half of the estimated amount) was actually spent on this sector. After three years of the second plan, only four per cent of total investments had been spent on the agricultural projects. Unlike the industrial sector which was financed largely by foreign suppliers' or governmental credits, the government had to rely almost entirely on local savings for financing agricultural projects and the funds available from this source were inadequate. It was also inadequate funds that were responsible for the failure of the state farms project and it prevented the state from importing adequate agricultural inputs such as insecticides, fertilizers, tractors and spare parts.

Another important factor was the failure of the Guinean regime to re-organize the unit of agricultural production in the rural areas. Most of the tractors imported between 1958 and 1963 (from 123 in 1957 the number of tractors rose to 223 in 1963) were distributed to the co-operatives of agricultural production but as these co-operatives disappeared the tractors were confiscated by a few individuals who constituted themselves into what Suret-Canale has described as a 'tractor bourgeoisie'.[16] As soon as this phenomenon became evident, the government reduced the import of tractors (inadequate funds, too, played a part). While 100 new tractors were imported between 1958 and 1963 only twenty-three were imported between 1963 and 1965. This meant that the government had abandoned the idea of increasing agricultural production through widespread mechanized farming in rural areas.

The failure of the commercial enterprises directly connected with the rural areas also played an important role in the poor record of the regime in the field of agricultural production. The major problems have been the virtual absence of incentive consumer goods for agricultural producers to purchase and the controlled prices at which they have to sell their products. Dissatisfied with the prevailing conditions in the state trading system, some farmers turn to the black market which buys at better prices and supplies some consumer goods. Because of the clandestine nature of the black market system its supplies have not reached such a level as to generate a real urge on the part of farmers to produce more. The serious challenge posed by the black market system to Guinea's programme for agricultural development is openly admitted by the ruling regime: in 1972, President Touré confessed that substantial proportions of coffee, groundnuts, palm produce and fruits were being smuggled out of the country annually.[17]

Finally, mention should be made of the attitude of Guinea's peasant farmers. Attention has already been drawn to how the traditional individualism which co-existed with communal life in rural areas contributed to the failure of the co-operatives. Although the ultimate aim of the regime's plan for the rural areas is in the interest of the farmers, they have not shown much interest in this long-term advantage; instead they have reacted to the prevailing failure of the regime's plan in a way that undermines the prospects for its future success: to avoid the state's prices for agricultural products some farmers sell to the black market where better prices are obtainable; to purchase the consumer goods that are rare in the official stores, some farmers turn to the black market; others who show no interest in the operation of the black market (largely because they cannot comprehend its operation) simply stop trying their hands at cash crop cultivation and remain as subsistence farmers. It was in order to combat these attitudinal problems that the regime decided in the late 1960s to develop a new generation of farmers who will both understand the plan for rural modernization and be prepared to work for its success. An adult literacy programme launched at about the same time is expected to help re-orient the mentality of the farmers.

As for the future, it should be mentioned that the programme of mechanized agriculture has been resumed and the plan is to provide each socialist community (the new units for rural modernization) with eighty tractors. By 1971, about 1000 animal-drawn ploughs, over 100 motor-powered implements and a small number of mechanical reapers and harvester-threshers had been distributed among the few socialist communities that had started to function. In addition, small-scale irrigation schemes have been constructed in some of these communities. From what the writer saw in two socialist communities in Maritime Guinea in March 1971, if this new programme of mechanized cultivation is successfully implemented, the Guinean regime could be on the threshold of a significant breakthrough in the agricultural sector by the end of this decade.[18] However, the slow progress that has so far been reported about the effective establishment of the socialist communities suggests that the prospects for this increased agricultural production should not be exaggerated. Suitable lands have been made available to the communities but the heavy financial investment for the necessary agricultural implements and the technical guidance required for the 'take off' stage constitute serious problems. Above all, the success of the regime in keeping the young generation of farmers on the land will depend to a great extent on whether or not their efforts are seen to be yielding good fruits.[19]

Infrastructures: Communications, Public Utilities and Others

Communications

At independence, Guinea inherited some basic transport facilities from the colonial administration: a port, an airport, a railway line and a small network of roads. In order to ensure the success of the development projects envisaged in both the Three-Year and Seven-Year Development Plans — transport of agricultural products from rural areas for export, supply of raw materials to the industrial units and the evacuation of their products and so on — the Guinean regime embarked on an expansion of the existing transport facilities.

Railway We have already mentioned that the only railway line in the country (from Conakry to Kankan) was not functioning at independence in 1958 because the rails were in a very bad state. Indeed it was the intention of the colonial administration to close it down. Because the Guinean regime considered the existence of this line to be of vital importance to the development of the economy, it was re-opened in 1959 and its management was entrusted to a national railway corporation called *Office national des chemins de fer*. Considering the very bad state of the rails, a study carried out under the Three-Year Plan recommended a re-construction that would cost thirty billion GF. This recommendation was turned down because of the huge cost and the regime decided to replace the existing rails with new ones. By 1967, 140 of the 662 kilometres-long rail had been replaced and there is an agreement with China for the completion of the remaining 522 kilometres.

Athough the continued existence of the railway line does make some contribution to the development of the economy, the fact that both its passenger and cargo traffics have fallen drastically since its re-opening (443,000 passengers in 1957 to 152,000 in 1966 and 96,000 tons of goods in 1957 to 58,000 tons in 1966) makes it open to question whether such contribution as it makes covers the annual deficits of between 100 and 250 million GF. It should, however, be mentioned that the bad management of the railway corporation, especially its numerous staff of more than 2500, contributes much to the corporation's annual deficit. The Fria railway line (Fria-Conakry, 145 km) is exclusively reserved for the transport of bauxite and alumina. In contrast, the Boké railway line (Kamsar-Boké-Sangaredi, 137 km) is used for local passenger and cargo transport. More significantly, there is a plan to construct a Trans-Guinea railway line (about 1000 kms) linking Conakry with N'zérékoré as part of the MIFERGUI project to transport iron ore from Mount Nimba and this line is expected to be open to passengers and cargo. Until the renovation of the Conakry-Kankan line is completed and until the Conakry-Nzérékoré line is constructed it will be difficult to say that Guinea possesses a railway network that makes a substantial contribution to the development of the country's economy.

Roads Compared to the progress made in improving rail communication, the Guinean regime has achieved a greater success with regard to the country's network of roads. In 1958, there were 8000 kms of classified national roads (that is, all-season roads) of which only 187 kms were tarred. By 1970 there were about 15,000 kms of classified roads of which nearly 1000 kms were tarred. Although the record of performance still falls far short of the target in the Seven-Year Plan (2400 kms of tarred road by 1970), the existing road network represents a considerable improvement on the colonial heritage. But it should be mentioned that the heavy investment in road construction has been seriously under-utilized as traffic density is very low. The writer obtained a first-hand experience of this under-utilization when he travelled on the Conakry-Mamou-Labé route in March 1971: between Mamou and Labé, there were less than ten vehicles throughout the return trip. An attempt to organize regional transport companies between 1961 and 1963 failed woefully and the existing national enterprise for road transport is unable to provide adequate transport throughout the existing network of roads. The result of all this is that, while the maintenance of the roads would require substantial sums of money, their under-utilization means that road transport for the evacuation of agricultural products and the distribution of consumer goods, some basic necessities and food crops, is inadequate.[21]

Sea and Airports The facilities of the port of Conakry have been improved and there has been a steady increase in both the number of ships that berth there and in the volume of cargo handled. A new subsidiary port has been developed at Kamsar to handle the export and import requirements of the Boké bauxite industrial unit. Since independence, Conakry airport has been expanded and renovated and the biggest planes can land there, unlike the situation in 1958 when only small and medium-sized planes could land. An embryonic internal air service created in the 1950s by the colonial administration has been expanded and it now covers fifteen centres instead of the original five. But the cost of maintaining both the external and internal air services (the former has two Russian Illyushin — eighteen passenger planes and the latter has a number of smaller planes and helicopters) has been very high; Air Guinea, a public enterprise which has responsibility for both services is, run at a loss — as much as 852 million GF in 1963/64 and an overall average of about 70 million GF. However, considering the keen demand for the internal flights, it appears that the services of Air Guinea represent a useful public utility despite its commercial unprofitability; the case for the external service is closely connected with national sovereignty and it is difficult in the circumstance to raise the question of commercial profitability.

Telecommunications   Here, again, there has been a considerable improvement on what was inherited at independence. There has been a great expansion in urban telephones, inter-urban telephones and telegraphs, international telephone and telegraph service, radio-telephone and radio telegraph service to Dakar, Abidjan, Bamako, Kinshasa, Freetown and via Dakar to Paris, New York and Moscow. The small radio transmission station inherited from the colonial administration has been replaced by a more powerful one and one can clearly follow the programmes of the 'Voice of the Revolution' (Guinea's national radio) in Ibadan (Nigeria) especially in the mornings and evenings. Unfortunately, because of the topography of Guinea, it is difficult for Guineans in some areas (parts of Middle and Forest Guinea) to hear the radio programmes clearly.

Public Utilities

As was the case in other French colonies in West Africa, the rudimentary public utilities that were established under colonial rule in Guinea were run by French capitalist interests. The French companies that controlled the supply of water and electricity to Guinea at independence were among those that embarked on a systematic transfer of their capital to France following the abrupt break of relations between France and Guinea in October 1958. The creation of an independent

Guinean currency in 1960 intensified this flight of capital. The Guinean government drew the only logical conclusion from the action of these companies, namely, that they have no confidence in their investments in Guinea. In January 1961, both companies were nationalized.

Since electricity became state-owned in 1961, considerable progress has been made in extending its supply especially in Middle and Upper Guinea. This has been achieved by the construction of a number of small dams with Yugoslav, West German and Chinese assistance on the Fouta Djallon Highlands and on the river Niger. However, the greatest hope of Guinea for an abundant electricity supply, the Konkouré hydroelectric power project, still remains untapped.[22] This project is expected to produce 6000 million kilowatts per hour (kwh). The French colonial administration had carried out a preliminary study of this project before Guinean independence but all the relevant documents were taken away to France at the time of the abrupt break in 1958. An agreement was signed with Russia in 1965 for the reactivation of this project. No concrete result came out of this agreement and in 1971 it was announced that Italy would construct the dam.

In 1968, electricity production in Guinea was estimated at 202 million kwh compared to 20 million kwh in 1958. This constitutes a remarkable achievement and it is also significant that three-quarters of this production was consumed by Guinea's industrial plants, compared to the situation in 1958 when nine-tenths of the production was for domestic consumption. In the meantime, the Guinean regime is hoping that the Konkouré project will soon materialize so that it can hasten the industrialization of the country.

Although the progress made in extending the water supply has been less spectacular than in the case of electricity, the progress made is still impressive compared to the situation in 1958 when a pipe-borne water supply was a luxury for some parts of Conakry, Kankan and Labé. By 1971, pipe-borne water had been extended to most of the regional administrative headquarters and there were plans to extend this to other towns and villages.

Other Infrastructures

A critical factor in carrying out any development project is the fund for financing it. Because of the acute shortage of capital in most of the new states of Africa, development projects are financed through bank credits. At the time of Guinean independence in 1958, the country's financial institutions were in the hands of French capitalists. Like the other French interests in Guinea, these financial institutions betrayed their unwillingness to co-operate with the Guinean regime and within eighteen months of the creation of the national currency they were all replaced by a number of national financial institutions. These were a central bank, *Banque centrale de la République de Guinée* (BCRG), a bank for external trade, *Banque guinéenne du commerce extérieur* (BGCE), a credit bank, *Crédit national,* a bank for agricultural development, *Banque nationale pour le développement agricole* (BNDA) and an insurance enterprise, *Société nationale d'assurance* (SNA).

These financial institutions have provided the bulk of the local funds for financing both the Three-Year and Seven-Year Plans. While it is correct to say that this source of finance was very useful, it is also important to mention that the high rate of inflation in the country is partly due to this system of financing development projects. Having tried in vain to limit the extent of dependence on deficit financing of development projects, the regime now appears to be resigned to an open acknowledgement of its inflationary consequences.[23] It appears that the Guinean leadership is anxiously waiting for the expected profits from the mining enterprises, especially the Boké project, as the surest means of escape from this predicament.

Social Sector: Health, Education, Sports and Culture

As in the other sectors of development, the Guinean heritage at independence in the social sector was just rudimentary. In health, for example, there was only one fully-fledged hospital, an average of one doctor for 70,000 inhabitants and one nurse for 8300 inhabitants.[24] And in education the whole country could only boast of about a dozen graduates and about 45,047 pupils in school (roughly equal to ten per cent of the school-going age) in 1958. The following account shows the progress that has since been made in the three areas of health, education, sports and culture.

Health

At the end of the Three-Year Plan in 1963, there were four fully-fledged hospitals, seventeen hospitals with moderate equipment (only one existed in 1958), one hundred and sixty dispensaries (ninety-nine in 1958), twenty maternities, and sixty-four health centres. In all, there were 6843 hospital beds against only 1383 in 1958. To meet the personnel needs of these institutions, six schools were established to provide the necessary specialized training for the middle-level staff while qualified Guineans were sent abroad to train as doctors, dentists, pharmacists and so on.

The programme of expansion was continued under the Seven-Year Plan and by 1970, each of the twenty-nine regional headquarters had at least one moderately equipped hospital and about 200 new dispensaries had been built. In 1967, it was estimated that Guinea had one physician for every 37,000 inhabitants, and this means that the inherited proportion of 1:70,000 had almost been reduced by half. This ratio as well as the personnel position in general will be greatly improved as more qualified personnel are produced by the specialized training institutions. In particular, mention should be made of the establishment of a School of Medicine and a School of

Pharmacy under the Seven-Year Plan. In the 1970/71 academic year, there were 146 students (including twenty-five girls) in the medical school and seventy students (including twenty-four girls) in the School of Pharmacy. The first sets of students in both schools were expected to pass out in 1973.

Finally, the Guinean regime has also decided to integrate the traditional methods of healing with the modern approach. This led to the creation of an Institute of Traditional Medicine in 1967 where some attempt is being made to assemble and develop all traditional methods of healing that are found to be effective. In all, the Guinean regime can be said to have done much to improve upon the rudimentary health facilities that existed in the country in 1958 after more than sixty years of colonial rule. Like other public institutions in Guinea, however, the hospitals have been adversely affected by bad management: incompetent administrative officers, some of whom steal drugs in the same way as their colleagues in the commercial and industrial enterprises embezzle funds. There is also the problem of inadequate equipment due to the limited foreign exchange resources of the government. These are the problems that the regime must tackle during the third plan in order to derive the maximum benefit from the considerable investments made during the past fifteen years.

Education

The following table showing the figures of educational enrolment in Guinea in 1957/58 and 1972/73 helps to sum up the achievement of the Guinean regime in the field of educational development since independence.

In reality these figures only tell part of the story of the programme of educational development which the Guinean regime has pursued. Besides the astronomical growth in numbers, the regime has also introduced a philosophy of education that is radically different from that which underlay the France-oriented educational system inherited at indepen-

Table 2 *The Progress of Educational Development in Guinea Since Independence*

Level of Education	1957/58	1972/73
Primary School	42,543	201,578
Secondary School and Technical School	2,547	76,386
Higher Education	–	3,995
Grand Total	45,090	281,959

dence. This new educational philosophy has been given several names by the Guinean leaders themselves but the one that sums it up best is the expression 'association of education with life' (*l'école liée à la vie*) meaning that there should be a close liaison between the country's educational system and the political, economic, social and cultural life of the nation. The salient features of Guinea's educational system can all be explained in terms of this underlying philosophy.

In 1961 the Guinean government nationalized all the private educational institutions in the country thereby bringing the 13,000 or so pupils in these institutions under the state-controlled educational system. This idea was considered necessary as a means of ensuring that the regime would have a completely free hand in orienting the education of the youth without any interference from any private, especially religious, interests. Two other measures announced in 1961 indicated how the Guinean regime intended to associate education with the political life of the country. First, from 1 to 15 July, all secondary school pupils were made to undergo a compulsory course in political education during which they learnt about the history of the PDG, its struggle for Guinean independence and the post-independence developments in Guinea under the PDG-led regime. Second, it was announced that the award of scholarship to secondary and post-secondary students would henceforth be based on the degree of their 'fidelity to the PDG and the country'. This is to be determined by the extent of the applicants' militancy within the PDG's youth organization, the *Jeunesse de la révolution démocratique africaine* (JRDA). In subsequent years, these two requirements were synthesized into an independent subject called ideology and it became a compulsory subject at all levels of education from the primary school to the university.

With regard to the desire to associate education with economic and social life, the Guinean regime's attention has been focused on how to use the educational institutions in rural areas to achieve the dual objectives of promoting increased agricultural production, and of establishing a new social relationship in the rural areas that would be characterized by a communal life where the exploitation of man by man is unknown. We have already described the way in which this programme is linked to the second cycle schools (lower secondary) which are expected to become socialist communities which in turn would absorb the PRLs in their respective areas. (See Chapter 3, pages 67–68). In addition, it should be mentioned that in the second cycle schools which are not in rural areas as well as in the third and fourth cycles (upper secondary and higher education respectively), great emphasis is placed on the need to introduce a vocational content into the educational curricula.

Another significant point to mention is the fact that, as a means of preparing all the students for the future life of self-management that will characterize the future socialist communities, all educational institutions of second cycle and above are administered by a council of administration composed entirely of elected representatives of the students, except for the post of president that is held by the head of each institution. The students' representative with the largest vote acts as the vice-president. The academic life of each institution is left to a council of teachers but this council must have periodic consultations with the student-dominated council of administration. This system of administration was introduced in 1968/69 and after one year of operation it was declared a huge success. Two problems were identified: failure of school directors to co-operate and a tendency of councils of administration to become 'institutions for making petitions'. The writer observed the council of administration of the Conakry polytechnic at work during four months in 1970/71 and felt that it worked fairly smoothly.

In 1962, the Guinean regime established a polytechnic in Conakry (with Russian assistance) to provide post-secondary education. In 1968, the teacher training institution at Kankan called *Ecole normal Julius Nyéréré* was upgraded to constitute with the Conakry polytechnic (called *l'Institut polytechnique Gamal Abdel Nasser de Conakry*) the national university. While the emphasis at the second cycle level is on the evolution of life in rural areas, higher education is oriented towards the production of the technical, specialist and administrative high-level manpower needed by the nation's industrial and commercial enterprises and the civil service with a great bias for the specialist and technical components. The following figures of the distribution of students between the eight faculties of the Conakry polytechnic in 1970/71 help to illustrate this point: social science, 262; advanced school of administration, 340; electrical and mechanical engineering, 185; civil engineering, 114; natural science, 195; pharmacy and medicine, 265; agriculture, 116; and geology and mining, 67. This bias for science and technology also characterized the scholarships awarded to 1381 Guineans who were studying abroad in 1973.

In the light of the above, it is easy to understand what President Touré meant when, at the height of the developments described above, he declared:

The heavy industry suitable for the qualitative transformation of the people, for the rehabilitation of its history and the constant uplifting of its civilization and of the whole set of material and human values on which the latter is founded, this heavy industry is the education and instruction perfectly adapted to the exigences of historical efficacy and the social utility of the people and of man.[25]

Naturally, the Guinean regime has encountered a number of problems in its attempt to carry out the above educational programme. One major problem has been the size of the national teaching staff which has not kept pace with the growth in the number of pupils and students. Until 1969 the regime made up for this deficiency by relying heavily on foreign assistance. Thanks to this approach it was possible to achieve a ratio of one teacher to forty-one pupils in the primary schools and of one teacher to thirty-three pupils in secondary and higher levels combined. During the academic year 1969/70 the Guinean regime cancelled the contract of almost the entire teaching staff from Western bloc countries for their alleged interference with the 'revolutionary culture' which the existing educational system was inculcating into the youth. For example, while there were about 170 French teachers in Guinea in 1965, only two of them remained in 1970.[26] The result of this was that by 1972 the ratio of students to teachers was very poor at all levels of education, about one teacher to sixty pupils in the primary schools. In the primary schools and the lower secondary schools, there were cases of untrained primary school leavers being employed as teachers[27] while in the third and fourth cycles the regime resorted to an extensive use of civil servants as part-time teachers, and students in their final years (except those in the Schools of Medicine and Pharmacy) at the Conakry and Kankan polytechnics are made to teach some courses in the third cycle schools in these two towns.

Another aspect of the teaching staff problem is how to ensure that the teachers themselves are capable of inculcating the regime's ideology into the students. According to President Touré:

> The ideological formation of teachers becomes pre-eminent because the politics of teaching must precede the technique of teaching. The revolution prefers a bad teacher, politically committed, devoted and honest, to a perfect teacher who is reactionary and anti-popular.[28]

It was the desire to measure the performance of some foreign teachers by this standard that resulted in the mass departure of 1969. As for the national teaching personnel, the regime has concentrated essentially on exhorting them to accept its viewpoint. According to President Touré the regime has successfully won over only a small proportion of the teaching personnel to its point of view especially with regard to the emphasis on vocational education.[29]

The ideological dimension in education also poses an important problem at student level. While at the end of secondary school education about ninety-five per cent of the students are said to reason both in the vocabulary and in the spirit of the Guinean ideology,[30] at university level some questioning begins. In order to combat this unsatisfactory regression (as the regime's leadership sees it), a system of an annual post-university ideological seminar was embarked upon in 1968. The following observations made by the director of the party school who conducted the 1969 seminar help to illustrate this point.

> The essays produced by students who have ended their university studies are in general inferior in quality to the essays produced by pupils at the end of secondary education.

> Several young comrades have acquired some stubborn knowledge in certain 'classical' theories of socialism and

were not easily able to understand that most of these theories were *a priori*.[31]

Both the teaching personnel and the students are faced with the serious problem of an inadequate supply of books — both textbooks and general reading material. The primary and secondary schools have some basic textbooks for the different established subjects but there is no general reading material in either the libraries or the book stores apart from party and government publications. The most serious problem at the secondary school level is the almost total lack of any teaching material on the vocation orientations that are in theory to be accorded about sixty per cent of the total number of hours per week: agriculture, livestock, fishing, building, construction of small dams and irrigation. Until something concrete is done about this problem the products of these schools are not likely to be as well equipped as the regime's leadership expects.

At the post-primary level, only the students in science and technology can be reasonably expected to manage with the basic textbooks at their disposal. The other students (social sciences and advanced school of administration) possess a few textbooks and the only other reading material available in the libraries (national as well as those for the two polytechnics) are a few old books and party and government publications. The journals that are taken regularly are less than ten and the majority deal with science and techology. The Guinean regime is against exposing its students to what it considers as foreign ideas that can influence the minds of students against the party ideology, and this factor is partly responsible for the absence of foreign books in the country. However, judging by the few old books that are found in the libraries, it is also likely that the serious problem of foreign exchange that has faced the country for most of the post-independence period is also partly responsible for the inadequate reading material in the country. In the meantime, it is the education of the students that suffers and they are likely to be seriously handicapped in carrying out the gigantic task of constituting 'the heavy industry suitable for the qualitative transformation of the [Guinean] people' (*supra*).

Finally, the regime's determination to promote the use of the country's major languages in the educational institutions has raised a number of problems. The regime has decided on developing eight national languages instead of the three widely spoken – *Mandika*, *Fula* and *Soso* – that belongs to the three largest ethnic groups in the country accounting for thirty-four, twenty-nine and seventeen per cent of the total population respectively. In addition to these three languages, there are five others (*Kpélé, Loma, Kisie, Wammey* and *Oneyann*) each of which is spoken by a proportion of the population that ranges from 0.5 to 7 per cent. This decision is already being implemented as pupils in the third year of their primary education in 1973/74 are expected to use national languages up to the sixth year, those in the second year to use them up to the seventh year and those in their first year to use them up to the eighth year (that is including the first two years of the lower secondary).[32] (French is taught as a subject from the third year in school.) At the post-primary level, each student is expected to learn another national language in addition to his mother tongue and French.

Although a National Academy of Languages was created in 1972 to produce manuals, to translate scientific terms and to find out the most effective methods of teaching these languages, it seems reasonable to doubt whether the progress of the Academy in these difficult research activities can keep pace with the programme described above. It should be mentioned here that the Guinean regime's decision to develop its national languages benefited from UNESCO assistance at the beginning and the emphasis then was on their use for promoting functional literacy among adults. The adult literacy programme, too, has made some progress but it also suffers from the inavailability of teaching material in the different languages. The Guinean programme is a very bold one indeed but one wonders whether the regime has the necessary material and human resources to carry it out. Considering the proportion of international educational material that is published in English the decision to delay the study of English until the post-secondary level is likely to have some adverse effect on the Guinean intellectual community. Perhaps the best attitude to take is to assume that as the regime's leadership becomes aware of these serious problems it will, as it has often done in the past, revise the entire programme during a session of 'criticism and self-criticism'.

Sports and Culture
At independence, football was virtually the only sport known to Guinean citizens and the rudimentary facilities for it existed only in Conakry and a few centres in the interior. Since 1958, the Guinean regime has embarked on a programme of making sporting facilities available throughout the country, down to the village level. Football and basketball are the most popular sports. The organization of the JRDA which groups together students, workers and farmers of both sexes (that is, those who by virtue of their ages belong to the JRDA) serves as the framework for the sporting competitions.

In basketball, there is an annual competition for determining the leading male and female teams. PRL teams compete for the selection of the section team. The section teams within a federation compete for the selection of the federation team. The federation teams within the same local development administration areas (the four natural regions) compete for the selection of the best teams to compete at national level. The writer witnessed the 1971 competitions held at Mamou to determine the teams to represent Middle Guinea. The matches were played under floodlight.

Football competitions are organized between competing

clubs. Each federation has a football club whose members are recruited as a result of preliminary competitions held within each federation along the same lines as those for basketball. The national football team is selected from among the best members of the federation teams. There is an impressive national sporting complex called the Stadium of 28 September (named after the date that the Guinean people voted to ask for their independence from French colonial rule). It was built under the Three-Year Plan with Russian assistance. In addition to facilities for football and basketball, there are also facilities for athletics, volley ball, judo, hand-ball, table tennis, boxing and swimming.

The greatest successes achieved in the sporting field to date have been in football. Both the national team and the leading clubs have distinguished themselves in international competitions and have won a well-deserved reputation for their country as one of the leading football-playing countries in Africa.[33] It should be mentioned that the coaching and training assistance provided by Eastern bloc experts have been most effective. But the greatest credit should go to the Guinean leadership for realizing that the provision of recreational facilities is also an aspect of development.

The attention paid by the Guinean regime to the development of the national cultural heritage helps further to underline the broad interpretation that the Guinean leadership gives to the term 'development'. Considering the fact that one of the reasons advanced for French colonization in Guinea (and in other African territories) was the need to bring French culture to them — this was referred to as the 'civilizing mission' — it is obvious that the colonial administration could not have bothered about Guinean culture which did not exist as far as they were concerned. All this means that the Guinean regime had to start from scratch. Predictably, the objective of Guinean leaders has been to develop the national cultural heritage which the French colonialists said did not exist. It is their belief that culture is 'the supreme method of national unification, of ideological progress, of the intellectual and material development of the people'.[34]

In 1959, a Guinean national ballet (*Ballet national guinéen*) was created. Within a few years this ballet had won an international reputation and its members were allowed to turn professional. Since the mid-1960s the ballet has spent the greater part of every year abroad in Europe, America and China. For example, the ballet was in America and Canada from 4 January to 4 June 1973 and they made 115 appearances! As the national ballet was winning an international reputation abroad, a systematic programme of developing other aspects of artistic manifestation — theatre, traditional music, modern music, painting and decorative designs, folklore — was embarked upon. Each of these forms of artistic expression is expected to be fully committed to the party ideology as the theory of art for art's sake is formally and categorically rejected.[35] As in the case of sports, the regime has relied on the party structure especially the JRDA. There are competitions at the levels of the PRLs, the sections and the federations. Finally, the best groups in the different areas compete at national level annually (since 1964) during an arts festival lasting for two weeks and called the *Quinzaine artistique*. At the end of each festival medals are awarded to the best groups in each competition.

The quality of the results achieved from the cultural development programme described above was brought to international attention in 1969 when Guinea won the *Grand Prix* (prize for the first position) at the first Pan-African Cultural Festival held in Algiers. Guinean artists won a gold medal in ballet and four silver medals in theatre, traditional music, modern music and singing. It should be mentioned that twenty-six independent African countries (including Nigeria which was placed in seventh position) and representatives of six African nationalist movements took part in this competition. Since 1969, the Guinean *Quinzaine artistique* has attracted an ever-increasing number of foreign delegations. The 1973 competitions were watched by delegations from Liberia, Gambia, Zaire and many Eastern bloc countries.

It is important to mention that the Guinean regime has achieved the above successes at very little cost. The artists practise in any available building or in the open air and the national festivals are held in the Palace of the People (built with Chinese assistance during the Three-Year Plan) which serves other purposes such as meetings of the National Assembly, the Party Congress, the Central Committee, the National Council of the Revolution and other national meetings of an administrative, political or economic nature. On the other hand, the regime has created a civil society called *Syliart* which has responsibility for the 'protection of the moral and material rights of artistic authors and producers of the Republic of Guinea'. The society was granted a capital of ten million GF and is to derive its revenue from authorship rights, receipts from productions, artistic and cultural shows and state grants. Perhaps the most important responsibility of the society *vis-à-vis* its members is the provision of pensions for retired artists.[36] In an obvious reference to *Syliart* in 1972 President Touré declared: 'We are ahead of all other African countries with regard to the material and moral conditions of our artists.'[37] To the writer's knowledge, this claim is quite valid, at least by 1973. In May 1973 *Syliart* was replaced by another institution called *Agence Guinéenne de Spectacles*. The new agency preserves the functions of *Syliart* with the only difference being that unlike its predecessor, it is not a civil society but a public institution under the Ministry of Youth, Arts and Sports.[38]

Because of the popularity of Guinea's modern music outside the country (especially in the neighbouring countries) a record production enterprise called *Sily-phone* was established to handle the production and sale of records composed by

Guinea's seven modern bands. In 1969, *Sily-phone's* account showed a profit of 24,682,701 GF. The Guinean regime, with Chinese assistance, is currently trying to base an industry on the production of traditional musical instruments such as *balafons, tam-tams, coras,* flutes and *toums.*

Finally, mention should be made of the existence of a flourishing cinema. The development of cinema began in 1965 and a cinema enterprise called Syli-cinema has been established. The personnel in charge of the enterprise were trained in Russia at the National Institute of Cinema and there is a close co-operation between the two countries in this field. Since 1969 a Week of Guinean Films is held in Russia every two years and a Week of Russian Films is held in Guinea in the intervening year. The emphasis in the production of films in Guinea is on ideological education; the cinema is regarded as an excellent instrument for inculcating ideological education into the masses.[39] The decision that private traders should manage the cinemas in 1972 is not expected to affect the ideological message of the films; the measure is aimed at improving the quality of administrative management.[40]

Economic and Social Development and the Nation Building Process

One important point that emerges from the above examination of the performance of the Guinean regime in the field of economic and social development is the fact that the leadership's conception of 'development' is broad-based. President Touré summed it up in 1971 as follows: 'Development is not only economic, it is at the same time political, social, cultural, technical, technological . . .'[41] In this chapter we have concentrated on these different aspects of development with the exception of the political. The purpose of this concluding section is to relate the performance of the Guinean regime in the field of economic and social development (including the 'cultural', 'technical' and 'technological') to the nation building effort.

In Chapter I, it was pointed out that the Guinean leadership shares the view that the promotion of economic and social development contributes positively to the nation building effort. For reasons of convenience, we shall first examine the way in which the Guinean regime's performance in the economic field has contributed to the nation building effort, and then turn to the contribution made by the performance in the promotion of social development.

In order to pass a fair verdict on the progress made by the Guinean regime in the promotion of economic development on the basis of the facts produced in this chapter, it is important to distinguish between two reference points: the level of development in 1958 and the country's potential for development. Compared to what existed at independence, it is correct to say that the Guinean regime has made considerable progress in promoting the country's economic development. On the other hand, it will also be correct to say that the Guinean regime has not done much in realizing the developmental potentials of the country. Abundant facts have been provided in this chapter for justifying the first verdict. In order to buttress the evidence on which the second verdict is based, we should like to stress that the Guinean regime's leadership more or less shares this opinion. President Tourés talks of 'the present state of economic undevelopment' from time to time. However, he always qualifies this by attributing it to the colonial experience.

> If we are underdeveloped, we should not be ashamed because we have undergone, by virtue of foreign domination, an eclipse in the existence of our national communities. The oppression and exploitation which characterized this domination is reflected today in the low standard of living of our peoples.[42]

An observer of the Guinean scene who is generally sympathetic towards the Touré regime, British socialist writer, L. Barnes, also concurs with this verdict of underdevelopment:

> Potentially, Guinea is one of the most prosperous of African countries. Actually it is still a disoriented agricultural economy with eighty-five per cent of the population scratching a living on the land.[43]

How has all this affected the nation building effort in Guinea? The Guinean leadership has tried to concentrate the attention of the masses on the positive verdict and whenever circumstances force it to admit the second, it attributes it to two factors which serve as scapegoats: the colonial experience and 'imperialist and neo-colonialist machinations' against the regime. By focusing attention on the positive verdict, the Guinean leadership hopes that the masses will feel grateful to a regime that has brought about some improvement in their condition of living (better roads, more water, more electricity, some industries) and that this will increase their sense of loyalty to the state. The practice of blaming the colonial experience for economic underdevelopment further helps to magnify the little that has been achieved — which is presented as an achievement in the face of formidable odds. By 'imperialist and neo-colonialist machinations' the Guinean leadership means that there are some imperialist and neo-colonialist powers (referred to also as 'capitalist') that seek to hinder the economic progress of Guinea. However, this forms part of a grand strategy designed to arouse patriotic and nationalist feelings in Guineans through the invocation of a permanent external threat which is discussed in the next chapter.

With regard to the social sector, the achievement of the Guinean regime measured against both the level of the colonial heritage in this field and against what might be described as reasonably attainable within fifteen years is, on the whole,

Economic and Social Development 113

fairly impressive. It is in reference to these achievements that the Guinean leadership proudly speaks of the 'gains of the revolution' (*'les acquis de la révolution'*). In health, there is one physician for every 37,000 inhabitants instead of the inherited proportion of 1:70,000 and health facilities now reach the rural areas instead of the situation at independence when they were found only in a few urban centres. In education, school enrolment has risen from a total of 45,090 in 1958 to 281,959 in 1973 and this figure includes about 4000 students at the post-secondary level where there was no single enrolment in 1958. (There were, however, about fifty Guineans studying for post-secondary diplomas abroad in 1958, mostly in France.) In sport, Guinea is widely acknowledged as an African football 'power' and in culture, Guinean artists have won world-wide fame.

All these achievements are constantly publicized in Guinea in order to arouse a feeling of loyalty on the part of the masses towards the state that has made these achievements possible. The progress made in health and education directly benefits the masses while the successes in sports and culture serve the purpose of helping to arouse their nationalism. The Guinean leadership consciously exploits the latter point as shown by the following statement made by President Touré in 1972: 'Among the factors that contribute actively to establishing and developing the prestige of a nation, the cultural factor is one of the most important.'[44]

However, when it comes to the shortcomings of the regime in the social sector the leadership allows the minimum publicity possible. Thus, for example, no publicity is given to the poor housing conditions in the country, especially in Conakry where virtually no improvement has been made in the town planning position inherited at independence. No publicity, too, is given to the serious inadequacy of teaching material and book supplies in the schools. Whenever any shortcomings are openly admitted during a session of 'criticism and self-criticism' it is either in order to announce the measures aimed at removing them (for example, the poor quality of teachers in 1972) or in order to denounce those allegedly responsible for the shortcomings.

In all, then, the Guinean leadership has managed to present its record in the field of economic and social development in such a way that the Guinean masses see it as justifying their loyalty to the state. To achieve this, the Guinean leadership has skilfully exploited the art of propaganda which it uses to focus attention on the positive aspects of its achievement while the negative aspects are either unpublicized or the responsibility for them is attributed to the external factors of the colonial experience and imperialist and neo-colonialist machinations. The success of the approach adopted by the Guinean leadership is due largely to the fact that about ninety per cent of the population are either illiterate peasants or young men and women who are very susceptible to this propaganda: the peasants have not travelled outside Guinea to know what prevails elsewhere and the only information to which they have access is the regime's propaganda which emphasizes the evils of the colonial experience (of which they had first-hand experience) and extols the post-independence achievements; the young people, too, readily accept that the colonial experience was a disaster while they have benefited from some of the post-independence regime's achievements, especially in educational and sporting facilities.

This leaves a minority of about ten per cent consisting of traders, intellectuals and bureaucrats (civil and military). Some of them disagree with the view that the colonial experience was an unmitigated disaster and more importantly, some of them are conscious of the fact that the ruling regime has done very little to realize the country's rich potentials. The 500,000 or so Guineans who have emigrated from the country since independence are largely drawn from this group.[45] The others constitute a clandestine opposition group inside Guinea. In the meantime President Touré continues to lead the remaining faction of the élite group which constitutes the PDG leadership. So far, this group has successfully prevented the opposing élite from making its viewpoint known to the masses. Can one, then, talk of nation building when some of the nation are abroad in voluntary exile and when some others (however small their total number might be *vis-à-vis* the entire population) feel alienated from the nation? This aspect of the Guinean approach to nation building will be discussed in some detail in the next two chapters.

5. The Quest for a National Identity

Like most other post-colonial states in Africa, the boundaries of Guinea were arbitrarily fixed by the colonizing power. As a result of this action, these states are composed of differing ethnic, religious and linguistic groups. The need for formulating a common national identity for the inhabitants of each state is widely recognized as an important task for the post-independence leadership. Referring to this problem, President Touré described the Guinean state that became a member of the international state system at independence as a 'juridically constituted state without historical entity'.[1] He then went on to say that the task of the post-independence regime was to build a 'nation' on to the framework of the state.[2] The purpose of this chapter is to describe the methods adopted by the Guinean regime for formulating a national identity and to assess their effectiveness.

Nationalism and Neutrality

In stating the case for Guinean independence in 1958, Sékou Touré, in his capacity as the PDG leader declared: 'We, for our part, have a first and indispensable need, that of our dignity. Now, there is no dignity without freedom. ... We prefer freedom in poverty to riches in slavery.' On 28 September 1958, 1,130,292 Guineans (about ninety-six per cent of the registered voters) endorsed the PDG's viewpoint by rejecting the Franco-African Community proposed by President de Gaulle.[3] When the French government reacted to the Guinean option for independence by considering it as an act of 'secession', it unwittingly produced a nationalist feeling among the inhabitants of the new sovereign state. It is important to narrate briefly the historical background to this incident.

As we have already mentioned, Guinea was, until 1958, one of the French colonies in West Africa which were administered from about 1900 onwards within a federal administrative set up called French West Africa (FWA). The headquarters of the federal administration was based in Dakar (Senegal) and there was a territorial headquarters in each of the constituent colonies. When, as a result of the liberal provisions of the French Fourth Republic's 1946 Constitution, political activities were allowed all over FWA, the African nationalist leaders that emerged saw the federation as the unit of their activities. It was not until the disappearance of this federal unit in 1956 as a result of the *loi-cadre* (*supra*) that many of these leaders limited themselves to their respective territories. Even then, some of these leaders, including Sékou Touré, still campaigned for an independent federal state consisting of the members of the former FWA between 1957 and 1958. However, the final say was the responsibility of the French government.[4] In May 1958 General de Gaulle became the leader of the French government and one of his first actions was to re-organize the relationship between France and her territories in Tropical Africa. To this end he proposed a Franco-African Community which these territories were free to accept or reject through a referendum; any territory which rejected the community would automatically become independent. When the referendum was held, Guinea alone voted for independence.

The French government took the Guinean vote for independence as an act of 'secession' and within a few months it stopped all financial and economic assistance to Guinea. In addition, all the French administrative and technical personnel who dominated the senior and middle levels of the colonial administrative machine were hurriedly recalled to France. It is also said that as some of these officers withdrew from Guinea they destroyed vital files and documents and took some away as part of their baggage.[5] Abandoned by the former colonial power, the leaders of the new sovereign state were faced with the task of ensuring its survival. Since the other territories of FWA had voted to remain within the Franco-African Community, the old idea of an independent FWA federation was dropped and the Guinean leaders had to concentrate their attention on making the independence within one state a reality.

The enthusiastic support expressed for the Guinean independence by the eight independent African countries (Egypt, Ethiopia, Ghana, Liberia, Libya, Morocco, Tunisia and Sudan), the Eastern bloc countries and the other independent countries in Asia and Latin America was a source of great encouragement to the Guinean masses and their leaders. In addition, a sizable number of teachers and technically qualified personnel from Africa and France (in spite of the official position of the French government) offered their services to the Guinean government in order to enable it to survive the abrupt departure of French officials. Above all, within three months of Guinean independence, nine Eastern bloc countries had signed bilateral agreements with Guinea and the government of Ghana granted it a loan of ten million pounds. Finally, in December 1958, Guinea was formally admitted to the international community when it became the eighty-second member of the United Nations Organization.

Inside Guinea, these events at the international level had the effect of creating a sense of a common destiny for all the inhabitants of Guinea regardless of ethnic, religious and linguistic differences. The following song which was widely sung throughout Guinea shortly after independence helps to illustrate this new national spirit:

Good-bye, Europeans
Good-bye, Europeans
And without a grudge
I, myself am not offended
Good-bye every one to his own home.

Without any fuss
Good-bye provided you disturb us no more.

Let him follow you
He who believes you indispensable.[6]

The adoption of a republican constitution together with a national anthem and a national flag were some of the actions taken by the Guinean leaders to emphasize the new national spirit. In addition, they also introduced the following terms into their public speeches: 'liberty', 'dignity', 'sovereignty' and 'responsibility'. According to the Guinean leaders, these terms stand for great values which national independence won for all Guinean citizens; all other considerations (for example, material wealth) are to be subordinated to the possession of these values.[7]

The Guinean leaders extended their search for an international identity beyond the dissociation from the former colonial power to include a formal rejection of membership of the two power blocs: 'We shall not join either of the blocs, we shall determine our policy in advance and all those who wish, on the basis that we have defined, to co-operate with us, will be our good partners.'[8] This policy is called 'positive neutrality'.

Because of the cautious reception given to the Guinean independence by Western bloc countries, the Guinean government's numerous agreements with Eastern bloc countries led many observers to question the genuineness of Guinean neutrality and some of them described Guinea as 'an African bridgehead for world communism' between 1958 and 1961.

However, when, in 1961, the Guinean government expelled the Russian ambassador for alleged involvement in the country's internal affairs,[9] this verdict became untenable. Again, when as a result of an experiment with a free market economy, the Guinean government was receiving important economic and financial aid from Western bloc countries, especially the United States, the country's policy of positive neutrality was called into question and Guinea was described in some quarters as 'an American protectorate.'[10]

In 1966, when this viewpoint was most widespread, the Guinean government ordered the American ambassdor in Conakry to be put under house arrest because of the American government's refusal to secure the release of a Guinean ministerial delegation detained in Accra during a stop-over of the Pan-American Airways aeroplane on which it was travelling.[11] In addition, the government ordered the sixty or so American Peace Corps members who were engaged in agriculture and teaching in several towns and villages to leave Guinea within a few days.

These two confrontations with the leading representatives of the two power blocs were skilfully used by the Guinean leadership to arouse patriotic fervour among the masses. This was particularly true of the 1966 incident when the members of the party's youth wing, the JRDA, spontaneously attacked and destroyed the American cultural centres in Conakry and other big cities of the country.[12] At international level, the two incidents helped to demonstrate that Guinea was not prepared to be anybody's puppet. Similarly, in reacting to the quarrel between Russia and China which assumed serious proportions in the 1960s, the Guinean leadership carefully avoided expressing support for either side; instead, it successfully maintained good relations with both sides. Clear evidence of the Guinean leadership's success in pursuing a policy of positive neutrality is the fact that since the late 1960s, China, Russia and the other Eastern bloc countries on the one hand and America and the other Western bloc countries on the other have joined the government as partners in establishing mining and manufacturing industries in Guinea.

A special dimension of Guinean nationalism and neutrality is provided by what the Guinean leaders refer to as the 'permanent plot'. According to them, since the vote for independence in September 1958, there has been a permanent plot against the PDG-led government of the state. The editorial of the party organ, *Horoya,* of 12 September 1971 put this point as follows:

> If we won our independence without any violence, it still remains true that the threats and attempts at colonial reconquest constituted since 1958 a sword of Damocles suspended over the young Guinean nation.

The first report of a 'plot' against the Guinean government was in April 1960. Some nationalist French soldiers based in Senegal and the Ivory Coast who were bent on making Guinea 'French' planned to overthrow the PDG regime and replace it with a new government led by men who would announce the return of Guinea to the French community. To achieve this objective, these soldiers established contacts with some Guinean ex-servicemen and some anti-PDG elements inside Guinea. According to the French journalist, G. Chaffard, the French soldiers hoped that a successful operation in Guinea would help to brighten a little the woeful balance sheet of French anti-independence campaigns which have failed in Vietnam (Dien Bien Phu) and in North Africa.[13] The plot was uncovered and President Touré used the occasion of announcing the discovery of the plot as an opportunity for appealing to the patriotic sense of the Guinean masses. An American research student who was doing field work in Guinea at this time summed up his impression as follows:

> Whether the plot was legitimate or not, its effect was to weld the Guinean people together against what they

considered to be a threat to their country. Differences between Soussou, Foulah and Malinké were temporarily forgotten; everyone was a Guinean. With a welter of resolutions swearing fealty to the National Political Bureau and unswerving faith in the Party, patriotic fervour reached a pitch of near delirium.[14]

Although the degree of French involvement in this plot is not exactly known, it is important to mention that relations between Guinea and France had remained strained since 1958. For example, the French government tried to prevent the admission of Guinea into UNO in December 1958. In January 1959, the two countries signed three protocols of agreement dealing with cultural, financial and technical matters. Guinea agreed to remain in the franc zone and France promised to send teachers to Guinea. Furthermore, both countries agreed to exchange diplomats. But in March 1960, Guinea voluntarily opted out of the franc zone and by that date, neither country had bothered to send an ambassador to the other's capital.

In 1961, the Guinean government announced the discovery of a second plot called the 'Teachers' Plot'. The origin of this plot was a dispute between the Guinean government and the country's Teachers' Union over better working conditions. However, in the document of claims presented by the teachers, there were some left-wing ideological criticisms of the government and this prompted the government to arrest the leaders of the Teachers' Union. In the tract distributed by the pupils who were demonstrating in support of their teachers was the following: 'It is impossible for a country to be neutral between the East and the West. It is necessary to choose one bloc or the other.'[15] The Guinean leaders interpreted this to mean that the government was asked to become a member of the Eastern bloc. The Russian ambassador who was believed to have been in support of the idea was expelled as a demonstration that the government was resolutely committed to the policy of positive

The Quest for a National Identity 123

neutrality. Naturally, public attention was not drawn to the fact that the incident allowed the incumbent PDG leadership to ward off a challenge from the left-wing of the party.

The next two 'plots' — the 'Traders Plot' of 1965 and the 'plot of the military' of 1969 — are said to have been essentially aimed at overthrowing the incumbent PDG leadership in Guinea and replacing it with a France-oriented government:[16] the new leaders to be installed in 1965 were traders while in 1969 the new leadership was to be drawn from the military. There is an independent corroboration of the Guinean allegation that France was involved in the 1965 plot. This was provided by a French journalist writing in *Le Monde* of 6/7 March 1966. It is important to mention that the French government did not formally deny this allegation.[17] As in the case of the 1960 plot, the announcement of these two plots was used as an occasion for arousing the patriotism of the Guinean masses in support of the legitimate national government smarting under the unwarranted challenge of the former colonial power.

Finally, in November 1970, Guinea was the victim of a Portuguese-led sea-borne invasion of which the writer was an eye-witness. While the Portuguese elements in the invading force concentrated their attention on the release of the Portuguese soldiers kept as prisoners of war by the Independence Party of Guinea and Cape Verde (PAIGC), the Guinean dissidents who were members of the invading force were expected to join forces with internal dissidents to overthrow the PDG leadership. A new government was to be installed that would expel the PAIGC from Guinea and would radically modify the existing policy of positive neutrality by being extremely friendly with some Western bloc countries especially Western Germany which were in support of the invasion. Although the PAIGC prisoners were successfully released and taken away, the plan to overthrow the Touré-led PDG regime failed. The open battle that ensued between the invaders and

Guinean soldiers, militia members and ordinary citizens turned out to be an unprecedented opportunity for involving the masses in the defence of national independence, dignity, responsibility and sovereignty. This was followed by a spontaneous nation-wide contribution of money, food and clothes for the victims of the aggression. It was later announced that about 150,000,000 GF were collected.[18]

All this has enabled the Guinean regime to present a self-image of a patriotic and nationalist regime. The masses accept this image to a great extent. As a means of constantly reminding the masses of this self-image, Guinean leaders punctuate their speeches with references to Guinea as 'The country of 28 September', and to the people as 'The valiant people of 28 September and of 22 November', 'The heroic people of Guinea', 'The invincible people of Guinea'. This image of a 'proud', 'valiant' and 'heroic' people is reflected in the content of Guinean history developed since independence. Of pre-colonial Guinea, the national history emphasizes the orderly administration and the modernizing efforts in Samory Touré's Ouassoulou Empire and in Alfa Yaya Diallo's Foutah kingdom. In the accounts of the confrontations between the French colonialists and these Guinean traditional rulers, the former are cast in the role of villains and the latter are portrayed as heroic victims. This nationalist history is of course not merely an imaginary tale as these two Guinean traditional leaders were actually exiled by the French colonial administration and they died in foreign lands, Samory Touré in Gabon and Yaya Diallo in Mauritania. In 1967, the Guinean regime brought back the 'remains' of these two national heroes to rebury them in the mausoleum in Conakry where the busts of both men now feature prominently. By teaching this nationalist history to Guineans from the primary school to the university, the regime hopes to inculcate nationalist feelings into the youth.[19]

On the whole, it appears that the strategy of the Guinean

The Quest for a National Identity 125

leaders has paid off handsomely. All visitors to Guinea that I know — including scholars, journalists and members of official delegations — are unanimously agreed that the Guineans are a proud people. Another factor that has made this single national image possible is the fairly high degree of ethnic integration achieved by the Guinean regime.

Ethnic Integration

Prior to 1958, Guinea was notorious among FWA territories for its intense ethnic rivalries. 'Throughout [French] West Africa Guinea was the most profoundly [ethnically] divided country between 1946 and 1958.'[20] In 1947, the Guinean Territorial Assembly could not agree on the location of a secondary school for which the colonial administration had made money available. Each of the four major ethnic groups wanted the school in its area: the Soussou wanted it in Conakry, the Foulahs in Dalaba, the Malinkés in Kankan and the forest people in N'zérékoré. After five years of continuous wrangling the money voted for the school was used for another purpose.[21]

In May 1958, Conakry was the scene of bloody riots between Foulahs and Soussous. Official figures put the number of the dead at sixteen and those wounded were estimated at about 100. Eye-witness accounts claim that the actual figures were much higher.[22]

During its struggle against the French colonial administration in the 1950s, the PDG leadership realized that ethnic particularism was a key weapon of the other political parties inside Guinea against the mass orientation of the PDG. Although a number of ethnic associations were allowed to integrate with the PDG,[23] the party leaders were determined to de-emphasize ethnic loyalty in political participation. The first action taken in this direction was the nomination of five PDG leaders in 1956 to contest municipal elections outside their regions of origin. The list included Sékou Touré, a Malinké, who was elected the Mayor of Conakry (a Soussou city). All the other PDG candidates won their elections. A similar step was taken in 1957 after the PDG had won fifty-six out of the sixty seats in the Territorial Assembly. The party leadership decided that all the deputies (title of the members of the assembly) from Middle Guinea (inhabited by the Foulahs) were to give account of their stewardship in Upper Guinea (inhabited by the Malinkés); deputies of Upper Guinea were to be responsible to the electorate of Maritime Guinea (inhabited by the Soussous); deputies of Maritime Guinea were to be responsible to the electorate of Forest Guinea (inhabited by the forest ethnic groups); and, finally, deputies of Forest Guinea were to be responsible to the electorate of Middle Guinea.[24]

Although the PDG leadership did not specifically interpret its decision of December 1957 to abolish the chieftaincy institution as an act designed to promote ethnic integration, it can now be said in retrospect that this decision has helped to destroy an important symbol of ethnic particularism. In exercise of the powers conferred on it by the *loi-cadre* of 1956, the PDG-controlled Council of Government approved a ministerial order of 31 December 1957 which formally abolished 'the chieftaincy of *cantons* called "traditional chieftaincy" all over the territory of French Guinea'.[25] The argument of the PDG then was that the chiefs had oppressed their fellow Africans in their enthusiasm to serve the colonial administration.[26] It is significant to mention that the decision to abolish traditional chieftaincy was taken at a meeting attended by French commandants (district officers), Guinean ministers and the French governor who was the chairman.[27] More importantly, the decision was enthusiastically welcomed by the vast majority of Guineans. With the abolition of the chieftaincy institution, a traditional centre of power which was also a rallying point for ethnic solidarity was destroyed;

this action can now be described as important groundwork for the PDG's post-independence programme of ethnic integration.

Another important pre-independence step taken towards ethnic integration was at the party's third Congress in January 1958 where the leaders became convinced that the mass orientation had become well established and they announced the abolition of ethnic-based party committees. This decision was followed up in June 1958 by the creation of a single youth movement of the PDG called the *Jeunesse de la révolution démocratique africaine* (JRDA) as a means of discouraging ethnic-based youth associations. When the PDG leaders assumed the full exercise of state powers as a result of the famous 'No' vote, they pursued the fight against ethnic particularism by including an article in the newly independent country's constitution aimed at discouraging it: 'Any act of racial discrimination as well as all propaganda of a racial or regional character shall be punishable by law.' (Article 45 of the Guinean constitution.) In February 1959, the relevant law was enacted.[28] In it, an 'act of racial discrimination' was defined as:

> Speeches, slogans, threats, proffered in meetings or public places tending to favour the predominance of one race or tribe in the nation.
>
> Writings, printed matters, sold or distributed, put on sale or exposed in meetings or in public places, notices or placards exposed to the public sight, aiming at ends defined in the preceding paragraph.

An 'act of regional discrimination' was defined as:

> Positive acts carried out by one of the methods enumerated in the preceding article, having as direct or indirect goal to place the interest of one or several men in one specific

region of the territory above the imperative of national unity determined by the central government.

Any offender against this law is liable to punishment of two to five years imprisonment and 70,000 to 700,000 francs fine, 'without prejudice to the provisions relative to attempts detrimental to the internal security of the state if that is the case'.

Although there has been no occasion when this law has been invoked (at least, as far as available sources went), its usefulness appears to be its deterrent effect. Compared with the pre-independence period of intense ethnic conflicts, the immediate years after independence were marked by a remarkable inter-ethnic harmony.[29] President Touré was so impressed by this achievement that in 1962 he declared;

> There is no more in the Republic of Guinea the Malinké race, the Soussou race, the Foulah race, the Guerzé race, the Landouma or Kissi race. The Soussou, Malinké, Toma, Guerzé, Foulah, Landouma or Kissi have taken up their language differentiation as a means of communication between men. Thus, every youth of Guinea, every adult of Guinea asked about his race will reply that he is African.[30]

It was not long before President Touré openly admitted that he had exaggerated the progress made in combating ethnic particularism. In May 1964, he corrected his 1962 assessment as follows:

> Regionalism and racism have not completely disappeared. They still exist with many of us, but less with our militants than with others. Our great victory, however, is that the people, in an official manner, can no more believe in regionalism and racism.[31]

Later in the same year, President Touré appealed to his countrymen:

The Quest for a National Identity 129

> Let us accept to become new men; let us accept to kill in us the Malinké man, the Soussou man, the Toma man, the Guerzé man, let us accept to be transformed into new men fit to rehabilitate Guinea and Africa, fit to serve the universal cause of man.[32]

In the late 1960s, President Touré came up with the idea that the Guineans who have remained devoted to ethnic particularism are the 'counter-revolutionaries', that is, those opposed to the PDG regime.

> And how can we detect the hidden accomplices [of imperialism] within the revolution . . . they are those who still think as a Foulah, a Malinké, a Toma, a Guerzé instead of as a Guinean and an African or better still, as a revolutionary . . .[33]

On the whole, there is abundant evidence that inter-ethnic relations in Guinea since independence are characterized by a fairly high degree of cordiality and harmony that was unknown in pre-independence Guinea. Most observers of post-independence developments in Guinea who have paid attention to this subject are likely to endorse the following verdict passed by the French scholar, Claude Rivière, after four years of teaching, research and extensive travel inside Guinea:

> In Guinea, integration is less formal, and therefore more solid, than in any other African country. We believe that it is impossible to envisage a future similar to that of the Congo [now called Zaire] or of Nigeria [affected by Civil War]; it is impossible to think of the emergence of tribal nationalisms similar to those of the Masai in Kenya and Tanzania, of the Ewes in Ghana and Togo. While conserving a certain strength at the regional level, ethnic particularism has given place to the idea of a nation . . . the majority of the élite — and it is this group that will lead the nation —

has been able to relegate its ethnic consciousness to an almost subliminal level, in any case, to a level much inferior to that of its national consciousness.[34]

The secret of the Guinean leaders' success in this task lies in their consistent pursuit of practical steps aimed at reducing the citizens' allegiance to ethnic particularism.[35] We have already seen that they started to tackle this problem prior to independence by emphasizing mass membership of the PDG. The positive result achieved — as shown in the tremendous increase in party membership which rose from 300,000 in 1953 to 800,000 in 1957 — must have been a great encouragement. The political institutional framework established after independence, consisting of a single party with nation-wide structures including special parallel structures for the youth, women and workers and a nation-wide administrative machine, has played a critical role in this task of placing allegiance to the national community above allegiance to an ethnic group.

Another practical step that has been taken in Guinea is something close to what political scientists commonly refer to as 'ethnic arithmetic' in the distribution of key posts and amenities. In his study of the ethnic origin of the holders of the top political and administrative posts in Guinea between 1958 and 1967, a French scholar, B. Charles, confirms that some attention has been paid to 'ethnic arithmetic'. Charles draws attention to the fact that the Malinkés (President Touré's ethnic group) have been more favoured than the others considering their share of the total population.

Perhaps the point to emphasize in the following table is the extent to which there is a fair representation of the different ethnic groups. And if any case deserves special mentioning, it should be the under-representation of the Forest People rather than the over-representation of the Malinkés. Of course, it is easy to see why it is the latter point that makes a more interesting story. President Touré does admit from time to

Table 3: *'Ethnic Arithmetic'* in the Distribution of Key Political and Administrative Posts in Guinea, 1958–1967*

Ethnic Group	Percentage of Total Population	Percentage of Total Key Posts
Foulah	29	26
Malinké	34	37
Soussou	17	18
Forest	18	8
Others	2	11†
Total	100	100

Notes: *The posts on which this analysis is based are ministers, secretaries of state, ambassadors, the majority of senior civil servants in the central government administration at headquarters, regional governors, the secretaries to regional governors, some commandants of arrondissements, directors and deputy directors of national and regional enterprises. This added up to 1200 individuals.
†This large discrepancy between the population classified as 'Others' and the percentage of posts they occupy is due to the fact that while Charles included ethnic groups 'assimilated' by the larger groups in the percentages for the latter, the calculation of posts held is based on a stricter definition of the ethnic groups. Furthermore, all cases of doubt were classified as 'Others'.

Source: Adapted from B. Charles, 'Cadres guinéens et appartenance ethnique'. Thesis for the *doctorat et recherche 'Etudes politiques'* (Paris 1968), pp. 18, 122.

time that some 'ethnic arithmetic' is practised but he clearly does not see a case for proportional representation or a strict quota system. On the contrary, he is positively against such an idea. Thus, in an obvious reference to some underground complaints about the ethnic composition of the military leadership in 1973, he said:

> Did the people have to vote for military officers? We found some of you as officers [at independence] and because you were officers, whether there were more Malinkés than Guerzés, or more Guerzés than Soussous, or more Soussous than Conniaguis or Foulahs, whose fault was it? In any case, it is not our fault.[36]

With regard to amenities, the Guinean leaders have shown concern for even distribution as much as possible. After the first development plan (the Three-Year Plan) had been completed, there were underground complaints that practically nothing had been done in Middle Guinea, the home of the Foulahs. President Touré openly explained that the government was aware of the need for even development but that there were certain economic factors that could not be disregarded.[37] Fortunately for the regime, the mining explorations carried out during the second plan revealed an important bauxite deposit in Middle Guinea — the Tougué deposit mined by Alusuisse. The geographical areas inhabited by the four major ethnic groups are covered by the intense mining activities that are now going on in the country: Fria and Boké bauxite deposits in Maritime Guinea; Tougué bauxite deposit in Middle Guinea; the Mali cement in Upper Guinea; and the Nimba-Simandou iron ore in Forest Guinea.

Attention has already been drawn to the fairly uniform distribution of social amenities such as health, educational and recreational facilities. Mention was also made of the language policy of the regime which is seeking to develop all the eight national languages spoken by sizable proportions of the population. While the outside observer might question the wisdom of this language policy considering the problem of language development, President Touré sees it as evidence of the regime's commitment to 'observe a strict equality between the ethnic communities ... the development of the national culture by the rebirth of our written languages'.[38]

Finally, the constitutional provision that Guinea is a secular state provides a written guarantee for the fifteen per cent or so of the total population who are not Muslims. These people are found almost exclusively in Maritime Guinea and Forest Guinea. The majority of the people in the former area are Christians (mostly Catholics) while in the latter area traditional forms of religion predominate. By adopting a religious reform programme that affected all the three forms of religious expression, the regime has successfully prevented religious differences from giving rise to ethnic conflicts. First, the regime abolished the particularisms of the Catholic and Islamic religions by taking over all religious schools (since 1961) and by africanizing the Catholic clergy in 1967. Second, it has led a fairly successful campaign against some evil practices associated with Islam (fanaticism, inter-sect conflicts and the exploitation of the masses by some religious leaders called *marabouts*) and against the irrational beliefs associated with traditional forms of worship (magic, long periods of initiation in sacred forests and human sacrifice). Although some Malinkés (Muslims) still despise the forest ethnic groups (worshippers of traditional religions) and many Soussous (most Catholics) still regard the Foulahs (Muslims) as enemies, in neither case is the religious factor emphasized. The grounds of competition are now those of political and economic powers.

In all, the ethnic factor which is widely recognized as a major cause of political instability in many African states has been successfully prevented from playing this negative role in Guinea. This means that the Guinean regime has achieved a fair measure of success in its quest for a national identity for all the inhabitants of its territorial area regardless of their ethnic, religious and linguistic differences. We shall now turn to two other factors that have helped to make this remarkable achievement possible: the concept of a party-nation and the role of a charismatic and flexible national leader.

The Party-Nation

In his book called *Guinée, la marche du peuple* (Dakar, 1968), Alpha Diawara who writes as a participant-observer of Guinean affairs uses the concept of party-nation to describe his viewpoint that the past, present and future of Guinea is inseparably tied to that of the PDG. Although Diawara does not elaborate on this concept in his book, it seems to be useful for summing up the contribution of the PDG to the task of formulating a national identity for all Guineans. President Touré has provided the following definition of this concept: 'Today, the PDG has become a party-state.... Our party and our state are fused in the same way as our party is fused with the people.'[39]

One of the earliest actions taken by the Guinean leaders after the proclamation of national independence was the announcement that the PDG-controlled government was committed to a Democratic African Revolution (*Révolution démocratique africaine*). The national radio was baptized the 'Voice of the Revolution' and the word 'revolution' was frequently mentioned in the speeches and writings of all the leaders of the new regime. Consciously or unconsciously, the Guinean leaders were confirming the view of Professor S. Lipset that 'in most post-colonial nations, it is revolutionary ideas, not conservative ones, that are associated with the national image'.[40]

As a logical follow-up of this revolutionary national image, the PDG was christened a revolutionary party and all its policies and orientations (i.e. its ideology) were described as revolutionary. This party ideology is also the national ideology.

> There is no problem that is beyond the comprehension of our party, there is no problem which it cannot control, analyse or solve in a fit and just manner ... The party constitutes the thought of the people of Guinea at its highest level and in its most complete form ... Not only is it the party which has thought, but it is it which 'is' thought. It is it which must determine the forms of the use of techniques in function of the political goals which it has fixed. It is the party which indicates to the engineer, the doctor, the magistrate, the teacher as well as to the worker and the peasant, the objectives that they must achieve in their own fields, conditions in which they must achieve them and the reasons which have led the party to choose one objective instead of another.[41]

According to a participant-observer, A. I. Diallo, in his study called 'L'Evolution des institutions administratives de la République de Guinée de 1958 à 1968', the claims made for the party are not gratuitous: 'No human activity takes place outside the party whether it is baptism, marriage or any other ceremony. Food supply for civil servants or militants is carried out through the channels of the party committee.'[42]

The Guinean regime relies on the nation-wide party structures as the means of ensuring that the claims made for the party are effectively translated into practice. The base committees (the PRLs) occupy the critical position here. The entire administration of the affairs of each PRL is left to the PRL executive and to some other members that are called upon to help, notably within the brigades. Birth, marriage and death certificates are received from the PRL president; he presides over the administration of justice; he supervises the distribution of food and of mail. In the Muslim areas, the PRL headquarters serves as the mosque and in many cases it is the PRL president who presides over the Friday worship. To crown all this, PRL members meet once a week at the party headquarters to participate in a session of political education. In these circumstances, it is easy to see how, for the ordinary Guinean, the party and the nation are synonymous.

The party sections and federations do not have the same effects on the life of Guinean masses as the PRLs for the reason explained in Chapter 2 (see pp. 31—33). However, as a means of providing a permanent party leadership above the PRL level, the leaders of party federations called federal secretaries were made permanent and paid party officers in 1967. In each administrative region of Guinea, (the borders of a party federation and an administrative region are coterminous except in the case of Conakry) it is the federal secretary rather than the regional governor who is described as the local chief executive. During a visit to five regions in 1971, the writer saw that the centre of regional power was the party headquarters, not the administrative secretariat. Party headquarters and residential accommodation for the federal secretaries were constructed between 1968 and 1971 to match the facilities provided for the administration under colonial rule. The federal secretary helps to maintain the image of a party-nation through his position as the local chief executive. He presides over all regional ceremonies of a political, economic or cultural nature. In particular, he joins the regional imam to preside over the important Muslim ceremonies such as the festivities marking the end of the Ramadan.

In 1964, the four natural regions of the country were constituted into politico-administrative units called ministerial delegations (renamed as Ministries for Rural Development in 1973) and placed under political heads who, among other things, were to provide overall political leadership. By 1973, it was found that their effectiveness in the political sphere had been very limited and henceforth they were to concentrate their energies on promoting rural development, hence the new title of Ministries for Rural Development. But it was still considered necessary to provide another party authority above the federal level. For this purpose, the party's ninth Congress held in 1972 decided to make every member of the newly elected twenty-five member Central Committee with the exception of the secretary general into a kind of political commissar 'charged with the organization, stimulation and co-ordination as well as the control of the different political, economic, social, cultural and administrative activities of one or several regions'. In a manner reminiscent of the pre-independence method of combating ethnic particularism, the Central Committee's political commissars are assigned to a region or regions inhabited by people of a different ethnic group from their own.[43]

Finally, at national level, everything is done in the name of the party: the party's Congresses lay down the broad outlines of national policies; the National Council of the Revolution (CNR) follows up these policies in between the sessions of the Congress; the Central Committee and its executive, the BPN act as the effective ruling bodies of the nation. This arrangement is underlined by the fact that the secretary general of the party who is the leading member of the BPN is also the president of the republic, and he shares with the other members of the BPN responsibility for the entire work of the government.

The only important qualification of this picture of a total party control of national life in Guinea is the position of the administrative machinery which is in theory considered as an 'instrument' of the party. In practice, the administrative machinery has played a more important role than the party ideology suggests and in certain areas such as the maintenance of the central authority and the implementation of development plans, it emerges clearly as an individual personality. This distinctive existence of the administrative machine is further underlined by the repect of the Guinean regime's leadership for the basic principles of a career system of administration —

permanency of tenure, fixed salary, recruitment by qualifications or through competitive examinations and regular promotions — in the management of its personnel with only a few modifications. However, the constant de-emphasis of the role of the administrative machinery together with the involvement of many of its leading officers in the party structures (the partisan bureaucrats) has had the effect of leaving the image of a party-nation intact in the eyes of the Guinean masses.

Another important factor that has contributed to the image of a party-nation in Guinea is the way in which the regime's leadership has sought to resolve all major national conflicts within the party structures: inter-ethnic; religious; the young versus the old; men versus women; rural versus urban; mass versus élite; soldiers versus civilians. The nation-wide party structures emphasize a common allegiance to a national authority and thereby undermine the appeal of ethnic particularism. There are cases where the federal secretary does not belong to the dominant ethnic group of his area. This was the case in Mamou in 1971 (during the writer's visit there) when a Malinké was the federal secretary of a predominantly Foulah area. We have already mentioned the deliberate policy of appointing the Central Committee's political commissars to serve outside their native areas.

As already mentioned, religious conflict has been avoided in Guinea by the adoption and implementation of a reform programme that uniformly affects all the forms of religious expression within the country. This reform programme was adopted in the name of the party and carried out under its supervision and in many cases with its active participation. For example, in the arrondissement of Bofossou in Forest Guinea, it was a party meeting that decided after a public debate to destroy all the magical objects used for traditional worship in the area. The long period of initiation into adulthood among the Tomas (it lasted for about three years in 1958) was first reduced to three months in 1959 and was later abolished altogether by the national leadership of the PDG. Because of the large size of the Muslim population, special attention is paid to the Islamic religion. Since the late 1960s, party dominance over the Islamic religion is expressed by the fact that BPN leaders preside over the national Muslim festivals side by side with the imams and on ordinary praying days, the federal bureau, the section executive and the PRL executive share prominence with local imams. Many PRL headquarters serve as mosques. And as a general (unwritten) rule, prayers to Allah are accompanied by prayers for the progress of the PDG regime.[44] The particularism of the Catholic religion was destroyed by the Africanization of its clergy in 1967 and since this date, it is the PDG leadership that recommends the appointment of a Catholic archbishop and bishops.

With regard to the generational conflict between the youth and the elders, the PDG leadership has itself created a virile youth organization, the JRDA, which has been allowed to watch over the interests of the youth. However, the party leadership makes it clear that the JRDA is not an autonomous pressure group but an integral part of the nation-wide party structure; it is formally called a 'parallel institution' of the party. For example, a BPN delegation presides over the periodic elections to the JRDA's National Executive. In March 1959, the party leadership declared the JRDA as the single national institution for all Guinean youth. One of the reasons for this decision was the leadership's desire to abolish the existing ethnic — and religious-based — youth associations. Although there were some protests against this decision, it was not seriously challenged and it seems to have contributed much to the fairly high degree of ethnic harmony inside Guinea. As a watchdog of the interests of the youth, the JRDA has concentrated its attention in three major areas of activity: culture and sports, national defence and 'revolutionary' moral.

The party programme of cultural revival embarked upon

after independence has relied heavily on the JRDA and the impressive results achieved to date (*supra*) are a tribute to the energy and dynamism of the JRDA. The achievements of the JRDA in the field of sports are equally considerable (*supra*). Between 1961 and 1965 the JRDA proposed to the party's national leadership various programmes aimed at mobilizing the youth; first, in 1961, there was a plan to create youth camps (*chantiers-école*) for post-primary students who failed to qualify for secondary school; nothing came out of this decision which was followed by the creation of five revolutionary camps (*chantiers révolutionnaires*) in 1964; again, this project was shortlived and finally, it was decided in 1966 to create a civic brigade and a popular militia. The former was to consist of seventeen to thirty year olds and each arrondissement was to have one. An arrondissement civic brigade was to consist of 100 to 150 members who were expected to help in the 'defence of the revolution' and in 'economic production'.[45] Less than half of the arrondissements successfully established their civic brigades which did not function effectively; in 1971, all the members of civic brigades (about 8000 of them) were incorporated into the Guinean popular army.

The decision to create the popular militia was influenced by a combination of a number of developments in the internal and external political environments: the 'Traders' Plot' of October 1965, the overthrow of President Nkrumah of Ghana in February 1966, and the activities of the Chinese Red Guards which began in August 1966. The functions of the militia were defined as follows:

> the protection of the national frontiers, of the big economic installations, the security of the towns, ports, airports, banks, radio, petrol reservoirs and other points of strategic importance, etc., patrols of public morality in the

towns, struggle against black-marketeers, prostitution and economic fraud.[46]

In order to ensure that the members of the militia would perform their functions well, it was stipulated that they were to be recruited from the 'élite cadres of the JRDA'. Those recruited were to undergo 'an intensive, complete and continuous military training'. 'Discipline, dignified behaviour, physical and moral courage, discretion must constitute the dominant qualities of the popular militia.'[47] About 8000 people were recruited and they were trained by a Cuban military delegation as well as by the Guinean national army. The overthrow of Modibo Kéita of Mali in 1968 and the 'Military Plot' of 1969 further led the regime to intensify the military training of the militia. During the 1970 invasion, the militia played a significant role in the defence of Conakry. Special mention should be made of a contingent of the Conakry Polytechnic's militia which played a significant role in the liberation of the Boiro military camp (situated at a distance of about three kilometres from the polytechnic) from the hands of the invaders.[48]

In March 1971, President Touré announced the regime's decision to train all students of upper secondary and of higher educational institutions (about 30,000) as members of the popular militia. In addition each arrondissement is expected to recruit about 1000 members; the national total is to be about 300,000.[49] This means that a large proportion of the JRDA will be involved in national defence. The JRDA's role as the defenders of 'revolutionary' morale has also been given considerable attention. The dance halls and hotels are regularly patrolled and prostitution has been effectively banished in these places. The JRDA prescribes the dress, make-up and the kind of music that are allowed and they are responsible for ensuring that their prescriptions are obeyed. For example, at its sixth Congress held in 1971, the JRDA decided that in any area where 'Yeye' music is played during a dance, the local JRDA executive will be dissolved. Judging by past performance, this 'Yeye' ban will become effective.

In addition to the above methods of involving the youth in the national political process, there is a youth representation in the party's Congress, the CNR and the Central Committee. Some youth leaders, too, are appointed as ministers, ambassadors, regional governors and directors of national and regional enterprises. However, one cannot say that there is a conscious policy of preparing the younger generation for political succession as only about five out of the twenty-five-member strong Central Committee elected in 1972 were below thirty-five years of age.[50] On the other hand, there is no real sign of intergenerational conflict. The clashes reported between the students of the polytechnics and the regime's leadership (in 1970, 1972 and 1973) have been connected with demands for improved campus facilities without any political overtones.

The women's organization, like the JRDA, is a pressure group within the PDG whose major responsibility is to watch over the interests of women. Like the JRDA, too, it is called a 'parallel institution' of the party. The existence of this single women's national organization with nation-wide structures that cuts across ethnic, religious and linguistic barriers is one of the factors that has helped to promote national integration in Guinea. As a pressure group, the women's organization's central task has been to mobilize support for the PDG's programme of women's emancipation. The objective of this programme is to replace the subordination of women to men within the traditional social systems of the country by a new social order in which men and women are treated as equals. To achieve this objective, the regime reformed the traditional practices related to marriage which to a great extent, accounted for the subordination of women to men. A civil marriage became compulsory, a minimum age of seventeen was fixed for the female partner, dowry was reduced to a symbolic sum payable to the female partner before a civil authority, and in 1968, polygamy was abolished. Although these measures have not been fully applied — the law on polygamy has proved very difficult to enforce — they have considerably improved the social standing of women.

Three other activities which the women's organization has actively supported have also contributed to the improved social standing of women. First, there has been a tremendous expansion in female education: the percentage of girls of school-going age in school rose from four in 1958 to twenty in 1967 and, in 1971, eleven per cent of the students in the Conakry Polytechnic were female. Second, the regime has paid some attention to the development of women's co-operatives for sewing, dyeing, embroidery, hair dressing and so on. In March 1972 these co-operatives were named Centres of Female Progress and their number was considerably increased: one for each party federation and a national centre in Conakry. Each centre was granted 120 million GF and they are now expected to function as commercial enterprises. (It is likely that some women's leaders actually lobbied for the 1972 grant.) Third, and finally, all professions are open to women. In 1973, in addition to a female member of the government (since 1958), there was a woman ambassador (at the UN), over twenty of the seventy-five members of the National Assembly and about 140 of 8000 members of regional assemblies were women; the women's organization was represented in the CNR and the Central Committee; and there were women in the army, the militia, the police, the administration and so on. Although some problems are still being experienced by both men and women in adjusting to the changes enumerated above — and these changes are indeed revolutionary in a predominantly Muslim society — the idea of equality between men and women has become established in Guinea and the current

Women's Liberation Movement in America and Western Europe will certainly make the regime feel proud of its achievement in this field.[51]

The problems of rural-urban and of mass-élite dichotomies are, like the other problems mentioned above, tackled within the party structure. The major factor here is that party membership is presented as a social equalization agent; all party members are equal regardless of whether they inhabit a rural or urban area and regardless of professional differences; the minister, the skilled worker, the civil servant, the teacher and the peasant are all equals. A number of additional practical steps have been taken to emphasize this commitment to social equality. At the introduction of higher education in Guinea in 1963, the regime's leadership decided that all polytechnic students must spend a month of every long vacation working in rural areas. This practice was also extended to Guineans studying abroad who were brought home at the government's expense and has continued ever since. Starting with the first graduates of the Conakry Polytechnic, every Guinean graduate must spend three months (the duration was at first only one month) working with a PRL after the successful completion of the compulsory ideological seminar. With the exception of a few graduates (for example, those qualified to pursue research and medical graduates) this three-month rural experience is a prerequisite for obtaining employment. In addition to exposing the young graduates to rural life, they are also specifically required to supervise the proper functioning of the PRLs and to organize literacy classes for PRL members.

In 1969, the regime's leadership announced a plan according to which the holders of key positions in the government and administration were to spend a brief spell in the rural areas annually. 2226 national cadres were involved — BPN members (excluding the head of state), ministers and all senior civil servants. They were divided into groups of ten to twelve and each group spent two weeks within an arrondissement where they were attached to the PRLs. The programme was organized for the period April—May which coincided with the harvesting of agricultural products. The national cadres joined the peasants in harvesting during the daytime and in the evening they discussed the proper functioning of PRLs. This programme was repeated in 1970 in exactly the same form. The aftermath of the 1970 invasion which has been marked by a large-scale purge of national cadres has so far prevented the continuation of this programme. Taken together, the students' compulsory rural experience and the rural stint for the national cadres constitute an effective method of promoting convergence between rural and urban and between mass and élite.

As a long term measure, the regime is relying on its programme aimed at making rural life attractive, namely, the creation of socialist communities throughout rural Guinea. Although these measures have produced some positive results, there is still an important problem of élite-mass gap within the party with the party officers as the 'élite' and the ordinary members as the 'mass'. However, as already mentioned, this new gap is not as wide as that which is found in other West African countries, although one cannot say whether the gap is widening or closing up.

Finally, the regime has also sought to resolve the military-civilian conflict within the party structure. In the mid-1960s, party committees were created within the armed forces. After the discovery of the 'Military Plot' of 1969, the regime's leadership felt that the integration of the military within the party structure had not prevented some army leaders from planning a *coup d'état*. It was then decided that the status of civil servant be extended to the members of the armed forces. There was also the additional provision that members of the armed forces could apply for admission to civil posts just as civil officers could apply to join the military ranks.[52] The soldiers were then baptized 'workers in uniform'. The November 1970 invasion has led to a reversal of this de-militarization policy. The strength of the army which was estimated at about 5000 in 1969 was increased to about 13,000 in 1971.

However, the regime's leadership still believes that the incorporation of the military within the party structure is not an adequate guarantee for army—civilian harmony. The solution adopted is the expansion of the popular militia which is to rise to the very high figure of about 300,000. Although the regime's leaders claim that the militia is essentially a complementary force to the armed forces, the military leaders see the militia as the potential allies of the civilian leaders in case of a confrontation between them. (Military-civilian conflict is discussed here only at the élite level where it really matters.) The following statement by President Touré in December 1970 (that is, shortly after the invasion) confirms this point:

> Every soldier who opposes the militia is an immediate or a potential recruit of imperialism which seeks to establish neo-colonialism within the armed forces everywhere; also, every soldier who opposes the militia is in fact opposing the democratic revolution.[53]

Unlike the other national conflicts examined above, the party structure has so far failed to resolve the military—civilian conflict.

On the whole, the attempt of the Guinean regime to formulate a national identity by presenting the party as the nation has proved fairly successful. Of the two outstanding problems mentioned above — the élite-mass gap within the party and the military—civilian conflict — neither appeared in 1973 to be a serious threat to the overall image of national harmony.

The Role of a Charismatic and Flexible National Leader

The central thesis of this study with regard to the role of President Touré in general is that in his dual capacity as the leader of Guinea's single party and the Head of State, he has practised flexible politics behind a façade of an inflexible and rigid ideology. In the task of formulating a national identity, President Touré has applied this same style of leadership.

On the basis of some statements made by President Touré, one gets the impression that he is a rigid unitarian who would like to will away the fact of ethnic, religious and linguistic differences. This rigid unitarianism is seen, for example, in such a statement as 'In Guinea, there must be no Soussou, no Malinké, no Kissi, . . . but only human beings who would have no personal responsibility to their places of origin'.[54] In a practical way, President Touré was the leading spirit behind the abolition of ethnic associations within the PDG and the creation of single national organizations for youth and women cutting across ethnic, religious and linguistic barriers. He has also been the most ardent advocate of the mass character of the PDG ('a single party for a single nation' as he sometimes puts it) as well as the chief exponent of the idea of unitary 'popular' power (in the place of the doctrine of the separation of powers) exercised by the party (*supra*). He summed up all this in 1970 as follows: 'The philosophy of the PDG is founded on the oneness of the state and the party in the service of the people.'[55]

But it was also the same President Touré who in 1968 considered it worthwhile to address the first set of graduates of the Conakry Polytechnic on what he called 'ethnic groups, the party and the national question'. The address started with the following significant sentence: 'Tribes, ethnic groups are social units which are historically constituted and characterized by geographical and linguistic community and an identity of behaviour and customs.'[56] At the end of this address which almost qualifies as a learned treatise, President Touré recommended three methods of creating a national identity. First, the existence of ethnic and social differences should be openly acknowledged. Repression should be rejected as a method of solving the problem; instead, these differences should be taken into account in the determination of national policies. Second, emphasis should be placed on the development of the different ethnic groups within the framework of the national community. Finally, it should be constantly stressed that 'no ethnic group can survive if the entire nation perishes under the dissolvent action of ethnic particularisms'.[57]

Just as President Touré has been the champion of the unitarian approach, he has also championed the application of the pragmatic and realistic methods summarized above. It is this combination that we have characterized as the Touré style of leadership, the practice of flexible politics behind a façade of a rigid and inflexible ideology. As the Head of State, it is President Touré who has always appointed people to the key political and administrative posts. This means that he is the brain behind the 'ethnic arithmetic' mentioned above in regard to the ethnic origin of the holders of these posts. Special mention should be made of Touré's particular concern about drawing public attention to one Foulah (Saifoulaye Diallo) and one Guerzé from Forest Guinea (Lansana Béavogui) who have been members of the BPN since 1958 (Diallo was dropped in 1972 but he is still a member of the Central Committee and of the government). In 1968, President Touré decorated both men with the Medal of Fidelity to the People and the Revolution for their 'very positive contribution to the work of national construction'. According to Touré, they have caused the failure of:

> the deviationist manoeuvres which the corrupt and racialist elements of their groups of origin have vainly tried with the

objective of dividing the party and the people on the reactionary basis of tribalism. In fact, if very early on the populations of the Lower Coast [notably the Soussous] banished tribalism from their political behaviour, this has taken longer for the Foulah and Forest intellectual elements.[58]

President Touré has also personally supervised the even distribution of social amenities throughout the country — health, educational and recreational facilities. Furthermore, he has watched over the creation and development of both the youth and women's organizations. These two organizations combine a unitarian aspect with a pragmatic mission. Their unitarian aspect lies in the fact that they are single national organizations cutting across ethnic and other barriers. But each organization also has a pragmatic mission: the youth organization is to watch over the interest of the youth and has so far prevented the emergence of an inter-generational conflict (youth versus age) inside Guinea; and the women's organization is charged with the care of women's interests with special reference to the abolition of the traditional role of women as subordinates to men. Another important illustration of Touré's resort to a pragmatic solution, despite the existence of an inflexible ideological position, is the way in which he has promoted the creation of a popular militia when the integration of the army within the party structure did not appear to be solving the military—civilian conflict. Of course, the formal appearance of ideological purity is still preserved as the army remains integrated within the party.

A critical factor in the Touré style of leadership described here is his charisma. As already mentioned, before Guinea became independent in 1958, Touré had become a charismatic leader. He acquired this quality on the basis of the leadership talent that he demonstrated between 1945, when he created the first trade union movement in Guinea, and 1957 when he became the leading nationalist in the territory. Operating on the platforms of the largest Guinean trade union movement (the local branch of the French Communist *Confédération générale du travail*, CGT) of which he was the leader and of the PDG of which he became the leader in 1952, Touré succeeded in impressing himself on the Guinean masses. He travelled extensively throughout Guinea and obtained a first-hand, almost 'clinical' knowledge of his people and their problems. He seized every opportunity provided by his trade union and political party platforms to attack the French colonial administration for not paying adequate attention to these problems. Perhaps the most notable success achieved by Touré during this period was the seventy-day strike he led in 1953 which resulted in a twenty per cent increase in the minimum wage and the introduction of a forty-hour week throughout FWA. From 1953, the ranks of the PDG began to grow and this was translated into good electoral results, again due largely to Touré's efforts. When, in 1957, elections were held for the purpose of establishing the territory's first local executive, the PDG won a landslide victory and Touré became the Vice-President of the Council of Government. For the masses, he had become 'syli', a local name for an elephant and this nickname was intended to signify that Touré, the elephant, could not be destroyed by the colonial administration. By this time, too, he had graduated from the colonial prison (in 1950) thus benefiting from the prestige that this 'honour' bestowed in colonial territories.

The full development of Touré's leadership talent has been made possible by his intuitive intelligence and great capacity for work, his sincerity, simplicity and transparent honesty. He is also a mob orator who can hold his audiences spellbound for about five hours of continuous speech-making. The new challenges posed by Guinean independence have served to bring Touré's leadership qualities into greater prominence. By the late 1960s he was generally expected to make wise

The Quest for a National Identity 151

decisions in all realms of political, social and economic affairs. Although he has not been able to live up to this infallibility demand,[59] his charisma still remains and each time he appears before a crowd either in Conakry or elsewhere in the country there is a spontaneous communion between the leader and the masses.

There is, however, one important negative aspect to Touré's style of leadership. It has generated the opposition of a small minority of Guineans consisting essentially of businessmen, intellectuals and members of the civil and military bureaucracies. This opposition is expressed with respect to the political, economic and social policies which the Touré-led PDG regime has pursued since independence. The cumulative effect of this opposition is that this bourgeois minority feels alienated from the national identity that the PDG regime is formulating and some of them have in fact left Guinea in voluntary exile. Can we still talk of an emergent national identity in Guinea while there exists a number of Guineans who feel completely alienated from it? From the titles given by the PDG regime to the 'plots' of 1961 ('Teachers'), 1965 ('Traders') and 1969 ('military'), it is clear that this minority is capable of challenging the PDG leadership. The alleged presence of a cross-section of this minority within the 'fifth column'[60] that was a party to the Portuguese-led invasion of 1970 further confirms the danger represented by this minority.

While recognizing the fact that a successful take-over of power by the bourgeois minority would certainly lead to significant modifications of the existing image of national identity which the PDG regime is formulating, we can still validly describe this existing image as national. The only important thing to do is to stress that it is a special kind of national identity — one that excludes a potentially dangerous faction of the society. It seems reasonable to say that there are only two possible outcomes to the problem mentioned here.

Either the PDG regime succeeds in planting the existing national identity very firmly in the minds of the vast majority of Guineans who seem to accept it at present, thereby leaving the bourgeois minority with a choice between a reluctant acceptance of the same or voluntary exile. Or the bourgeois minority may succeed in overthrowing the PDG regime and embark on a drastic modification of the existing national identity. All this adds up to the following question: what is the future of the Guinean experiment? The next chapter examines this question on the basis of an overall balance sheet of the experiment.

6. Balance Sheet of the Guinean Experiment and the Prospects for the Future

In order to situate the Guinean experiment examined in the preceding chapters in the correct historical perspective, it is important to emphasize that when the Guinean masses in response to the mobilization order of the PDG voted for independence in September 1958, very serious doubts were raised in certain quarters as to the ability of the new state to survive as a sovereign member of the international community. Indeed, about thirteen months after the historic vote, General de Gaulle who was then the President of France referred to Guinea as follows in his press conference of 23 October 1959:

> Guinea is for us a growing entity and we do not know into what it will develop. We shall watch what it will become and do under its present Council of Government, from the point of view of its policies and external contacts and *from the point of view of its capability, as a state, if it happens that a state can really be established there*... We shall establish our relations with Guinea in the light of what happens in these different fields. We shall do that without acrimony, but *without having, I should say, the certainty that what is today could continue tomorrow*... (italics added).[1]

It is now clear that Guinea has demonstrated its capability to survive as an independent member-state of the international community. However, in a somewhat different sense, one can still use the last part of General de Gaulle's statement in reference to Guinea after fifteen years of independence: is

153

there any certainty that what exists today in Guinea will continue tomorrow? Put differently, will the Guinea of Sékou Touré portrayed in the preceding chapters still preserve the same basic features after Touré has departed from the scene? Before attempting to answer this important question about the future of the Guinean experiment, we should like to draw together the major findings of the study.

Achievements

In the context of the framework within which this study has been conducted, there is a sense in which one can say that the Guinean experiment in nation building has been successful. This real achievement is the fact that fifteen years after the PDG took over the exercise of sovereign powers in Guinea, one can talk of an emerging national identity. The idea of a Guinean nation which made no sense in 1958 now has meaning. Of course, we are aware of the time dimension of nation building and there is therefore no suggestion here that the process of nation building has been completed in Guinea. In fact, there is hardly any nation about which one can make such a claim. As one American scholar has put it, 'The existence of a nation is a daily plebiscite.'[2] We shall now briefly recall the political, socio-cultural and economic achievements of the PDG regime.

Political Mobilization

The achievements of the PDG regime in the political sphere can be summed up by saying that the regime has successfully mobilized the Guinean society politically. The major instrument for achieving this effective political mobilization is the political institutions which the regime has developed as the framework for carrying out the basic political functions of the society. The PDG structure has responsibility for the authoritative allocation of values within the state and it relies on an administrative machinery as an 'instrument' for performing some of its functions.[3] The entire political process is operated in such a way that some form of participation is allowed to the population and attention is paid to the need to keep the governors as close to the governed as possible. Special mention should be made of the political education that has been carried out by the regime. The result of this effective political education is that it has produced such a high level of political consciousness that abstract political concepts like 'sovereignty', 'liberty' and 'imperialism' really mean something to the average Guinean. The writer was able to confirm this at political rallies and meetings and in private conversations with a cross-section of Guineans (traders, students, civil servants, workers, academics, men and women) during his two study visits in 1968 and in 1970-71. For example, in Guinea today, children, young people, men and women, repeat anti-imperialist slogans as Christians recite the 'Lord's Prayer' and, one would venture to say, with more or less the same degree of conviction.

> Today, the small baby at the breast of its mother, at the slogan 'imperialism?' responds 'down with it!'. . .
>
> Shout at two o'clock in the morning in any remote village: 'imperialism?' You will hear the reply 'down with it!'
>
> Henceforth, all the people know that its enemy number one, that which incarnates the Satan of the Koran, is none other than imperialism, colonialism and neo-colonialism.[4]

There is some exaggeration in this assertion but it contains a lot of truth.

It is important to mention that the three methods in the Guinean approach to nation building have proved suitable for promoting political mobilization. The idea of a mobilization-oriented single party as the central piece of the political institutional framework has worked out well even though a few problems have been encountered. Similarly, the doctrines that underlie the political institutions — the doctrine of party supremacy, the doctrine of the withering away of the state and the principle of democratic centralism — are broadly related to the objectives pursued by the party structure despite some important contradictions within them. Finally, in his dual role as the party leader and the Head of State, President Touré emerged as the chief operator of the political institutions and he clearly deserves some praise for the achievement of the mobilization effort. In particular, he has successfully managed to handle the conflicts and contradictions that arise from his different roles, thanks to his commitment to the principle of practising flexible politics behind a façade of ideological inflexibility.

Socio-cultural Changes

The achievement of the Guinean regime in promoting socio-cultural changes is very remarkable. There has been a real qualitative transformation of some important aspects of socio-cultural life in Guinea. First, the serious and sometimes violent inter-ethnic rivalries that characterized pre-independence Guinea have given way to the idea of a nation thanks to the impressive efficacy of the regime's policies aimed at combating ethnic particularisms. These policies include the mass membership of the party, the nation-wide political institutional framework and respect for some 'ethnic arithmetic' in the distribution of key posts and amenities.

Second, vigorous efforts have been made to resolve or at least contain a number of important conflicts that affect social relations within the nation: religious; the young versus the old; men versus women; rural versus urban; mass versus élite. A party-sponsored secular reform programme has been used to destroy the existing religious particularisms. By giving the young generation a sense of purpose which includes a significant role in cultural development and national defence as well as some degree of involvement in the national political process, there has been no danger of an intergenerational conflict. Guinean women have become closely integrated within the social life of the nation as a result of the women's emancipation policy which the regime has used to smash the subordination of women to men that characterized the traditional social systems in the country. There is now a new social order in which men and women are equals and this order is largely respected throughout the country.

To solve the problems of the dichotomies between the élite and the mass, the rural and the urban, the regime has pursued a policy of social equality — notably the shared membership of the PDG by every Guinean — combined with a number of programmes aimed at bringing into close contact the élite and the mass, the rural and the urban. At the psychological level, the importance attached to nationalism and neutrality in Guinea's foreign policy has also contributed to the emerging national identity — adding to it the specific quality of national pride. The abrupt break with France generated the first feeling of national solidarity, and afterwards the feeling was sustained by some spectacular actions aimed at demonstrating the nationalist and neutral content in Guinea's foreign policy as well as by periodic moments of patriotic fervour generated by real or imaginary 'plots' and 'aggressions'.

All these socio-cultural changes are supported by an educational programme whose guiding philosophy seeks to inculcate into the school-going population the ideas and outlook that would help to make them readily accept the essential features of the emerging new society. The large expansion in the school population that has taken place since independence means that a reasonable proportion of the youth is now imbibing these new values.

As in the political sphere, the three methods in the Guinean approach to nation building have proved suitable for promoting socio-cultural changes. The party structure and the party ideology have played a dominant role in bringing about the socio-cultural changes summarized above. President Touré's contribution has also been significant. He has provided positive leadership for the party programmes that have made these changes possible and, wherever he found it necessary, he has not hesitated to ignore the official ideology in order to do what practical politics dictated.

Economic Development

Contrary to the prevailing opinion in the existing literature on Guinea, according to which the post-independence period has witnessed economic regression rather than economic progress,[5] we think that it is quite valid to talk of the economic achievement of the PDG regime. Measured against the level of development achieved by the French colonial administration after about sixty years of continuous rule, the PDG regime could be said to have made considerable progress in promoting the country's economic development. But judged on the basis of the development objectives which the regime fixed for itself in the light of the country's resources, one would have to say that the regime has only made a little progress. The industrial base of the country has been expanded especially in the mining sector. By the time the different bauxite projects enter into full production (Boké and Kindia have already joined Fria) and the MIFERGUI iron ore takes off the ground, Guinea would rank among the leading industrialized states in West Africa. The progress made in the provision of infrastructures such as communications and public utilities is quite substantial and they will most certainly expand with the growth of the industrial sector.

However, in contrast to the political and socio-cultural

spheres where the methods in the Guinean approach to nation building have, on the whole, proved suitable for coping with the relevant tasks, this harmony has been absent in the economic sphere. Why is this so? In the next section we shall examine this problem as well as other problems that have emerged from the Guinean approach to nation building.

Problems

The Slow Rate of Economic Development

It was pointed out above that the methods in the Guinean approach to nation building have not proved suitable for promoting economic development. From the analysis provided in Chapters 3 and 4 of this study, it is clear that the mobilizing capability of the PDG has been of very little use in the economic sphere. In fact, there is evidence to support the view that the mobilization character of the party has actually hindered economic development. Because of the effectiveness of the discipline within the party, Guineans respond in very large numbers to any mobilizing order of the party leadership. These orders are usually connected with events marking national festivities and historic anniversaries (Women's National Day, Youth Day, Workers' Day, 14 May — PDG'S anniversary, 22 November — Victory Day and so on); welcome of foreign Heads of State; and welcome of PDG leaders to lower levels of the party structure. In an average year, this can amount to the loss of several working hours per adult with obvious adverse consequences for the national economy. By 1967, the situation had become sufficiently alarming to warrant the following warning from President Touré.

> We ask the responsible cadres to stop henceforth demobilizing the comrade peasants by taking them away from their

occupations at the slightest excuse in order to make them participate in demonstrations at the (regional) headquarters. It is in their fields, in their places of work that the responsible cadres must go to meet the comrade peasants in order to participate effectively and concretely at their sides, at their effort for production. That is the veritable demonstration. If not, it is a question of political mystification . . . you even mystify the political leader you welcome by this inopportune mobilization by making him believe that all is for the better in the best of all federations. Political mobilization must be the climax of work well done.[6]

The attempt to use this mobilization system to promote economic development has also failed despite President Touré's effort to strengthen it by extolling the 'mystique of work'. (A presidential decree of July 1964 and a presidential circular of December 1970 deal with the 'mystique of work'.) By 1973, the remark made by President Touré in 1967 about the failure of economic mobilization was still largely true. He said:

The paradox is that the slogans of economic mobilization have been translated into deeds, not only by stagnation and, in some extreme cases, by a regression of production, but also by a constant increase of consumption.[7]

The second method in the Guinean approach is the role of party ideology. Here, too, the economic policies that were adopted in the light of this ideology have so far failed to produce impressive results. In the field of rural development where the regime has kept fairly strictly to the party ideology we saw that despite the creation of an institutional framework for achieving the stated objectives success was still very far from sight. As a result of the practical difficulties encountered in translating into practice the ideological position of the party on planning and on the respective roles of the public and private sectors in the economy, a number of important modifications were introduced. This point leads to the third element in the Guinean approach which is the role of President Touré. Because of his overall commitment to the Smelser principle of practising flexible politics behind a façade of an inflexible ideology, he was able to introduce some significant modifications to the economic policies dictated by the party ideology.

The most important of these changes is the fact that while the Guinean economy continues to be described as 'socialist' or 'non-capitalist', we find that in practice capitalist America and socialist Russia together with their respective allies have established important industrial and manufacturing enterprises in the country. Considering the fact that the Fria bauxite enterprise owned entirely by foreign capitalists until 1973 was the greatest foreign exchange earner for Guinea for most of this period (to the tune of about sixty per cent), it can be said that the Guinean economy could have been in a serious mess if the regime had tried to adhere strictly to the 'non-capitalist way' to development.

In the policy areas where the party ideology was respected the consequences for the economy were, on the whole, negative. The party structure proved unable to play a leading role in plan preparation and implementation. The refusal to use foreign planning experts when there were no national experts meant that the regime was trying to operate a planned economy without planners and the result was that very few concrete results were achieved. By 1973, it appeared that the regime had significantly modified the role of the party in plan preparation and implementation: the idea of a leading role was abandoned and replaced with the idea of an important role. This conclusion is based on the role of the party in the preparation of the third plan, the Five-Year Plan launched in October 1973. Another important development is that there now exists in Guinea a crop of national planners who can effectively operate a planned economy.

In all, then, it appears that positive steps are being taken to solve the problems that have been largely responsible for slow economic progress in Guinea. But as the above account shows, the economic policies that promise a better tomorrow for Guineans demand some radical modifications of the methods used in the political and socio-cultural spheres. In a sense, it appears that the experience in the economic sphere suggests that an additional method should be introduced into the Guinean approach, namely, administrative machinery staffed by 'specialists in the various fields of knowledge, technology and experience'.[8] This will naturally have consequences for the 'mobilization-oriented single party' as well as for some elements in the party ideology.

The Opposition Bourgeois Minority and Class Struggle

The other major problem that has arisen from the Guinean experience is the existence of a bourgeois minority that feels alienated from the emerging national identity. This bourgeois minority is particularly critical of the fact that the PDG regime has done very little to realize the economic potentials of the country. And in their opinion, the record of the regime in the political and socio-cultural spheres is unimpressive when the positive aspects are weighed against the negative ones.

There are two important reasons why the bourgeois minority is dissatisfied with the economic record of the PDG regime. First, its members belong to that group of post-colonial Africans of whom some social scientists have talked of 'the revolution of rising expectations'. They hoped that with the departure of the French, there would be a tremendous increase in the range and volume of the bourgeois comforts within their reach. Rather than relate the level of development within the country to what existed at independence, they compare it with what is happening in neighbouring countries like the Ivory Coast and Senegal where the post-independence developmental strategies have produced more comfort for their counterparts. Naturally, they are not bothered by the great inequalities that characterize the Ivorian and Senegalese societies.[9]

The second reason is that they disagree with the party ideology that has led to the adoption of economic policies aimed at creating a socialist or non-capitalist society. From the available evidence, this bourgeois minority became convinced around the mid-1960s that they had to strive to take over power in order to establish a capitalist economic system diametrically opposed to that of the PDG regime. Although the PDG regime began to adopt some aspects of the capitalist system from about the same time, this has not dampened their enthusiasm for re-orienting Guinea towards a fully-fledged capitalist society.

In the political and socio-cultural sphere, their main criticism of the PDG regime is that it does not in practice allow some of the basic rights guaranteed by the constitution: 'the right to elect and to be elected'; 'freedom of speech, of the press, of meeting, of association, of procession or of demonstration'.[10] They are dissatisfied with this virtual absence of law and legality. For example, one aspect of the 1965 'plot' was that some of the people allegedly involved in it had made public their intention to form an opposition party. Even within the 'mass' party, their members are formally excluded from contesting elections to leadership posts. However, it should be said that there is no guarantee that if the bourgeois group came to power they would allow these freedoms to opposition elements.

As the bourgeois minority became more vociferous in its opposition in the late 1960s, the regime's leadership realized that it could no longer continue to claim that all Guineans were united within the single mass party, the PDG. It was at this point that President Touré articulated the idea of a class struggle within the PDG which still preserved its mass character — 'the PDG' said Touré in September 1970, 'is the entire people of Guinea'.[11] On the one hand, there is the class of 'the laborious masses', 'the working class, the peasants and the truly progressive elements' and, on the other hand, there is the class of 'the reactionary elements of the bourgeoisie, the bureaucracy and capitalism'. The former is referred to as 'the people's class' and the latter as 'the exploiting class'. For our purpose, the leadership of the people's class will be called the people's élite while the leadership of the exploiting class will be referred to as the bourgeois élite.

In practical terms, the PDG leadership describes itself as the leadership of the people's class. This means that the people's élite is synonymous with the PDG leadership. Until the November 1970 invasion, President Touré believed that the ranks of the bourgeois élite could still be depleted by integrating some of them within the people's élite (yet, another evidence of his flexibility). One of the results of the 1970 invasion now appears to be a strong polarization between the two élite groups. In the meantime, the invasion had also shown that some members of the bourgeois élite had successfully camouflaged themselves within the people's élite. The extensive purge that followed the invasion (it lasted from 1970 to 1972) was aimed at identifying those who really belonged to the people's élite. It seems that some members of the people's élite are in favour of a physical extermination of the opposition bourgeois élite. Thus, in the editorial of the party organ, *Horoya,* of 17 August 1971, one finds the following reasoning:

> History is rich with examples where a minority of monopolists has disappeared for the benefit of the vast majority of the people. The failure or disappearance of a negative minority has never hindered the march towards progress and the conquest of new heights by the great people.

While a policy of physical extermination rationalized along the lines indicated in the *Horoya* editorial could take care of the members of the bourgeois élite inside Guinea, a sizeable number of this élite is outside the country and the seriousness with which the PDG leadership has consistently denounced their activities since the 1970 invasion (it reached a climax in 1973) suggests that the struggle would not be over with the 'disappearance' (what a euphemism!) of the internal bourgeois élite. To a very great extent, the future of Guinea depends on the outcome of this struggle between two competing élite groups.

Prospects for the Future

Any realistic attempt to discuss the probable course of future events in Guinea must be based on the premise that there are two major possibilities arising from the élite struggle mentioned above. If the bourgeois élite wins the struggle, the future of Guinea will be radically different from what it would be if the PDG leadership, the people's élite, remains in power. But what are the chances of each group?

Prospects for the Bourgeois Élite

The fundamental factor to remember about the bourgeois élite is that they are in two parts: one part is found inside Guinea and the other is outside the country. The internal bourgeois group does not appear to have much chance when one compares its resources with those at the disposal of the PDG leadership.

It appears to have a strong ally in the army but there is a faction of the army leadership that supports the regime. More importantly, the army in Guinea does not enjoy a monopoly of military skills; it has been disseminated to the militia and a considerable proportion of the civilian population — party leaders at all levels of the party structure (including the BPN), workers, civil servants and teachers. Any attempt at a violent overthrow in Guinea is likely to lead to some kind of civil war. (The dissemination of military skills for the civilian population was introduced after the 1970 invasion and the writer witnessed some of the military training that took place in Conakry and some parts of the interior between February and March 1971.)[12] Although the bourgeois group can count on the support of America whose economic interests continue to expand in Guinea, the high concentration of Eastern bloc countries and other revolutionary regimes (notably Cuba) in the capital is likely to make an American-backed operation similar to the one which occurred in Chile in 1973 difficult if not impossible. Above all, the denial of any facilities for organization and publicity to the bourgeois group contrasts with the monopoly of these facilities enjoyed by the PDG leadership. (This aspect, too, contrasts sharply with the Chilean experience about which one observer has remarked 'the almost anarchical situation of press liberty' under Allende.)[13] For all these reasons it does not appear that the internal bourgeois group can successfully challenge the PDG leadership single-handedly. But suppose they successfully team up with the external group?

The grand strategy of the Guinean bourgeois élite since 1970 has been to achieve a combined assault on the PDG leadership. The external group is able to organize and publicize its activities. The leading members are pre-independence opponents of the PDG (for example, the Christian trade unionist David Soumah based in Dakar), former PDG ministers and ambassadors who have deserted the regime (Naby Youlah, Dr Saidou Conté etc.), professionals, businessmen, dissident military leaders (commandant Diallo Thierno and a few others), ex-servicemen, academics and students,[14] This *emigré* bourgeois group is based mainly in France, Senegal and the Ivory Coast. Its campaign is directed towards the fairly large number of Guineans who are either traders or migrant labourers in the neighbouring countries of Sierra Leone, Gambia, Liberia, Senegal and the Ivory Coast.

Balance Sheet of the Guinean Experiment 167

The Guinean *emigré* bourgeoisie is faced with two serious problems. The first is the disunity within its leadership and the second is the problem of how to effectively link up with the internal bourgeois group. The basic reason for disunity is the lack of agreement on the policies to pursue after taking over power. There is a strong body of opinion among the group that supports the full return of Guinea into the company of West African countries that maintain a 'special relationship' with France. The protagonists of this viewpoint were either the leaders of the Socialist Democratic Party of Guinea of the pre-independence era or people who would more or less have supported the views of that party. The following quotation from the party's newspaper, *Le Populaire de Guinée* of 15 September 1956, reveals the extent of this attachment to France.

> Africans by blood and flesh but Frenchmen at heart, we intend to remain French in our actions, our thoughts, and in the achievement of our ideal: the rapid attainment by Africa of cultural, economic, social and political emancipation within the bosom of the great French Republic, one and indivisible.[15]

It is alleged that this French-oriented faction of the *emigré* bourgeoisie provides the bulk of the fund used for building up support for the movement. The Secretary-General for African and Malagasy Affairs at the Presidency in France, M. Jacques Foccart is alleged to be the major source of finance.[16] In opposition to this faction is a number of academics and students in Paris who would like the PDG regime overthrown in order to end 'American imperialism' there (reference to the idea of Guinea as an 'American protectorate' already mentioned above). Instead of substituting 'French imperialism' for 'American imperialism' as advocated by the France-oriented group, they would like the adoption of some kind of socialist policies – based on certain principles derived from French, Russian, Chinese and Cuban socialist thoughts.

The problem of linking up with the internal bourgeoisie is a real one. Because of the effective control exercised by the PDG leadership all over the country the question of infiltration is ruled out. Until 1970, the best that the external bourgeoisie could do was to maintain some kind of contact with the internal faction through emissaries from their two important centres in Dakar and Abidjan. Then, in 1970, some of them made contact with the Portuguese colonialist rulers of Guinea-Bissau (maybe it was the other way round) who were desperately trying to inflict a mortal blow on the Independence Party of Guinea and Cape Verde (PAIGC) which had its operational headquarters in Conakry where the PDG leadership granted it unconditional freedom to use Guinean territory as a base for prosecuting its liberation struggle. The Portuguese wanted to kill Amilcar Cabral (who was then the PAIGC leader) and to release a number of Portuguese soldiers captured and kept in prison in Conakry by the PAIGC leadership. The vast majority of the Guinean *emigré* bourgeois leaders gladly resolved to integrate their own plan of overthrowing the PDG leadership with the Portuguese plan. For the Portuguese, this combined operation had two important advantages. First, they would be able to carry out their attack on the PAIGC under the cover of an anti-PDG invasion led by Guinean dissidents. Second, if the Guinean dissidents succeeded in overthrowing the PDG regime, the Portuguese would be able to destroy the Conakry base of the PAIGC which would amount to a great set-back for the liberation movement.

The Portuguese provided the material facilities for the sea-borne invasion and the Guinean *emigré* bourgeoisie had some of its members trained for the purpose of carrying out the operation of overthrowing the PDG regime. The white Portuguese leaders of the invading force had with them a number of black recruits from Guinea Bissau. On 22 November 1970 the invading force arrived in Conakry. The Portuguese successfully freed their fellow countrymen held as prisoners but could not kill Cabral because he was abroad.

But the plan to overthrow the PDG regime failed. In the early hours of the operation, the invaders failed in two critical areas: they failed to capture the radio and to capture or kill President Touré. In the bitter struggle that ensued the Guinean military, the militia and the PAIGC effectively combined to put the invaders to rout. Although the internal bourgeois élite knew of the invasion plan and had promised to mobilize internal support, the critical failures of the first few hours prevented them from organizing any support. In his first broadcast to the nation on the morning of the invasion, President Touré described it as an external aggression aimed at violating the sovereignty and territorial integrity of Guinea. From what the writer saw in Conakry, the average Guinean reacted with a sense of wounded pride and saw himself as being called upon to defend his fatherland against external aggressors.[17]

For our purpose, the 1970 invasion demonstrates the great difficulties that the component parts of the Guinean bourgeois élite face in trying to link up for a combined attack on the PDG leadership. By agreeing to ally with Portuguese colonialist rulers they greatly discredited themselves in the eyes of the Guinean masses as well as in the eyes of progressive people throughout the world. The tremendous external support expressed for the PDG leadership throughout the world and especially in Africa following the news of the abortive invasion constitutes a real defeat for the Guinean bourgeois élite. Although the PDG leadership has been raising alarms that new aggressions are being planned with the assistance of some foreign countries (notably Portugal, France, Ivory Coast and Senegal), the 1970 experience suggests that the bourgeois élite is not likely to plan a repeat performance of 1970. One critical factor in their calculations appears to be the personality of President Touré. They seem to believe that his disappearance from the Guinean political scene (through assasination or natural death) would create an opportunity for them to successfully challenge the remnant of the PDG leadership which they expect to be seriously divided over the question of succession. But how, in fact, is the PDG leadership preparing for the succession to President Touré?

The PDG Leadership and the Succession Problem

Since Sékou Touré emerged as the most prominent nationalist leader in Guinea around 1957 his personal life became inextricably linked to the history of his country. Today, many people who wish to distinguish between Equatorial Guinea, Guinea-Bissau and the Republic of Guinea simply refer to the Republic of Guinea as Sékou Touré's Guinea and this assimilation of leader and country is widely accepted. It is hoped that adequate evidence has been adduced in the preceding chapters of this study to explain the origins and the manifestations of Touré's dominant role in post-independence Guinea. The important question that we wish to consider here is whether or not the PDG regime can remain in power after his departure from the scene. Although there are some achievements of the PDG regime which are likely to remain permanent features of Guinea even if the regime is displaced by an entirely different one (*infra*), the preservation of the existing political, economic and socio-cultural features of Guinean life will depend on a smooth and peaceful succession to President Touré.

There are some important factors that are likely to facilitate a smooth and peaceful succession in Guinea. First, the PDG has been successfully established as a national institution inside Guinea. The pre-independence agitational nationalist politics which it championed turned it into a household word. When, in September 1958, ninety-six per cent of the adult population voted 'No' in the referendum on the Franco-African Community, they were responding to an

Balance Sheet of the Guinean Experiment 171

order of the PDG. Since independence, the PDG has become more firmly institutionalized as a result of its position as the central political institution in Guinea. Its structures are nation-wide and about 300,000 Guineans are involved in running its affairs. The national ideology which has been in the main articulated by President Touré is formally called PDG ideology.

Similarly, the writings of President Touré on the history and ideology of the PDG are called 'The Works of the PDG'. Above all, President Touré has consistently used his dual role as the Head of State and PDG leader to attribute all the post-independence achievements in the country to the action of the PDG: the expansion of the country's industrial base, the tremendous growth of educational facilities and the successes achieved in sports are all 'gains of the revolution' led by the PDG. From the writer's experience in Guinea, the history of post-independence Guinea is synonymous with either Sékou Touré or the PDG. It is this confusion of the nation with the PDG that we have called the concept of party-nation.

However, if the PDG has become institutionalized to a great extent, the dominance of Touré's leadership suggests that his departure from the scene might weaken the party. This possibility appears to have dawned on the PDG leadership around 1967. To avert this danger, the party's eighth Congress held late in 1967 decided to de-emphasize the image of a single party leader and to substitute for it the image of a collective leadership. The fifteen-member party executive, the BPN, was reduced to a seven-member body which was consituted into the cabinet of the government. These seven men thus became the effective rulers of both the party and the state. As a means of emphasizing the new collective leadership, it was decided that the photographs of the six other BPN members should be added to that of President Touré in the party headquarters. This idea of an image of a collective leadership was reaffirmed by the party's ninth Congress of April 1972.

However, despite the effort that has so far been made to establish this image of a collective leadership, (on most occasions President Touré claims to speak in the name of the BPN rather than in his own name as party leader or Head of State), the dominance of President Touré still remains. This is perhaps not surprising as he cannot will away his charisma. Furthermore, as party leader, Head of State and the Commander-in-Chief of the Armed Forces (since the 1970 invasion), he enjoys powers that are only comparable to the powers of Stalin during the last decade of his rule in Russia. Also, simultaneously with the attempt to establish the image of a collective leadership a mild form of 'personality cult' was developing around President Touré. At every public rally, the closing slogans are usually; 'Long Live the Revolution', 'Long Live President Sékou Touré'. Party resolutions, the press and the radio refer to him affectionately with two or more of the following titles: 'The Faithful and Supreme Servant of the People', 'Our Well-beloved Secretary General', 'The Helmsman of our Revolution', 'The Great Son of Africa', 'The Strategist', 'The Liberator of Oppressed Peoples', 'The Terror of International Imperialism, of Colonialism and Neocolonialism', 'The Doctor of Revolutionary Sciences'.[18]

In all, then, collective leadership cannot really work in President Touré's lifetime. But can it be used to solve the succession problem after his departure from the scene? From the available evidence, it appears that Touré would like the question to be answered in the affirmative. At the party's ninth Congress he obtained the right to nominate the members of the BPN, and the composition of this body suggests that he sought to select a group of men who are committed to the perpetuation of the regime and who are at the same time likely to be acceptable to the country when he disappears from the scene. Two of them, Mamadi Kéita and Moussa Diakhité, can be described as the defenders of the left-wing image of the regime. The former is a brilliant and articulate philosophy graduate from Europe and he was teaching at the Conakry Polytechnic before he was co-opted to the ruling body of the party in 1968. The latter was one of the few senior civil servants in Guinea at independence but he was also a front-line member of the PDG. He became a member of the BPN in 1958, was dropped in 1967 only to re-enter it in 1972. He played a critical role in organizing the defence of Conakry during the 1970 invasion.

Lansana Béavogui and Ismael Touré (half brother of President Touré) are stabilizing figures as they represent continuity in the full sense of the term. Since 1958, they have been top members of both the party and government. Béavogui established himself internationally when he was Foreign Minister for about six years in the 1960s and he was appointed Prime Minister in 1972. Ismael Touré has been closely involved in all the economic negotiations with both Western and Eastern bloc countries and he has been in charge of the *Domaine* of Economy and Finance since 1969. The two other members, Dr Barry Oumar and N'Famara Kéita, are essentially in the BPN to uphold Touré's commitment to the need for some ethnic balance. Dr Oumar is the only Foulah in the BPN just as N'Famara Kéita is the only Soussou. Although Dr Oumar was a deputy (member of the National Assembly) in 1958 and later became a regional governor (a political post in Guinea), he did not become a minister until July 1971. He is a political light-weight who was brought into the BPN in 1972 as the representative of the Foulahs. In contrast, N'Famara Kéita who was a junior civil servant under colonial rule was one of the early leaders of the PDG and could rightly be described as a political heavy-weight before 1958. Since independence he has been a member of both the BPN and the government. He enjoys the reputation of a solid administrator but his commitment to the regime does not appear as strong as is the case with Béavogui and Ismael Touré. (For example, he was allegedly mentioned in one of the lists of prospective ministers to be appointed after the hoped-for success of the 1970 invasion.) It is likely that President Touré trusts him personally and, in any case, his presence in the BPN gives the Soussous a representative.

The three criteria identified above as representing the basis for BPN membership — ideological activism, stability and continuity and ethnic arithmetic — also appear to have influenced the composition of the Central Committee. The only additional criterion that President Touré also considered was the representation of the three 'active forces' that constitute the 'parallel institutions' of the party: the youth, the women and the workers. There are two women, about five youth and about three workers' representatives in the Central Committee.

The writer's belief is that the PDG will survive President Touré and it will be led during the crucial early months by a collective leadership composed of the other BPN members. Eventually, a leadership struggle is likely to ensue and whoever manages to enlist the majority support within the Central Committee will emerge as the *primus inter pares* of what would then be known as PDG Regime Phase Two. If this happens, the essential characteristics of what we have presented in this study as Sékou Touré's Guinea will be preserved with certain modifications (a greater dose of socialism or more capitalist remedies depending on the preference of the new leadership).

Although the verdict of this study is that the PDG will survive President Touré and that what exists today is likely to continue tomorrow with only some modification, we are prepared to admit that there is no scientific basis for this verdict. Certain unforseen circumstances in either the internal or external environments or both may introduce new factors that we have not taken into consideration. In such circumstances, the élite struggle in Guinea may be resolved in favour of the bourgeois élite. However, regardless of whichever élite group rules Guinea after the departure of Touré, there are certain features of present-day Guinea that will most probably

Balance Sheet of the Guinean Experiment   175

remain unchanged. President Touré himself described these permanent gains as follows in 1967:

> Statisticians, carried away by a violent passion for figures, and having nothing else in their heads except 'plus' and 'minus' signs, would not understand the significance for our people of the reconquest of its freedom, the liquidation of the fear which paralyzed it, the restoration of its human rights, the liberation of its energies and the sovereign exercise of its historic responsibilities.

In 1970, he added: 'The whole world knows that if Guinea is a poor country, a small country confronted with serious problems, it is also a country of dignity.'[20]

National pride and a high degree of political consciousness that makes ordinary citizens appreciate the profound significance of such abstract concepts as 'sovereignty', 'liberty' and 'dignity' are the important achievements of the Touré-led PDG regime that are likely to remain permanently. With these invaluable assets, Touré's successor(s) should be able to mobilize the Guinean people for the important task of raising their standard of living from its present low level.

7. Conclusion: Some Theoretical Reflections on the Guinean Experiment in Nation Building

As a conclusion to this study, we should like to relate the Guinean experiment to the existing theories of nation building. First, let us briefly examine what these existing theories are:

Theories of Nation Building

The most striking feature of the existing literature on nation building is the variety of approaches adopted by analysts. A large number of analysts have followed what Lucian Pye has described as 'the tradition of dichotomous schemes.'[1] According to this tradition, all societies can be classified within a dichotomous scheme of two categories variously labelled as: 'traditional and rational, rural and urban, agricultural and industrial, primitive and civilized, static and dynamic, sacred and secular, folk and urban, *societa* and *civitas*, *Gemeinschaft* and *Gesellschaft*, communal and associational, traditional and modern'.[2]

The theorists of the dichotomous scheme approach present composite pictures of their two categories as follows. On the one hand, the traditional society is characterized by affective relationships, ascriptive standards, functional diffuseness and particularistic norms. On the other hand, the modern society is characterized by achievement standards, rationality, functional specificity and universalistic norms. In the opinion of these analysts, the development of any society involves its transition from a traditional to a modern state and such a society is called a transitional society. The transitional society combines some of the characteristics of both the traditional and modern societies with a few distinctive qualities such as a charismatic form of authority compared to a traditional form and a rational-legal form for the traditional and modern societies respectively.[3]

The dichotomous scheme approach suffers from two important limitations. First, it does not provide a clear picture of transitional societies. How, in fact, does a society move from one category to the other and what constitutes the ideal 'mix' of traditional and modern characteristics that qualify a society for the label 'transitional'? This critically important question has not been tackled in the existing literature and it appears that it defies an easy answer. This problem seems to suggest that the static analysis of the dichotomous scheme approach is inadequate for conceptualizing the evolution of a society which is clearly a dynamic process. The second limitation of this approach is that the two basic typologies, the traditional and modern societies, do not exist in the real world. All political systems have mixtures of the characteristics of the two typologies.[4]

Another approach to nation building interprets the term to be synonymous with national integration. There are three dominant themes in the integration literature: territorial integration, political integration and ethnic integration.[5] 'Territorial integration' refers to the maintenance of an effective central authority over the entire territory under a state's claimed jurisdiction. 'Political integration' emphasizes the question of linking government with the governed (sometimes referred to as bridging the élite-mass gap) and the development of a participant political community. Finally, 'ethnic integration' refers to the process of bringing together the culturally and socially disparate groups within a state and making all these groups share a single national identity.

There are two important problems in the integrative

approach. The first concerns the relative importance to be attached to each of the three dominant aspects of integration. In particular, there is a clear division between theorists who see political integration as the most critical issue and others who think that the utmost importance should be attached to ethnic integration. The second and more serious problem is related to the variety of ways — many of them confused and self-contradictory — in which theorists think that integration can be achieved. For example, while some theorists hold the view that increases in social communication and mobilization facilitate the development of a common national identity within an ethnically heterogenous society, others have argued that such contacts could intensify cultural awareness thereby exacerbating inter-ethnic conflict.

The third and final approach to nation building in the existing literature takes nation building to be synonymous with development. Two subjects feature prominently in the literature on the developmental approach: economic development and political development.[6] Broadly, economic development is interpreted to refer to measures aimed at promoting industrialization, agricultural development, the construction of roads, railways, and other transport facilities, and the provision of social and welfare services, especially in health and education. Political development is generally interpreted to mean the emergence of a functioning political system characterized by institutions for articulating and aggregating the interests of the members of the society which are then transformed into authoritative decisions, binding on all members of the society by the central governmental institutions. Two points are commonly emphasized; the effectiveness of the central authority and the extent to which there is popular participation in political life.

There are several problems in adopting the developmental approach. First, a large number of developmental theorists follow the tradition of dichotomous schemes by interpreting economic and political development to mean the economic and political arrangements that exist in the societies that the theorists of the dichotomous schemes label as modern. This category of theorists go further to use the term 'modernization' as synonymous with development.[7] In theory, the efficiency of the institutional arrangements which the new states are expected to establish should depend on the attributes of the modern society: clearly defined roles, or offices, based on universalistic norms, functionally specific relationships and rigid adherence to achievement considerations. In practice, the work of organization theorists has shown that the effective functioning of organizations depends essentially on a mixture of modern and traditional relationships.[8]

Another set of problems is related to the relative importance of the various factors which help to promote both economic and political development and the nature of the interaction between these different factors. On economic development, theorists are not agreed on the relative importance that should be attached to industrialization and agricultural production; there is argument over the effects of political factors on economic development; and there is controversy over the significance of growth (meaning increase in national income) which is not accompanied by a substantial improvement in the standard of living of the citizens of a state.

These conflicting interpretations are accompanied by divergent views on the extent to which the developmental activities carried out can promote or hinder the objective of nation building. Thus, for example, while some theorists emphasize the positive advantages that can accrue from a well-developed communication system which promotes intensive contacts between the different ethnic and religious groups within the state, others stress that such contacts can hinder the nation building effort by making the citizens of the state more conscious of the inter-ethnic, religious and other differences.

Similarly, while some theorists claim that the increase in the production of goods and services contributes to the attachment of citizens to the state that provides them, others argue that the competition for these very goods and services among the citizens contributes more to the instability of the state. But it should be mentioned that the dominant view in existing literature is that the promotion of economic and social development contributes positively to the nation building effort.

On political development the arguments for the creation of an effective central authority with limited general participation conflict with those for a political structure that permits wide participation; there are arguments between functional-systems theorists and their critics (who claim that the theories have a static or conservative bias and imply an equilibrium or harmony of parts); theorists are not certain about the relationship between economic development and political development; there are numerous typologies of the political regimes of the new states (radical/pragmatic, unitary/pluralistic, authoritarian/democratic, modernizing totalitarian/conservative totalitarian), with conflicting features sometimes attributed to the same state; and finally there is disagreement on what constitutes political development: single party or multi-party, effective representative institutions versus strong state bureaucracies and so on.

From the different interpretations given to the concept of nation bulding as shown in the above review of the existing literature on the subject, it is possible to highlight what most theorists of nation building consider to be the essential subjects of concern. First, the nation is expected to have a political institutional framework which provides for an effective central authority and for popular participation in political life. Second, the national leadership is expected to recognize socio-economic development as a primary objective whose realization could facilitate the task of nation building. Third, the national authority is expected to strive to create a national identity which can be shared by the diverse ethnic, language, racial, regional and religious groups within the society.

The three subjects highlighted in these theories correspond closely to what we have identified in the introductory chapter as the critical tasks in the Guinean approach to nation building. This coincidence is almost certainly accidental since one can safely assume that the post-independence Guinean leadership was not aware of the theoretical literature on the concept of nation building. But the coincidence should not really be surprising since the same broad meaning is given to the concept by almost every African leader who has clearly articulated views on the subject.[9]

Three Hypotheses on the Concept of Nation Building

The analysis of the Guinean experiment in nation building carried out in the preceding chapters of this study suggests three hypotheses that relate to the theories of nation building discussed above. The first hypothesis is that the process of nation building cannot be accomplished without the emergence of some divisions within the society; in other words, nation building and nation dividing go *pari passu.* A second hypothesis is that in the early stage of nation building, effective political mobilization and significant qualitative changes in the socio-cultural sphere can be used to forge a national identity despite a slow rate of economic development. The third hypothesis is that the methods used for nation building at the initial phase require periodic modifications which could be significant until the end of the early phase and less significant thereafter.

Nation Building and Nation Dividing

As pointed out above, while some theorists of nation building emphasize the positive contribution that certain factors can make to the process of nation building, others draw attention to the negative effects of these same factors. This dichotomous viewpoint was summed up recently in an article entitled 'Nation Building or Nation Destroying'.[10] The present study suggests that instead of a dichotomous proposition, we should talk of a congruent proposition: nation building and nation dividing go *pari passu*. However, the concept of nation bulding will be applicable only in circumstances where the nation building process is the major phenomenon with nation dividing as the minor. When the reverse is the case, one can talk of nation destroying.

The Guinean experiment examined in this study is a clear case of a process of nation building accompanied by a process of nation dividing where the former is the major phenomenon and the latter is the minor. The major instrument that the PDG regime used for forging a national identity is the mobilization-oriented single party. On the one hand, the fact that the entire people of Guinea are members of the party which has nation-wide structures helps to create a national image. On the other hand, the formal exclusion of certain Guineans from a leadership role within the party (traders, businessmen, industrialists and the other members of the 'exploiting class') clearly introduces a division within the nation. However, this division is minor because the number of Guineans excluded from the PDG leadership is very small.

Similarly, the Guinean regime's ban on associations based on ethnic, religious, or geographical grounds has made it possible to establish single nation-wide organizations for the 'active forces' of the society: the youth, the women and the workers. There is no doubt that the existence of these organizations has greatly contributed to the emerging national identity inside Guinea. On the other hand, it is also true that there are some Guineans who would have preferred a religious trade union organization, an ethnic youth organization or a region-based women's organization. Again, it will be correct to say that the vast majority of Guineans accept the steps taken

Some Theoretical Reflections 183

by the PDG regime and that only a small minority is dissatisfied.

In the economic sphere, too, we have seen that it is only the small-minded, bourgeois Guineans who have been suffering from the frustration of unfulfilled economic expectations (the so-called 'revolution of rising expectations') as a result of the PDG regime's relative failure in promoting economic development — a result of the part-socialist and part-capitalist economic policies that have been badly planned and poorly implemented. The majority of Guineans whose expectations are limited and specific (food, clothing and shelter) have not expressed any serious dissatisfaction with the regime's economic record even though they would certainly welcome a greater improvement in their standard of living.[11]

In short, it will be correct to say that when all the activities of the PDG regime during the past fifteen years are taken together, the majority of Guineans seem to have accepted both the positive and negative results without much complaint. It is only a small bourgeois minority that feels alienated from the emerging national identity in the country. Despite the potential threat that this minority was and still is, the regime has successfully laid the foundations of a new society in Guinea, especially in the political and socio-cultural spheres.

During the fifteen-year period covered in this study, then, the PDG regime in Guinea was engaged in a process of nation building. At the same time, a process of nation dividing was taking place because the activities that the regime was carrying out in the political, socio-cultural and economic spheres led to the alienation of some sections of the society. In all, this group constituted only a small minority and this means that the phenomenon of nation dividing was clearly a small subsidiary, an off-shoot, one might say, of the larger dominant phenomenon of nation building.

Nation Building, Political Mobilization, Socio-cultural Changes and Economic Development

One of the important conclusions reached in this study is that the rate of economic development in Guinea since independence has been rather slow. It is significant that while the methods in the Guinean approach to nation building have been quite suitable for promoting the tasks of political mobilization and socio-cultural transformation, they have proved less effective in the promotion of economic development. We have suggested elsewhere[12] that the problem of economic development in a post-colonial state such as Guinea can only be effectively tackled either by a 'root and branch' revolutionary strategy or by some degree of commitment to the operation of a neo-colonial economy. A high 'neo-colonial economy' is one that relies heavily on the participation of foreign capital (public as well as private) and on foreign technical skills (usually from the former metropolitan country) in the preparation and implementation of developmental plans. This point was summed up as follows: 'In the absence of a root and branch revolution, a colonial economy cannot become a modern economy without passing through a neo-colonial phase.'[13]

In reality, all post-colonial African countries can be said to have opted for a neo-colonial economy with only a difference of degree. The Ivory Coast in West Africa and Kenya in East Africa are examples of highly neo-colonized economies while Guinea in West Africa and Tanzania in East Africa are examples of small degree of neo-colonized economies. It is significant that while the Ivory Coast and Kenya are grouped among the more economically developed states, Guinea and Tanzania are grouped among the less economically developed states. In contrast to the situation in the economic sphere, the Guinean approach to nation building has achieved concrete results in the political and socio-cultural spheres. In other words, these results were achieved despite the relative failure in the economic sphere.

There are some theorists of nation building who regard economic development as *the* critical factor in the nation building process. With abundant goods and services, it is argued, it will be possible to secure the allegiance of the masses to the state that provides these good things of life. Similarly, the abundance of goods and services is expected to make it possible to reduce inter-ethnic tensions as there will be something substantial to share between the different ethnic groups. This same solution can be applied to the conflicts between the élite and the masses and the rural and the urban: the gap between the élite and the masses as well as that between the rural and the urban populations can be reduced by the existence of abundant goods and services to share between them. Although some other theorists have drawn attention to the important ways in which economic progress can in fact hinder the process of nation building, only a few writers have gone further to suggest that considerable progress can be achieved in the process of nation building despite a slow rate of economic development. The point that we wish to make here is that the Guinean experience is an example of a state that has achieved some progress in the process of nation building despite a slow rate of economic development.

By concentrating on political mobilization and sociocultural transformation, the Guinean regime has managed to forge a national identity. The factors that have made this achievement possible include a mobilization-oriented single party based on an ideology that emphasizes, among other things, popular participation in the political process; practical steps aimed at resolving a number of important social and cultural conflicts such as inter-ethnic, religious, the young versus the old and men versus women; and a charismatic and flexible national leader. We also saw the significant way in which the special circumstances of Guinean independence have influenced the course of events. All this adds up to a combination of factors that will be difficult to find in any other state. For example, if there is a mobilization-oriented single party, there is no guarantee that there will be a charismatic and flexible national leader to direct its affairs. Indeed, it appears that the most difficult factor in the Guinean approach to transplant to another state is the nature of the leadership. The post-independence history of African states to date shows that charismatic and flexible leaders are very rare; in the writer's opinion, President Touré is the only leader of this kind that has emerged in West Africa. (Nkrumah was a charismatic leader but he was not a particularly flexible man.) In other words, the Guinean experiment is not for export.

However, in a recent study of the nation building process in East Africa, Professor Ali Mazrui presents Tanzania as a state that has made considerable progress in nation building as a result of the importance attached to political mobilization and socio-cultural transformation while the rate of economic development has been rather slow.[14] Although Professor Mazrui does not explicitly state a proposition similar to the one illustrated above, it appears that the Tanzanian experience can be described as another good illustration of this proposition. It is interesting to point out that in Tanzania, as in Guinea, there is a mobilization-oriented single party whose ideology emphasizes some form of popular participation in the political process. Another important similarity is the fact that President Nyerere has provided Tanzania with a strong and positive leadership similar in some respects to the leadership that President Touré has provided in Guinea.

There are, however, some important differences in the approaches of the two countries to political mobilization and socio-cultural transformation. For example, the 'one-party democracy' in Tanzania is quite different from the one-party system in Guinea. Similarly, the content of the programme for cultural transformation in Guinea with its almost exclusive inward looking characteristics is different from the programme in Tanzania, which consciously seeks to enrich its local cultural resources with selected external influences, such as the translation of certain English classics into the national language, Swahili, by President Nyerere himself. A comparative study of the nation building processes in Guinea and Tanzania promises to be a most fascinating field for future research.

Another significant point that emerges from Mazrui's book is the fact that from his comparison of Tanzania, Kenya and Uganda, both Kenya and Uganda which have given priority to economic development have not made as much progress as Tanzania in nation building. However, Mazrui seems to suggest that in the long-run the Kenya-Uganda approach may achieve better results in certain aspects of nation building.[15] This finding can be summed up by saying that in the short-run, there is no direct correlation between economic development and progress in nation building (the Guinean experience supports this viewpoint) but in the long-run, there could be a direct correlation between the two processes. To sum up, in addition to providing an interesting illustration in support of the hypothesis discussed here, the East African experiences as presented in Mazrui's book suggest a number of interesting ways in which our hypothesis can be modified. These are clearly exciting prospects for researchers who would like to study the process of nation building in Africa on a comparative basis.

Time Dimension and the Methods of Nation Building

The third and final hypothesis deals with the critical influence of the time dimension of nation building on the methods used to pursue the objective. A good historical illustration of this point is the nation building process in the United States of America. From Professor Lipset's *The First New Nation* (New

York, 1963), we learn that charismatic leadership, nationalism and neutrality, and a revolutionary ideology were among the major factors that were used to forge a national identity during the early phase of nation building in America. Although the process of nation building in America still continues today (the process has been described as endless), none of these three factors now plays a significant role. For example, only one of the three presidents that have ruled America since the 1960s can be said to come close to a charismatic leader — John F. Kennedy. The fact that his successors have no charismatic quality has not significantly affected the sense of nationhood in America. More dramatically, the idea of nationalism and neutrality has been replaced by an international policeman's role while the notion of a revolutionary ideology is now taboo to the vast majority of Americans. Finally, the constitution that was established by the 'Founding Fathers' as the basis of the American governmental system was subjected to a number of important amendments during the early phase of the nation building process, but the number of amendments decreased as national consensus was progressively built around the constitution.

To some extent, it can be said that throughout the period covered by this study the Guinean regime relied on the three methods identified in Chapter 1 — a mobilization-oriented single party, an inflexible party ideology and a charismatic and flexible national leader — for pursuing the task of nation building. However, the analysis carried out in Chapters 2, 3, 4 and 5 shows clearly how these methods were being modified, sometimes radically, sometimes in minor details, as the years progressed and in response to developments in both the internal and external environments. Although the Guinean regime did not formally admit that these changes were taking place, this refusal does not alter the fact that the changes were actually taking place. For example, the idea of the PDG as the party of 'the entire people of Guinea' was a fairly accurate description of the political reality in Guinea during the first few years of independence. In fact, considering the atmosphere of national emergency created by the abrupt French withdrawal and the subsequent French efforts to literally kill the young state, one could say that a one-party system was a necessity. However, with the 'Teachers' plot' of 1961 (a left-wing unrest within the party) and the 'Traders' plot' of 1965 (a right-wing quest for self-assertion outside the party) it became clear that the entire people of Guinea were no longer voluntary members of the party. The one-party system had become inelastic to accommodate important differences of opinion.

When the party leadership eventually decided to acknowledge this important split within the party, it came up with the idea of a class struggle inside the single mass party. As we have already pointed out, what really exists in Guinea today is an élite struggle for the exercise of power. It appears that the regime is showing an increased awareness of the need to acknowledge this problem and deal with it. If the suggestion that the opposition bourgeois élite be physically eliminated is adopted, one will have to add Stalin-style purge and terror to the methods in the Guinean approach to nation building. But this writer feels that the PDG regime has neither the will nor the capability to carry through such a programme. A more humane approach would be for the regime to introduce a new electoral system that allows known bourgeois élite members to compete freely with members of the people's élite during the periodic elections to the National Assembly. This could produce a situation similar to the one-party democracy in Tanzania which, from all accounts, allows some healthy rivalry within the single party élite.[16] The fact that the National Assembly in Guinea has very few powers (the powers of the Tanzanian Assembly are not considerable either) means that this innovation will not unnecessarily hamstring the central authority.

Another important area where the method of the Guinean regime has changed significantly is the ideological position on economic development. In reality, we have seen that the Guinean economy is part-socialist and part-capitalist. In this case, it appears that what the Guinean regime should have done is to assert that the national objective is to operate a socialist economy but that in the meantime it allows some capitalist remedies. One of these capitalist remedies is the acceptance of substantial foreign capital and another is the important role of a state administrative machinery. With regard to the latter, the regime's leadership could claim to be following Lenin's counsel which states that 'without the guidance of specialists in the various fields of knowledge, technology and experience (this is what a state bureaucracy provides), the transition to socialism will be impossible'.

While the PDG regime has shown some reluctance in acknowledging that some changes have occurred in the methods it has adopted for nation building, it will be impossible for it to maintain this attitude with regard to the style of leadership when President Touré departs from the scene. None of the potential leaders in the incumbent élite or in the opposition has any charismatic quality and none of them possesses the same degree of integrity, sincerity, transparent honesty and patriotism which made it fairly easy for Touré to apply the principle of practising flexible politics behind a façade of an inflexible and rigid ideology. All this means that the style of leadership will change and it is likely to become a less significant factor in the process of nation building in Guinea after the departure of Touré. In all, it seems correct to say that the Guinean experience shows how in the early phase of the process of nation building, significant changes take place. As the American experience suggests, it is likely that subsequent changes will be less significant.

Some Theoretical Reflections 191

To sum up, we have tried in this study to examine the post-independence developments in Guinea in the context of the ruling regime's self-assigned task of nation building. After examining the different ways in which the regime sought to achieve its objective, we have come to the conclusion that significant progress has been made in the process of nation building; ethnic particularism has given way to the idea of a nation; the social groups within the society are being integrated and the average citizen has been socialized to such a point that he feels proud to identify himself as a Guinean.

On the other hand, the process of nation building was also accompanied by a process of nation dividing which was caused by the fact that the various activities carried out by the ruling regime led to the alienation of some sections of society. The most affected group is a small bourgeois élite which has consistently sought to wrest power from the hands of the incumbent PDG leadership. The continuing struggle between these two élite groups makes the future evolution of events in Guinea rather uncertain. However, regardless of the outcome of this struggle, there appears to be some measure of certainty about two points. First, it is most unlikely that the emerging national identity in Guinea will be called into question again. Second, the methods in the Guinean approach to nation building in future will be different in some important respects from those examined in this study. The changes will occur partly because of the limited effectiveness of the existing methods in promoting economic development and partly as a result of the new leadership style that is certain to emerge after the departure of President Touré from the Guinean political scene.

Notes

Chapter 1

1. When Charles de Gaulle came to power in France in 1958, one of his first actions was the re-organization of the relationship between France and her colonies in Tropical Africa. To this end, he proposed a Franco–African Community which these territories were free to accept or reject through a referendum; any territory which rejected the Community would automatically become independent while those who accepted would become autonomous states (without sovereign status) within the Community.
2. The expression 'one-party ideology' is used, for example, by A. Zolberg in his *Creating Political Order, The Party States of West Africa* (Chicago, 1966), pp. 43–7. For the description of PDG ideology as 'socialism', see B. Charles, 'Le Socialisme africain: mythes et réalités', *Revue française de sciences politiques*, xv, 5 (1965), pp. 856–84.
3. A. S. Touré, *La Lutte du Parti démocratique de Guinée pour l'émancipation africaine: la planification économique*, Vol. V. (Conakry, 1960), pp. 281, 285. The volume number in front of this book refers to its position in the list of President Touré's works which now run into eighteen volumes. Subsequent references to the volumes of these works will be given as: Touré, Vol.   p.   ; the details on each volume are supplied in the bibliography; translations are the author's.
4. Throughout this study, we shall frequently use the expression 'the Guinean leadership' as synonymous with President Touré. This is because of his dominant position as both the President of the Republic and Secretary General of the ruling PDG; he is also the most articulate exponent of party doctrines.
5. Touré, Vol. XII, p. 44.

6. ibid.
7. In *Bulletin du compte-rendu des activités du BPN* (occasional publication of the PDG), No. 22 (1963), p. 32. BPN is the abbreviation for *Bureau politique national*, the National Political Bureau of the PDG.
8. See, for example, Touré, Vol. X, pp. 349–62.
9. Touré, Vol. IV, p. 60.
10. Touré, Vol. XII, p. 35. The village committee, the steering committee, the federal bureau, and the National Political Bureau are the party executive bodies at the village, arrondissement, regional and national levels respectively.
11. The problems raised by this automatic membership of the PDG are referred to later on, especially in Chapter V.
12. The term 'a non-capitalist way' was used between 1958 and 1967 when President Touré did not want the term 'socialist' to be used for 'tactical' reasons.
13. Quoted in 'Rapport présenté par Ismael Touré, ministre du développement économique au CNR du 16 avril 1964', in Touré, Vol. XIV, p. 96.
14. Touré, Vol. V, p. 309.
15. Touré, Vol. XII, p. 32.
16. For Weber's views on a charismatic leader, see T. Parsons (ed.), *Max Weber, The Theory of Social and Economic Organization* (New York, 1964), pp. 358–92.
17. N. J. Smelser, 'Mechanisms of Change and Adjustment to Change', in B. F. Hoselitz and W. E. Moore (eds.), *Industrialization and Society* (UNESCO–Mouton, 1970), p. 47. I am grateful to Professor James Coleman of the Rockefeller Foundation Office, Lubumbashi, Zaire, who brought this important reference to my attention.
18. ibid.
19. This idea was defended by some members of the Guinean National Assembly in October 1963; see Touré, Vol. XII, p. 58.
20. For text of the Guinean consitution, see Appendix B.
21. Touré, Vol. XVI, p. 10.
22. op. cit., p. 9.

Chapter 2

1. Until the ninth party Congress held in April 1972 decided that elections to the PRLs should take place every two years, the elections were held annually. What follows

about the party organization takes into account the changes introduced by the ninth Congress but references are made to the pre-1972 arrangements wherever they are considered to be important.
2. Prior to 1972, the party Congress was summoned at least once every four years.
3. Until the ninth Congress in 1972, the Central Committee which was first created in 1967 by the party's eighth Congress acted as the supreme party institution between the sessions of the CNR while the BPN was the supreme executive of the party. This point is discussed in more detail later on in this chapter.
4. See Chapter 1, p. 8.
5. The *loi-cadre* was an enabling law which allowed certain measures which the French constitution reserved for the domain of law to be decided upon by decree. In other words, the administrative reform referred to here was carried out by decrees.
6. In every territory of French West Africa, the Governor was the President of the Council of Government until July 1958 when he relinquished the post to the African Vice-President as a result of tensions between the holders of the two posts in several territories.
7. Touré, Vol. XII, p. 35.
8. See *Compte rendu d'activités du BPN*, No. 11 (1963), pp. 123–4.
9. The civil servants who are elected to party posts combine party functions with their normal civil service duties and they are not paid; the other party officials at this level too are not paid.
10. The only difference is that the leading member of the federal bureau called the federal secretary is a full-time party official (since 1967). However, in 1971, twenty-one of the thirty federal secretaries were civil servants 'detached' from the civil service but with their promotion and pension rights intact.
11. The title was further changed to that of ministry for rural development in 1973 but again without any change in the role of the ministers.
12. 'Cabinet' is used here to refer to the ministers within a government who have responsibility for the major areas of government work.
13. The titles of the *domaines* were changed thrice between

1967 and 1972 but the number was always seven. The most significant change occurred in 1972 when the *domaine* of the Prime Minister was introduced. In 1973 a new *domaine* of Rural Development was created but there was no corresponding increase in the size of the BPN although it is reasonable to assume that the minister in charge of this *domaine* would attend cabinet meetings.

14. It is not clearly stated anywhere whether President Touré enjoys this right by virtue of his constitutional position as the President of the Republic or by virtue of his position as the Secretary General of the party. It is probably the latter since he obeys the party Congress' decision (the ninth Congress) to appoint the ministers for local development from among the members of the party's Central Committee. Also, the same Congress gave him the right to propose the names of BPN members.
15. See fn. 4 above.
16. *Horoya*, 25 April 1972.
17. See S. Camara, 'De l'action à l'idéologie', in *La RDA–PDG*, No. 27 (n.d.), p. 199.
18. This point is discussed in some detail in Chapter V.
19. S. Touré in *Horoya*, 21 March 1972. It is possible that the ideological inconsistency implied here has been dictated by practical political calculations: President Touré may have decided to exclude traders and industrialists from party posts as a means of incapacitating a group of potential challengers for power.
20. These are the people who ride in costly DS 21 (thirty-five were bought in 1965) and Mercedes (forty were bought in 1970). For more details on the relative affluence of this group of Guineans see Rivière, 'Comportements ostentatoires et style de vie des élites guinéens', *Culture et développement*, III, 3 (1971), pp. 415–43.
21. In *Horoya-hebdo*, No. 96, 14–20 November 1970. The Guinean belief in the ultimate withering away of the state has been strongly influenced by marxist theory on the subject. However, the process envisaged in Guinea differs substantially from the orthodox marxist formulation as set out by Lenin in *The State and Revolution*. For an attempt to reconcile the Guinean scheme with the orthodox marxist formulation, see M. Douno, 'Le Rapport du parti avec l'Etat guinéen', *Memoire de fin d'etudes*

supérieures, Institut polytechnique de Conakry (IPC), Ecole supérieure d'administration (ESA), 1969/70.
22. Touré, Vol. IV, pp. 83–4.
23. See Touré, Vol. IX. p. 198 and Presidential Circulars No. 004/71 PRG/SG of 30 January 1971 and No. 005/73/PRG of 30 January 1971.
24. Touré, Vol. XII, p. 30.
25. In *La RDA–PDG*, No. 41, August 1970, pp. 101–2.
26. Reports in *Horoya-hebdo* for 1969 and 1970 and interview with the Administrative Secretary of the PDG, Conakry, February 1971.
27. Published in *Horoya-hebdo*, No. 75, 20–26 June 1970.
28. This is particularly true of their judicial functions; see S. Touré in *Horoya-hebdo*, No. 86, 12–18 September 1970.
29. See Touré, Vol. IX, p. 42.
30. Except the regional governor and the federal secretary; the federal secretary is a national deputy (member of the National Assembly).
31. The statutory members of the federal conference are the members of the federal bureau, five members of every steering committee within the region, and the regional executives of youth, women's and workers' organizations. The federal bureau can, in addition, invite 'all persons judged useful'. See *La RDA–PDG*, No. 39 (n.d.), pp. 143–4.
32. Presidential Circular No. 004/71/PRG/SG of 30 January 1971.
33. Article 9 of the Guinean constitution.
34. République de Guinée, Parti démocratique de Guinée, Bureau politique national, *Le Cahier du militant*, No. 20 (n.d.), pp. 27–8.
35. This and other observations on the decision-making process in Guinea are based on information contained in the following sources: (a) *Bulletin d'information du BPN* (1962–1970); (b) *Horoya* (1961–1973); and (c) *Horoya-hebdo* (1969–1973). The *Bulletin d'information du BPN* which is purely for circulation within the party institutions is the most useful of these sources as many of its issues contain verbatim reports of CNR and Central Committee meetings.
36. See *La RDA–PDG*, No. 39 (n.d.), p. 155.
37. Presidential Circular No. 005/71/PRG of 30 January 1971.

38. See *Le Monde* (Paris), 6 January 1972.
39. The major problem in enforcing this criterion of party militancy is the difficulty of devising effective methods of testing political militancy in the absence of the membership criterion which is used in the one-party systems of Eastern Europe. The membership criterion is inapplicable in Guinea since every Guinean is automatically a member of the party. For more details, see O. O. Adamolekun, 'Central Government Administration in Guinea and Senegal Since Independence: A Comparative Study', unpublished D.Phil. thesis (Oxford, 1972), pp. 185–90. The application of the militancy yardstick has produced a fairly large number of bureaucrats who can be described as partisan bureaucrats. They owe their recruitment and, more especially, their promotion to party support and they simultaneously do party work either as activists or as leaders.
40. See *Horoya-hebdo*, Special No. 24, April 1972.

Chapter 3

1. Ambassade de France, Service de presse et d'information, *French Economic Assistance in West and Equitorial Africa: A Decade of Progress* (New York, 1958), pp. 18–19.
2. See La Documentation française, Notes et études documentaire, No. 1291, *L'Avenir de la Guinée* (Paris, 1950), p. 8.
3. According to Professor J. Suret-Canale, this mistake was responsible for a reduction in coffee plants from seventy million to between forty and forty-five million in 1964. See his *La République de Guinée* (Paris, 1970), p. 257.
4. The colonial governor in 1949 wrote as follows: 'If we could take the trouble, considering the extraordinarily favourable conditions for the cultivation of rice in Guinea, our territory could become tomorrow the rice granary of French West Africa.' See *L'Avenir de Guinée*, op. cit., p. 10.
5. Suret-Canale, op. cit., p. 119.
6. See Touré, Vol. XV, p. 5.
7. A former colonial governor in FWA gave the following advice to his successors in his memoirs: 'Always co-

operate with commerce ... it is the support of commerce that will constitute your strength at the same time as your eventual support with the [metropolitan] Government.' See A. Annet, *Je suis gouveneur d'Outre-Mer* (Paris, 1957), p. 101.
8. See Touré, Vols. I & II, p. 127.
9. See Suret-Canale, op. cit., p. 131.
10. See Touré, Vol. XIV, p. 96.
11. Touré, Vol. V, p. 309.
12. Suret-Canale, op. cit., p. 181. For many other writers, too, this decision is the chief criterion for describing the Guinean plan as 'socialist'. See, for example, M. Gaud, *Les Premières Expériences de planification en Afrique noire* (Paris, 1967), p. 138 and Y. Bénoit, 'L'Afrique en mouvement: La Guinée à l'heure du plan', *La Pensée*, No. 94, November–December 1960, pp. 3–36.
13. The Guinean franc was abolished in October 1972 and replaced with a new unit called *syli*. The value of one *syli* is ten Guinean francs and it is said to be equivalent to 0.036 gramme fine gold. There is a minor unit called *cauris* and 100 *cauris* make one *syli*. However, we shall use the old monetary unit, the Guinean franc, throughout this study. Officially one Guinean franc was equivalent to one cfa franc (currency used throughout francophone West and Central Africa) until the devaluation of the cfa in 1969. Prior to the international currency muddle of 1972, 200 GF was equivalent to $1 and 650 GF was equivalent to £1 sterling (N2).
14. See Ministère de la Fonction publique et du Travail, *Etat des fonctionnaires en service avant l'indépendance*, Conakry, August 1964, mimeo; and Assemblée nationale, *Exposé fait le 25 octobre 1963 par le Ministre de la Fonction publique et du travail*, Conakry, mimeo.
15. For the text of the plan, see 'Rapport présenté par Ismael Touré, ministre du developpement économique au CNR du 16 avril 1964', Touré, Vol. XIV, pp. 77–130.
16. 'The Seven-Year Plan must mark the entry of the Guinean economy into its industrialization phase', op. cit., p. 105.
17. In 1960, the regime claimed to have discovered a 'plot' in which France was allegedly involved. For an independent confirmation of this plot and of French involvement, see G. Chaffard, *Les Carnets secrets de la colonisation*, Vol. II

(Paris, 1967), pp. 218–44. In 1961, another 'plot' was uncovered in which the USSR and France were said to have been involved. For an eye-witness account, see *Jeune Afrique* (Tunis), No. 71, 6–12 February 1962.
18. For the text of this Circular, see *Horoya*, 25 June 1972.
19. See E. Berg, 'Socialism and Economic Development in Tropical Africa', *Quarterly Journal of Economics*, LXXVIII (1964), p. 557.
20. This was the total number of foreign experts in Guinea at this date outside teaching and medicine. République de Guinée, Statistique du travail au 15/12/67, Conakry, mimeo.
21. See M. Fainsod, 'Bureaucracy and Modernization: The Russian and Soviet Case', in J. La Palombara (ed.), *Bureaucracy and Political Development* (Princeton, 1963), p. 249.
22. Touré, Vol. V, p. 95.
23. Berg, op. cit., p. 558, fn. 8.
24. In this regard, Guinean officials distinguish between the projects of the People's Republic of China which they consider well-planned and well-executed and those of Russia and other Eastern bloc countries which are sometimes ill-planned and badly executed. Interviews, Conakry, 1970/71.
25. Touré, Vols. I & II, p. 332.
26. This expression was widely used in Western literature on Guinea between 1958 and 1961. See G. de Lusignan, *French-Speaking Africa Since Independence* (London, 1969), p. 24.
27. This incident is referred to in Guinea as the 'Teachers' Plot'. The Teachers Union presented a document to the government in November 1961 in which they asked for better wages. However, this document also contained some left-wing ideological criticisms of the government. In the tract distributed by pupils who took to the streets demanding the release of the Teachers' Union Executive members whom the government had arrested was the following: *'It is impossible for a country to be neutral between the East and the West. It is necessary to choose one bloc or the other'* (italics added). This statement probably gave the Guinean leadership the idea that Russia was behind the plot. For more details, see an eye-witness

account in *Jeune Afrique* No. 71, 6–12 February, 1962.
28. Quoted in B. Améillon, *La Guinée, bilan d'une indépendance* (Paris, 1964), p. 187.
29. See *Horoya*, 7 October 1963.
30. See A. S. Touré, *8 Novembre 1964* (Conakry, n.d.), *passim*, esp. p. 29.
31. A number of prominent traders were allegedly involved in this 'plot' (hence its label). It was claimed that the leaders of the plot planned to establish a fully-fledged capitalist system that would be more in accord with their personal interests. For an independent confirmation of this plot, see *Le Monde* (Paris), 6/7 March 1966.
32. The Guinean delegation was detained by the Ghanaian authorities because of the Guinean government's support for ex-President Nkrumah who was overthrown by a military *coup d'etat* in Febuary 1966. It was also alleged that the Guinean government was detaining about 100 Ghananians in Conakry against their will; these Ghananians landed in Conakry with ex-President Nkrumah. The American ambassador's house arrest lasted for only about twenty-four hours. For a detailed study of this diplomatic incident, see W. A. E. Skurnick, 'Ghana and Guinea, 1966 – A Case Study in Inter-African Relations', *Journal of Modern African Studies*, 5, 3 (1967), pp. 369–84.
33. In an apparent reference to the ideological contradiction implicit in this state of affairs President Touré provided the following explanation in 1972: '... there is no capitalist monopoly in Guinea and there never will be one.... [The people of Guinea] will however deal with private capital but on the basis of conventions that safeguard their interests. The Soviet Union has several agreements with capitalist countries.... We shall work with those who accept our conditions.' *Horoya-hebdo*, 20–26 February 1972.
34. See the Editorial of *Revue du développement économique* (Conakry), No. 2, March 1964.
35. This total of 1269 private traders is about half the estimated number for 1958 (2500) and about one-quarter of the number for 1964 (5000). For the 1958 and 1964 figures, see *Jeune Afrique*, No. 243, 1 August 1965.
36. See *Horoya-hebdo*, No. 139, 11–17 March 1972.

37. In *La RDA—PDG*, No. 40, May 1970, p. 19.
38. See Touré, Vol. V, p. 348.
39. Their full title was *Sociétés indigènes de prévoyance de secours et de prêts mutuels agricoles* which can be translated as Native Provident Societies for Mutual Agricultural Assistance and Loans.
40. Touré, Vol. V, p. 353.
41. Suret-Canale op. cit., p. 195.
42. It should, however, be mentioned that when the government was surveying an area of Upper Guinea for the purpose of establishing a state farm, a number of families who possessed cultivated plots there protested vehemently and their opposition contributed to the failure of the project. Suret-Canale, op. cit., p. 198, fn. 1.
43. In T. N. Diallo, 'Bilan et perspectives de la coopération dans le développement de l'agriculture guinéenne', Mémoire de fin d'études supérieures', IPC (ESA), 1967/68, p. 98.
44. See *La RDA—FDG*, No. 8, August 1966, pp. 127—30.
45. See *Horoya-hebdo*, No. 131, 24—30 July 1971. The abortive Portuguese-led invasion of November 1970 was responsible for this increased emphasis on the 'defence of the revolution'.
46. See *Horoya*, 7 January 1972.
47. See *Bulletin d'information du BPN*, No. 94 (1970), pp. 153—4.
48. ibid., p. 123.
49. This opinion is based on reading the reports on the progress so far made as contained in issues of *Horoya* and *Horoya-hebdo* for 1972 and 1973.
50. An indication of this manpower problem is provided by the fact that in 1967 there were only 148 middle-level agricultural officials in Guinea, fewer than the number of arrondissements (about 200).
51. In condemning this state of affairs in 1963, President Touré said that it was giving 'the masses the impression that political and administrative authorities are sharing the revenues of the state between them'. See *Bulletin du compte-rendu des activités du BPN*, No. 13 (1963), p. 108.
52. See B. Améillon, op. cit., p. 117.
53. See *Horoya-hebdo*, No. 86, 12—18 September 1970.

Chapter 4

1. S. Amin, *Trois expériences de développement: le Mali, la Guinée et le Ghana* (Paris, 1965), p. 158.
2. p. 291.
3. Amin, op. cit., p. 157.
4. This fifty-one per cent is shared out as follows: the United States (53%), Canada (27%), Western Germany (10%), and France (10%).
5. The projects are named after the principal towns in the areas where the bauxite deposits are located. The Kindia project began production in November 1973 several months ahead of schedule; See *West Africa* (London), 10 December 1973, p. 1735.
6. Suret-Canale, op. cit., p. 312.
7. In *Horoya*, 12 November 1963.
8. Suret-Canale, op. cit., p. 292.
9. Touré, Vol. XIV, p. 45.
10. In *Horoya-hebdo*, 5–11 February 1972.
11. Between 1960 and 1968, there was some similarity between the economic and social policies of Guinea and those of the Republic of Mali.
12. See Berg, op. cit., pp. 566–9.
13. ibid., p. 559.
14. In *Bulletin d'information du BPN*, No. 94 (1970), p. 75.
15. See President Touré's speech in *Horoya-hebdo*, Special No. 24, April 1972.
16. See Suret-Canale, op. cit., p. 273. President Touré himself admitted that this was what actually happened several years after the event; see *Horoya-hebdo*, 29 May–4 June 1971.
17. See *Horoya-hebdo*, Special No. 24, April 1972.
18. I visited the Banban Socialist Community on the outskirts of Kindia which had forty members including four girls. The Community is planned for 1000 members. I also visited the Yabandi Socialist Community in the same region with sixty-three members including five girls.
19. These observations are based on what I saw in 1971, on my discussions with some Guinean officials during this visit and on reports contained in issues of *Horoya* and *Horoya-hebdo* for 1972 and 1973. The cautious remarks made here contrast with the rather over-optimistic views

expressed by Xavier Leunda in his 'La Réforme de l'enseignement et son incidence sur l'évolution rurale en Guinée', *Civilisations*, XXII, 2 (1972), 232–59.
20. These figures are quoted from Suret-Canale, op. cit., p. 335.
21. There is reference to this problem in *Horoya-hebdo*, 22–28 January 1972.
22. It has been estimated that an annual output of 150,000 tons of aluminium can be achieved by establishing an aluminium smelting project with the aid of electric power from the Konkouré. At present, Guinea's alumina is exported to the Republic of Cameroon for smelting.
23. See Secrétariat d'Etat à l'idéologie, au Télé-enseignement et à l'alphabétisation, *Problèmes monétaires et courts des comptes*, (Conakry, 1970), mimeo. pp. 21–2.
24. See Touré, Vol. XIV, p. 42.
25. In *La RDA–PDG*, No. 27 (n.d.), p. 47.
26. In 1967 there were 6830 Guineans and 621 foreigners employed by the educational service. See *Statistique du travail... 1967*, op. cit.
27. President Touré's own words on this problem deserve to be quoted: 'Hundreds of young people are made to teach without any teacher training [education] and without the necessary qualifications and guidance. Thus, without any experience, without any professional ability and without any adequate provision, young people are charged with the responsibility for the intellectual, technical and cultural training of other young people! Also, we should like to point out that young teachers trained by teacher training colleges as ordinary pupil teachers or assistant pupil teachers are often found being used in lower secondary or even upper secondary schools.' *Horoya-hebdo*, 15–21 January 1972.
28. See *La RDA–PDG*, No. 27, p. 148.
29. *Horoya*, 4 January 1972.
30. See C. Rivière, 'Les résultats d'un enseignement révolutionnaire en Guinée', *Revue française d'études politiques africaine*, No. 52 (April 1970), p. 43. Mr. Rivière was a sociology teacher in the Conakry polytechnic between 1964 and 1968.
31. In *Horoya-hebdo*, No. 32, 23–29 August 1969.
32. See *Horoya*, 21 April 1973.

33. Guinea has won both the African nation's cup and the cup for the champion club (twice). And at the Second All-African Games held in Lagos (Nigeria) in January 1973 the Guinean national team won the silver medal.
34. Touré in *Horoya*, 9 March 1973.
35. ibid.
36. For the text of the decree setting up *Syliart*, see *Horoya-hebdo*, 24–30 July 1971.
37. In *Horoya-hebdo*, No. 139, 11–17 March 1972. A striking demonstration of the excellent 'moral condition' for Guinean artists was provided in April 1973 when the death of a leading member of the Bembeya National Jazz Band (through an accident in Dakar) was treated as a national tragedy with messages of condolence sent to the President of the Republic from all parts of the country and from foreign governments.
38. For details, see *Horoya*, 17 May 1973.
39. According to President Touré, 'The revenue obtained by the cinema is seen by us in political, ideological, moral and intellectual terms'. See *La RDA–PDG*, No. 27 (n.d.), p. 99.
40. See *Horoya-hebdo*, No, 139, 11–17 March 1972.
41. In *Horoya-hebdo*, No. 129, 10–16 July 1971.
42. Touré in *Horoya-hebdo*, 17–23 July 1971.
43. *African Renaissance* (London, 1969), p. 203.
44. In *Horoya-hebdo*, No. 139, 11–17 March 1972.
45. These *emigrés* are mostly found in Sierra Leone, Liberia, Ivory Coast, Senegal and France.

Chapter 5

1. Touré, Vol. XII, p. 44.
2. ibid.
3. The details of the Guinean historic vote can be found in Touré, Vols. I & II, p. 190.
4. For more details, see 'Ladipo Adamolekun, 'The Road to Independence in French Tropical Africa', *Tarikh*, 2, 4 (1969), 72–85.
5. A French observer has described the actions of her countrymen as 'an abusive confusion of small-scale individual gangsterism with patriotism': see Améillon, op. cit., p. 83.

6. See *Présence Africaine*, English edition, Vol. I (1960), devoted entirely to 'Independent Guinea', p. 103.
7. President Touré reaffirmed this in 1971 when he declared: 'For a people, there is no wealth that is superior to liberty, sovereignty and dignity', See *La RDA–PDG*, No. 43, January 1971, p. 205.
8. Touré, Vols. I & II, p. 332.
9. See footnote 27, Chapter 3.
10. See Chaffard, *Les Carnets secrets de la décolonisation*, op. cit., p. 256.
11. See fn. 32, Chapter 3.
12. See reports in *Horoya*, November 1966.
13. G. Chaffard, *Les Carnets secrets de la décolonisation*, Vol. II (Paris, 1967), pp. 218–44. See also *Nouvel Observateur* (Paris), No. 258, 20 October, 1969.
14. V. Du Bois, 'The Independence Movement in Guinea: A Study in African Nationalism', an unpublished Ph.D. dissertation at the Princeton University, U.S.A., March 1962, p. 181.
15. See *Jeune Afrique*, No. 71, 6–12 February 1962.
16. The French ambassador in Conakry was expelled (with a forty-eight hour quit notice) for alleged involvement in the 1965 plot. This marked the end of the diplomatic relations established in 1961 after numerous months of a wait-and-see attitude adopted by late President de Gaulle's government. Diplomatic relations have not been resumed since this break.
17. The Guinean version of these 'plots' is contained in *La RDA–PDG*, No. 38 (Conakry, 1970), *passim*. See also Touré, Vol. XV, pp. 24–42.
18. See *Horoya-hebdo*, Special No. 14 May 1971. I can testify that this contribution was considered by Guineans as a patriotic gesture and an act of national solidarity. I discovered that I became emotionally involved (having witnessed the whole incident) and donated 5000 FG.
19. The basic text is D. T. Niane and J. Suret-Canale, *Histoire de l'Afrique occidentale* (Conakry, 1960). A simpler version of this book was later prepared for primary schools.
20. Touré, Vol. X, p. 65.
21. Touré, Vol. III, pp. 409–10.
22. One account refers to 'several twenties dead and several hundreds wounded'. Améillon, op. cit., p. 30.

23. At its inaugural congress in 1947, almost all the 100 delegates were representatives of ethnic associations.
24. It is important to mention, in this connection, that Sékou Touré was elected a territorial councillor in 1953 in a by-election in Beyla, outside his region of origin.
25. See *Journal Officiel de la Guinée française*, 15 January 1958.
26. In the attempt to collect taxes and provide labourers for the colonial administration, many chiefs put their subjects under undue pressures. Furthermore, some chiefs hid under the protection of the colonial administration to exploit their subjects. In the 1950s, the chiefs were among the emerging local bourgeoisie riding luxurious cars and living rather sumptuously.
27. For an account of this meeting, see *Guinée, prélude a l'indépendance* (Paris, 1959), *passim*.
28. See *Journal officiel de la République de Guinée* (JORG), 1 March 1959.
29. The only incident of inter-ethnic conflict recorded during this period was in connection with the election to the executive of the PDG section in Mamou (Middle Guinea) in 1959. The national executive of the party, the BPN, nullified the result of the elections because it claimed that it was based on 'racial myth'. New elections supervised by the BPN were later held. See Touré, Vol. III, p. 276.
30. Touré Vol. VIII, p. 26.
31. Touré Vol. XIV, p. 197.
32. Touré, *8 Novembre 1964*, p. 67.
33. In *Horoya-hebdo*, 28 November–4 December 1970.
34. Rivière, *Mutations sociales en Guinée* (Paris, 1971), pp. 87–8. Rivière was in Guinea between October 1964 and July 1968.
35. Although the fact that President Touré is married to a woman whose mother was a Foulah (the father was French) is not given any publicity, it is nevertheless likely to be considered by some Guineans as an example of how to transcend ethnic particularism. But there is no deliberate policy to encourage inter-ethnic marriage in Guinea.
36. In *Horoya*, 17 June 1973. Rivière claims to have heard these complaints during his stay in Guinea; see *Mutations Sociales en Guinée*, op. cit., p. 74.
37. Touré, Vol. XIV, pp. 245–6.

38. Touré, Vol. XVI, p. 9.
39. *Horoya*, 16 June 1972.
40. S. M. Lipset, *The First New Nations* (New York, 1963), p. 74. It is important to mention that the national leaders of the majority of West African states have at one time or another sought to project a revolutionary national image. The only exceptions are Liberia, Gambia, Sierra Leone, Ivory Coast and Niger. Of the other countries that have sought to project a revolutionary national image, only Dabomey has followed the Guinean example of baptizing its radio network as the Voice of the Revolution (since 1973).
41. Touré, Vol. III, pp. 342–3.
42. Mémoire de fin d'études supérieures, IPC, 1967–68, p. 92.
43. For the details, see *Horoya*, 27 May 1972.
44. On the other hand, the PDG leadership has consistently allowed an important number of Guinean Muslims to go to Mecca annually despite the acute foreign exchange problem in the country. Allah's blessing for the PDG is not free of charge!
45. See *La RDA–PDG*, No. 8, August 1966, pp. 127–31.
46. ibid.
47. ibid.
48. For a detailed account of the role of these students, see *Horoya*, 22 November 1971. Shortly after the incident, I met the two leaders of the students' militia, Pivi Togba and Funuisiré Kondé, who were very proud of the achievement of 'The 90-Member Column' (the name that was later given to their rescue team).
49. See *Horoya-hebdo*, No. 116, 10–16 April 1971, pp. 17–18.
50. This is an approximate figure as I was unable to determine the ages and background of two Central Committee members. The whole question of political succession is discussed in some detail in the next chapter.
51. It is important to mention that Guinea has declared as a national heroine a woman called M'Baila Camara, a PDG militant who was accidentally killed during a violent confrontation between the PDG militants of the *Canton* of Tondon and the chief of the *Canton* who had responsibility for maintaining law and order. Her name is usually

mentioned in the class of Samory Touré and Alfa Yaya Diallo.
52. See *JORG*, 1 November 1969.
53. *Horoya-hebdo*, 28 November–4 December 1970.
54. Touré, Vol. III, p. 9.
55. *Horoya-hebdo*, No. 86, 12–18 September 1970.
56. Touré Vol. XVI, p. 5.
57. ibid., p. 10.
58. *La RDA–PDG*, No. 23 (1968), p. 65. Touré also does some ethnic balancing in the references he makes to Guinea's past heroes. As he mentions Samory Touré (his great-grandfather) he also mentions the Foulah ruler, Alfa Yaya Diallo. Although both Samory Touré and Yaya Diallo died in French-imposed exile, the former's offence was clearly because of his tough resistance to French conquest while the latter's banishment was a result of some administrative muddle by French rulers. In order to achieve some ethnic balancing, the qualitative difference between these two men is not mentioned.
59. Considering the fact that Touré's formal education ended at the primary school, his inability to live up to this infallibility demand is not surprising. Touré himself has described his limited schooling as an important handicap: 'Dismissed from school with the ordinary Primary School Leaving Certificate ... I have known the important handicap of the lack of any serious intellectual and professional training'. See Touré, Vol. XI, p. 5.
60. The Guinean regime refers to the dissidents inside Guinea who knew of the 1970 invasion in advance and were ready to join forces with the invaders as a 'fifth column'. The expression was first coined during the Spanish War of 1939 when General Franco claimed to be attacking Spain with five columns: one from each of the four cardinal points and the fifth from inside Spain itself meaning his collaborators in Spain.

Chapter 6

1. Quoted by J. Lacouture, *Cinq hommes et la France* (Paris, 1961), p. 362.
2. Quoted in S. M. Lipset, *The First New Nation* (New York, 1963), p. 16.

3. We accept David Easton's definition of 'politics' as 'the authoritative allocation of values' given in his *The Political System* (New York, 1953), pp. 130 ff.
4. Touré in *La RDA–PDG*, No. 42 (1970), p. 23.
5. See, for example, Rivière, *Mutations Sociales en Guinée*, op. cit., pp. 400–3. The only exception to this school of thought is provided by Suret-Canale's verdict which can be summed up as 'modest' economic success. See Suret-Canale, *La République de Guinée*, op. cit., pp. 159–399.
6. Touré in Republique de Guinée, *Huitième Congrès du Parti démocratique de Guinée (RDA) tenu à Conakry du 25 Septembre au 20 Octobre 1967* (Conakry, n.d.), p. 91. This exhortation was to no avail as President Touré had to formally prohibit these 'demobilizing' activities in 1972: 'all mobilizations for welcoming a commandant of arrondissement or a regional governor are henceforth absolutely prohibited.' See *Horoya-hebdo*, Special No. 24, April 1972.
7. Touré, Vol. XIV, p. 259.
8. By implication we are saying that the idea of direct popular administration is an illusion.
9. The writer obtained first-hand experience of the social inequalities in Senegal and the Ivory Coast as a result of fairly long study visits to both countries between 1965 and 1971. The situation in Senegal has been brilliantly portrayed by Sembene Ousmane in a film called *Le Mandat*.
10. Articles 39 and 40 of the Guinean Constitution; see Appendix B.
11. In *Horoya-hebdo*, No. 88, 26 September–2 October 1970.
12. This mass militarization is summed up in the following slogan which was coined early in 1971:
    'Beside the cutlass, a gun
    'Beside the pot, a gun
    'Beside the hammer, a gun
    'Beside the pen, a gun
    'Beside the industrial plant, a gun.'
At about the same time, I heard rumours of a plan to translate the handbook on guerilla warfare used in Cuba into French for use within Guinea. Presumably, the new emphasis on national languages could mean that the handbook will be translated into these languages too.

13. P. Collins, 'The Coup Against Chile's Allende', in *New Nigerian* (Kaduna, Nigeria), 11 October 1973.
14. In 1972, the number of Guinean students who were sent abroad by the PDG regime and who have refused to return home after completing their courses was officially estimated at 180. *Horoya*, 2 March 1972.
15. Quoted in Du Bois, 'The Independence Movement in Guinea . . .', op. cit., p. 96, fn. 3.
16. President Touré has consistently made this allegation since the late 1960s. See, for example, *West Africa*, 11th June 1973, p. 792. Mr Foccart's Secretariat was abolished in May 1974.
17. I arrived in Guinea a week before the invasion on 14th November 1970 and remained there till March 1971.
18. The award of a number of international prizes has also helped to boost President Touré's prestige. In 1961, he was awarded the Lenin Peace Prize (the first African leader to win it) and in 1970 he was awarded the Lambrakis Medal for Peace (the Eastern bloc equivalent of the Nobel Peace Prize).
19. *La RDA–PDG*, No. 14, February 1967, p. 38.
20. *Horoya-hebdo*, 30 January–5 February 1971.

Chapter 7

1. L. W. Pye, *Politics, Personality, and Nation Building: Burma's Search for Identity* (New Haven, 1962), p. 33.
2. ibid.
3. Pye provides a comprehensive review of the respective contributions of Sir Henry Maine, Ferdinand Toennies, Emile Durkheim, Max Weber, and Talcott Parsons to the dichotomous scheme approach in his *Politics Personality, and Nation Building* . . . , pp. 33–7.
4. Pye has argued this point in his book cited above; see especially pp. 38–40. In doing this, he acknowledges, in particular, the works of R. C. Wood, *Surburbia: Its People and Its Politics* (New York, 1959); W. Whyte, *The Organization Man* (New York, 1956) and D. Reisman, *The Lonely Crowd* (New Haven, 1950).
5. For a comprehensive review of the existing literature on the integration approach, see W. Connor, 'Nation-Building or Nation-Destroying?' *World Politics*, xxiv, 3 (April 1972), 319–55.

6. See, for example, G. Morrison and H. M. Stevenson, 'Cultural Pluralism, Modernization, and Conflict: An Empirical Analysis of Sources of Political Instability in African Nations', *Canadian Journal of Political Science*, V, 1 (March 1972), 82–103.
7. For example, this is the position taken by G. Morrison and H. Stevenson in their 'Cultural Pluralism, Modernization, and Conflict . . .' op. cit., p. 88: 'We define *modernization* as changes in the structure of nations that produce institutional arrangements like those found in the structure of industrial societies. In particular, we are concerned with the degree to which new nations develop greater measures of national income, industrialization, urbanization, enrolment in formal educational institutions, mass media consumption and political participation.'
8. Pye, op. cit., p. 40.
9. For example, the leaders of the three East African States of Kenya, Tanzania and Uganda have similar views on the subject. See, A. Mazrui, *Cultural Engineering and Nation Building in East Africa* (Evanston, Illinois, 1972), *passim*.
10. By W. Connor in *World Politics*, XXIV, 3 (April 1972), 319–55.
11. According to one account, the cost of living rose by 100–120 per cent in Guinea between 1960 and 1970 while the salary of the middle and lower-level workers rose by only ten per cent. See, Rivière, 'Les Consequences de la réorganisation des circuits commerciaux en Guinée', *Revue Française d'études politiques africaines*, 66, (June 1971), p. 94.
12. 'Ladipo Adamolekun, 'Some Reflections on Sékou Touré's Guinea', *West Africa*, 26 March 1973, pp. 403–4.
13. ibid., p. 404.
14. Mazrui, op. cit., *passim*, esp. pp. 87–261 and p. 282.
15. ibid., p. 282.
16. ibid., p. 128.

Appendix A

Prelude to the Ballot Box Revolution of September 1958: Resolution of the Territorial Conference of the PDG held on 14 September, 1958*

The extraordinary Conference of the PDG, convened in Conakry on 14 September 1958 to determine the position of the party in face of the referendum of 28 September 1958.

Unanimously *approves* the report of the Secretary General, salutes the Congressists with acclamation:

The Conference
Whereas all youth, trade union and political organizations of Black Africa have always fought for the total liquidation of the colonial regime and the affirmation of the African national reality;
Whereas these same organizations have constantly posed the problem of African unity as coming before any form of association with France;
Whereas the struggle of the RDA, in particular, since its creation, had as its finality the political, social, and economic liberation of the African masses;
Whereas these major objectives have been reaffirmed by the Conference of the Regrouping of African Parties, held in Paris on 15 February 1958, and by the memorandum prepared by these same parties on 18 July 1958;

Noting
1   that the constitutional bill submitted to referendum on 28 September 1958, far from satisfying the essential aspirations of African masses, consecrates the balkanisation of Africa and its integration into the French Republic;
2   that the exercise of the right to independence which it proposes to African states is left to the discretion of the French Republic alone;

*Translated by the author.

3   that the bill introduces inequality between the future states to the profit of the French Republic in the management of the community's affairs.

Taking note of the declaration of General de Gaulle, President of the government of the French Republic, made on 25 August 1958, before the Territorial Assembly of Guinea, in the following terms:

> The community, France proposes it. Nobody is forced to adhere to it. People have spoken of independence. I say here, louder than elsewhere, that independence is within the reach of Guinea. She can take it, she can take it on 28 September by saying 'No' to the proposal which she is offered and, in that case, I guarantee that the *Metropole* will not present any obstacle. She will, of course, give effect to the implications of that decision but she will present no obstacles and your territory could, as it wishes, and in the conditions which it will desire, follow the road that it wishes.

Whereas there cannot be, for a dependent people, the least hesitation in the choice between independence and the community proposed. The Conference DECIDES TO CHOOSE INDEPENDENCE BY VOTING 'NO' AT THE REFERENDUM OF 28 SEPTEMBER: (*sic.*)

INVITES African masses, political, trade union, youth and student organizations of Black Africa, to do everything in order to save the future of African by the triumph of 'No' in all of Africa under French domination.

THROWS a pressing appeal to the populations of Guinea, Europeans and Africans, in order that they can contribute to the realization in the calmness and dignity of our option, the best guarantee for the safeguard of our common interests;

GIVES THE MANDATE to the Political Bureau of the PDG to make contact immediately with the bureau of the Steering Committees and Territorial Sections of the RDA with a view to safeguarding African unity in the direction of independence.

Source: Territoire de la Guinée. *L'Action politique du Parti démocratique de Guinée pour l'émancipation africaine: par M. Sékou Touré* (Conakry n.d.) pp. 205–6.

Appendix B

The Constitution of the Republic of Guinea*
(Adopted on 10 November 1958 and modified on 22 October 1963)

Preamble

The people of Guinea by their overwhelming vote of September 28 1958 rejected domination and, in so doing, acquired their national independence and became a free and sovereign state.

The State of Guinea adheres fully to the Charter of the United Nations and to the Universal Declaration of Human Rights.

It proclaims the equality and solidarity of all its citizens without distinction as to race, sex or creed.

It affirms its will to utilize every means possible to realize and consolidate unity within the independence of all Africa. To this end it will fight against all tendencies and manifestations of chauvinism which it considers as serious obstacles to the realization of this aim.

It expresses its desire to form bonds of friendship with all peoples based on the principles of equality, reciprocal interests and mutual respect of national sovereignty and territorial integrity.

It upholds unreservedly all policies tending towards the creation of a United States of Africa and the safeguarding and consolidation of world peace.

The principle of the Republic of Guinea is: government of the people, by the people and for the people.

---

*Translated by the author.

Title I

On National Sovereignty

Article 1 — Guinea is a republic based on the principles of democracy, freedom of religion and social justice.

The national flag consists of red, yellow and green vertical stripes of equal dimensions.

The national anthem is: 'LIBERTY'.

The motto of the Republic is: Work, Justice, Solidarity.

Title II

On National Collectivities

Article 2 — National sovereignty shall belong to the people who shall exercise it in all matters through their deputies to the National Assembly, whose members are elected by equal universal suffrage, in direct and secret ballot, or by referendum.

Article 3 — The Republic of Guinea shall be composed of territorial collectivities which shall be: communes, arrondissements and administrative regions.

Title III

On Parliament

Article 4 — Parliament shall consist of one National Assembly whose members, elected on a national list for five years, bear the title of deputies.

Article 5 — The method of electing members of the National Assembly, the terms of eligibility and incompatibility, as well as the number of deputies, shall be ascertained by law.

Article 6 — The National Assembly shall be the sole judge of the eligibility of its members and the regularity of their election. It may accept their resignation.

Article 7 — The National Assembly shall meet in two ordinary annual sessions fixed respectively for the third and tenth month of the financial year which begins on the 1st October of the current calendar year and ends on the 30th of

September of the following year. The duration of these sessions cannot exceed two months.

The Assembly may hold extraordinary sessions if so called by its president, upon the request of the government or of two-thirds of its members.

The National Assembly elects from among its members a Permanent Commission.

The Permanent Commission sits during the intervals between the sessions of the National Assembly. It pronounces on bills whose urgent character admits of no delay.

The legislative texts adopted by the Permanent Commission are subject to the ratification of the National Assembly during its next session.

Article 8 – The Bureau and the Commissions of the National Assembly are elected for the duration of each legislature.

Title IV

On Relations between Parliament and Government

Article 9 – The National Assembly alone shall pass the law. The domain of the law is unlimited.

Article 10 – No member of the National Assembly shall be subjected to pursuit, investigation, arrest, detention or trial because of his opinions or votes during the exercise of his functions.

Article 11 – Unless apprehended *in flagrante delicto* no member of the National Assembly shall, during the length of his term, be pursued in criminal matters or minor offences except with the authority of the Assembly. Detention or pursuit of a deputy is suspended if the National Assembly so decides.

Article 12 – Members of the National Assembly shall receive, for the duration of the sessions, a daily allowance determined by decree.

The members of the Permanent Commission shall enjoy the same allowance during the sessions of the Permanent Commission.

Article 13 – The meeting of the National Assembly shall be public. The National Assembly can hold meetings *in camera* upon the request of the president of the government or of more than half of the members.

Article 14 – The President of the Republic and the deputies to the Assembly alone shall have the power to initiate and propose laws.

Article 15 – The National Assembly shall study drafts and proposals of laws which originate in its various committees whose numbers, composition and functions shall be determined by the National Assembly. Drafts of law submitted by the government and proposals accepted by it shall be studied with priority.

Article 16 – The National Assembly shall examine the estimate of the budget which when voted on by Parliament shall become law.

The general budget must be ratified at the latest on the last day of the eleventh month of the preceding financial year.

Article 17 – The deputies to the National Assembly shall possess the power of initiative for expenditures. No proposal tending to increase expenditures shall be presented without an accompanying proposal providing corresponding receipts.

Article 18 – The National Assembly shall regulate the accounts of the nation. A statement of expenditures shall be presented before it at the end of each semester for the preceding semester.

The final accounts of the preceding year shall be examined during the second ordinary session and ratified by law.

Article 19 – The National Assembly shall dispose of the following means of information concerning governmental action:

– oral questioning
– written questioning
– interpellation
– audition by committees
– investigation committees

The law shall establish the conditions and procedure according to which these means of information shall be executed. The law also shall fix the time limit for answers.

Title V

On the Head of State

Article 20 – The President of the Republic shall be the Head of State. He shall be head of the armed forces. Any citizen who is eligible and has reached the age of thirty-five years can be elected President of the Republic.

Title VI

On the Government

Article 21 – The powers of the government of the Republic shall be exercised by the President of the Republic assisted by a Cabinet.

Article 22 – The President of the Republic shall be elected for a term of seven years by universal suffrage with an absolute majority on the first ballot or a plurality on the second ballot. He may be re-elected for a second term.

Article 23 – The President of the Republic shall appoint the ministers by decree. No member of the government may be arrested or pursued without the previous consent of the President of the Republic.

Article 24 – In the exercise of their duties, the ministers shall be responsible for their actions to the President of the Republic who is responsible for the general policies of his cabinet to the National Assembly.

Article 25 – The President of the Republic shall ensure the execution of all laws. He shall make appointments to all posts in the public administration and to all offices and functions of a military nature.

Article 26 – Government acts shall be signed by the President of the Republic and countersigned by the ministers in charge of their execution.

Article 27 – During his term of office no government member shall hold any other obligation, professional or private.

Article 28 – In case of vacancy, the Cabinet shall remain in function to administer all current affairs until the election of a new Head of State.

Article 29 – Ministers may attend meetings of the National Assembly and of its committees. They shall be heard upon their request.

They may be assisted or represented in the discussions before the National Assembly or its Committees by civil servants assigned for this purpose.

Article 30 – In emergency cases the President of the Republic may delegate his powers to a minister.

Title VII

On International Relations

Article 31 — The Republic of Guinea shall conform with the rules of international law.

Article 32 — The President of the Republic shall negotiate treaties subject to the provisions of *Article 33*.

Article 33 — Treaties concerning international organization, treaties of commerce, treaties of peace, treaties which engage the finances of the state, those which relate to individuals, those which modify provisions of a legislative nature as well as those which entail assignments, exchanges, adjuncts of territory, shall not be ratified except by law and shall take effect after ratification.

Title VIII

On Inter-African Relations

Article 34 — The Republic may conclude, with any African state, agreements of association or community, comprising partial or complete surrender of sovereignty with a view to achieving African unity.

Title IX

On Judicial Powers

Article 35 — Justice shall be rendered in the name of the people of Guinea. The President of the Republic shall be the trustee of the independence of judicial authority.

He shall hold the power of pardon.

In the exercise of their judicial functions, the judges shall obey only the law.

Article 36 — The Court shall hold its sessions in public except in particular cases as set by law.

The accused shall be entitled to the right of defence.

Article 37 — Judicial authority, guardian of individual liberty, shall ensure the respect of the rights of citizens under conditions stipulated by law.

Article 38 — The judicial organization of the Republic shall be established by law.

Title X

On the Rights and Fundamental Duties of Citizens

Article 39 – All citizens of the Republic of Guinea, without distinction as to race, sex or creed, shall have the right to elect and be elected under the conditions established by law.

Article 40 – The citizens of the Republic of Guinea shall enjoy freedom of speech, of press, of assembly, of association, of procession and of public demonstrations under the conditions set by law.

Article 41 – Freedom of religion shall be assured to all citizens by the secularity of schools and state.

Article 42 – No one may be detained arbitrarily.

Article 43 – The domicile of citizens of the Republic of Guinea is inviolable. The privacy of citizen's mail is guaranteed by law.

Article 44 – The citizens of the Republic of Guinea shall enjoy the same and equal right to work, rest, social assistance and education.

The exercise of trade unionism and the right to strike are recognized for the worker.

Article 45 – Any act of racial discrimination as well as all propaganda of a racial or regional character shall be punishable by law.

Article 46 – The Republic of Guinea grants the right of sanctuary to foreign citizens pursued because of their struggle for the defence of a just cause or for their scientific or cultural activities.

Article 47 – All citizens of the Republic of Guinea shall conform to the Constitution and other laws of the Republic, pay their taxes and fulfil in an honest manner their civic duties.

Article 48 – The defence of the nation is the sacred duty of every citizen of the Republic of Guinea.

Title XI

On Constitutional Revisions

Article 49 – The initiative for revising the Constitution shall belong concurrently to the President of the Republic and to members of the National Assembly. The National Assembly by a vote of a two-thirds majority of its members may adopt or submit to referendum the draft of a constitutional revision.

Article 50 — The republican form of State shall not be put to any constitutional revision.

Title XII

On Transitory Provisions

Article 51 — The government functioning at the date of the promulgation of the present Constitution shall remain in office until the election of the President of the Republic.

Article 52 — The present Constitution shall be promulgated by the Head of State within forty-eight hours following its adoption by the National Assembly.

Article 53 — The first legislative session of the National Assembly of the Republic of Guinea shall begin from the date of promulgation of the present constitution.

Appendix C

Extracts from the Statutes of the Democratic Party of Guinea*

(The text reproduced below was prepared after the substantial modifications introduced by the party's eighth Congress of 1967. A few changes made by the party's ninth Congress of 1972 are incorporated into the text by the writer.)

Preamble

The PDG is the party of the African democratic revolution – the maker of the independence of the people of Guinea, it is resolved to remain a popular party, the effective agent of political, economic and social promotion based on the action of the masses, the inexhaustible source of creative energies.

On the basis of the mass line, the PDG is resolved, thanks to the cultural socialist revolution, to carry out a radical transformation of mentalities and to root out from the society all irrational practices, all alienating tendencies and the slightest inclination towards the exploitation of man by man.

The PDG recognizes class struggle as the only dynamic and historically just step towards the conquest of political, economic, social and cultural power by the entire people. This global power, will be exercised by the people of Guinea henceforth and for ever by the popular revolutionary authority deriving from the mass line which is the foundation of the political philosophy of the party. . . .

Conscious of its responsibilities to represent in all fields of human activities the entire working people of Guinea: the

---

*Translated by the author.

young, the old, men, women, workers of all kinds without distinction, the PDG organizes, orients and stimulates the young generation, the women, the salaried workers on the fundamental structures of the party. But because of the specialized activities and functions which they carry out within the Guinean society, these special organizations developing within the party, are represented in all the instances of the general organization and bring their specific contributions to it.

Within the party, they are administered by internal regulations which are the adaptation to the fields that concern them of the general statutes of the party.

Title I

Object

Conscious of its historical role at the national, African and international levels

Article 1 — The object of the PDG is, among others:

- to group all the citizens of the Republic of Guinea and to organize them within the national territory into a united, strong, democratic and socialist nation.
- to educate the Guinean popular masses in order to make them fully and exclusively responsible for their future.
- to work constantly for:
- the total liberation and emancipation of all African peoples and the affirmation of their personality.
- the rehabilitation and development of African culture.
- the unification of the African fatherland, the development of its riches for the benefit of African peoples.
- the building of a socialist society in a world of social justice, democratic progress and peace.

Head Office

Article 2 — The head office of the party is based in Conakry. It can be transferred to any other place in the Republic by a decision of the Congress.

Requirements for Admission

Article 3 — Membership of the Democratic Party of Guinea is the right of every citizen of the Republic of Guinea who is at least seven years old, who accepts its programme and the statutes, takes an active part in the realization of the objectives fixed in *Article 1* above and applies the decisions of the party and pays his dues.

Title II

Duties and Rights of a Member of the Party

Article 4 — The member of the party must:

(a) apply strictly and without failing the decisions of the party, participate actively in the political life of the state, in the building of the economy and in the development of its art and culture, show example in carrying out social duty, put the interests of the society above personal interests.

(b) foster criticism and self-criticism, courageously expose any shortcomings and be committed to their removal, fight against ostentatious spirit, self-sufficiency, laziness, racism, chauvinism, regionalism, liberalism; counter energetically any attempt to stifle criticism and self-criticism; oppose all acts that are detrimental to the party, to the revolution and to the state; and inform the bodies of the party about such acts right up to and including the National Political Bureau.

(c) apply without failing the line of the party in the choice of cadres on the basis of their political and practical qualities.

(d) respect the discipline of the party and the state.

(e) contribute by all means to the consolidation of the power of the Republic of Guinea, fight untiringly for peace and friendship among the peoples.

(f) remain permanently as an active, conscious and effective instrument in the service of the Guinean revolution and of African emancipation.

Title III

A member of the party has the duty and the right:

Article 5 — (a) to discuss freely in the assemblies of the base committee, conferences and congresses of the party before the organization takes a decision, the party's political problems and practical activities and to make proposals, to openly express and defend his opinion.

(b) to elect and to be elected to the directing bodies of the party.

(c) to pose questions, to make declarations and proposals within any instance or body of the party, up to and including the National Political Bureau in the framework of the established hierarchy and to demand an answer on the basic cause of any problem.

The following cannot be elected to the directing bodies of the Democratic Party of Guinea: (i) Persons who exercise private industrial or commercial activities or who are engaged in any activity involving the exploitation of man by man. (ii) Persons condemned since 1958 for theft, embezzlement, crime, irrational practices, abuse of confidence, subversion and racism during the five years following their liberation.

Article 6 — Admission to the party is exclusively on an individual basis. It is pronounced by the base committees.

Article 7 — Each member pays an annual due whose sum is fixed by the Congress or the CNR. He receives, in return, the card of the party signed by the president and treasurer of the base committee.

Article 8 — Membership right can be forfeited either by exclusion or by voluntary resignation.

Title IV

Principles

Article 9 — The guiding principle of the party is democratic centralism which means:

(a) Election of all the directing bodies of the party from the base to the summit.

(b) Periodic accounts of the bodies of the party before their respective instances and before the immediately superior directing bodies.

(c) Rigorous discipline in the party and submission of the minority to the majority.

(d) Strict obligation for the lower bodies to respect and apply the decisions of the superior bodies.

Article 10 – Democracy is ensured within the party through the election in Congress of all the directing bodies at every level, according to methods which ensure the expression of the free will of all the members.

The decisions of all the party's bodies are taken by the majority of the members present. They are not valid unless at least half of the members are present.

Article 11 – Each directing body is responsible:

(a) before the level that elects it.

(b) before the immediately superior body.

Title V

Organizational Structure of the Party

Article 12 – The structure of the party is at the same time horizontal and vertical. It is as follows:

(i) (a) At the base, corresponding to a village or a quarter, there is a committee grouping the whole of the militants of the geographical unit concerned and whose role consists of organizing the masses, educating them, directing their struggle for the realization of the objectives pursued by the party and ensuring the application of the decisions made in Congress or by the superior instances and bodies.

(b) Within the services, enterprises and societies grouping an important number of workers and which responds to the criterion of functional unity there shall be a Committee of Production.

(c) Within each military and para-military unit there shall be a Base Committee.

(ii) Several committees constitute the second level called the Section of the Party.

(iii) The Federation groups all the Sections within the same administrative region.

(iv) The whole of the Federations constitute the Democratic Party of Guinea.

Article 13 – These four levels of the party are in direct liaison. Each level of the party has a directing body.

Article 14 – Because of certain specific conditions recognized in the activities of the youth, the women and certain categories of workers, the following have been created:

(a) Within each Base Committee, a Special Committee of the Youth of the two sexes and a Special Committee of Women.

(b) At the level of each Section of the party, a Committee of the JRDA of the Section and a Female Committee of the Section.

(c) At the level of each Federation, a Regional Committee of the JRDA, a Regional Committee of Women and a Regional Committee of Workers.

(d) At the national level, a National Committee of the JRDA, a National Committee of Women and a National Committee of Workers.

Title VI

The Directing Bodies of the Party

The Executive of the Base Committee

Article 15 – The Base Committee Executive constitutes the organ of the Local Revolutionary Authority. It consists of thirteen members elected for two years among whom eleven should be elected in the General Assembly of the Committee. The first leader of the youth and the first leader of the women are compulsorily members. The presidents of the Committees of Production are members of the Base Committees in their places of residence.

Article 16 – The members of the Base Committee Executive are chosen exclusively from among the members of the Democratic Party of Guinea aged twenty-one at least and who have been party militants for a minimum of three years.

The Executive of the Section

Article 17 – The Executive of the Section is the Steering Committee composed of thirteen members among whom ten are elected in the Congress of the Section for two years.

It must include the first leader of the JRDA Section Committee and the first leader of the Female Section Committee.

The Commandant of Arrondissement who is a member by right is the thirteenth.

The members are chosen exclusively from among the leaders of the Committees composing the Section who have served for a minimum of three years as leaders with a Base Committee Bureau and of members of the out-going Steering Committee.

The Executive of the Federation
Article 20 — The Federation is directed by an Executive of thirteen members of whom nine are elected in the Congress and four are members by right:

- the Regional Governor
- the President of the Female Regional Committee
- the Secretary General of the JRDA Regional Committee
- the Secretary General of the Workers' Regional Committee

The elected members are chosen exclusively from among the leaders of the Steering Committees and the members of the out-going Federal Bureau.

Article 22 — The Federal Bureau meets at least twice a month.

The Secretary General of the PDG, Supreme Leader of the Revolution
Article 24 — The Secretary General of the PDG bears the title of Supreme Leader of the Revolution. In this capacity:

he is responsible for the life of the party

he can, at all moments:

— summon the Congress of the Party

— award the highest distinctions to every militant whose political behaviour would have been judged exceptionally remarkable

— exclude from the party any leader or militant whose behaviour is considered prejudicial to the party and to the revolution.

Title VIII

Functioning
Article 28 — The instances of the Democratic Party of Guinea

are:

- the General Assembly of the Base Committee
- the Conference of the Section
- the Congress of the Section
- the Federal Conference
- the Federal Congress
- the National Council of the Revolution (CNR)
- the National Congress

The General Assembly of the Base Committee

Article 29 — The General Assembly of the Committee groups the members of the PDG resident in the territorial area of the Base Committee . . .

The General Assembly of the Committee is compulsorily summoned every Friday. It can hold extraordinary meetings by the decision of the Committee's executive.

Conference of the Section

Article 30 — In-between two Congresses of the Section, decisions are taken in the Conference of the Section which is held at least twice a year. . . .

Congress of the Section

Article 32 — The highest political instance of the Section is the Congress of the Section.

It meets compulsorily at least once every two years. The notice of meeting and the agenda are made public at least fifteen days in advance. The reports to be discussed must reach the Base Committee ten days before the opening of the Congress.

The Congress of the Section deals with all the questions that relate to the life of the Section, fixes the objectives to be achieved within the period that follows the sessions and conducts the election of the Steering Committee of the Section.

Appendix C 231

Federal Conference

Article 34 — In-between two Congresses, the decisions are taken in the Federal Conference. . . .

Article 35 — The Federal Conference is summoned at least once every six months.

Federal Congress

Article 36 — The highest instance at the level of each Administrative Region is the Federal Congress.

The Federal Congress must meet at least once in every three years. It can be summoned in an extraordinary session by the Federal Bureau or at the request of half of the Sections within the Federation.

The notice of meeting and the agenda for the Congress are made public at least one month in advance. The reports to be discussed must reach the Sections at least fifteen days before the opening of the meeting. In case voting becomes necessary, each Section has a vote unless the Congress decides otherwise. . . .

Article 38 — The Federal Congress deals with all questions related to the life of the region in all fields (political, economic, social and cultural), fixes the objectives to be achieved during the period following the session and conducts the election of the members of the federal bureau.

The National Council of the Revolution

Article 42 — In-between two sessions of Congress, the decisions of the party are taken by the National Council of the Revolution (CNR) which is summoned at least twice a year.

The National Congress

Article 44 — The highest instance of the party is the National Congress.

Article 45 — The National Congress fixes the political line of the party, the objectives to be achieved during the period that follows its meeting and decides on all the modifications to be made to the party's statutes. *Its sovereignty is unlimited* (italics added). . . .

Article 46 — The National Congress must meet every four years. It can be summoned in an extraordinary session at the initiative of the BPN or at the request of the Central Committee or at the initiative of the Supreme Leader of the Revolution.

The notice of meeting and the agenda of the Congress are made public at least two months in advance. The reports to be discussed must reach the Federations at least one month before the opening session. Each Federation and each National Committee have a single vote in case voting becomes necessary.

The Central Committee[1]

The National Executive of the Democratic Party of Guinea is the Central Committee (CC). The CC has a membership of twenty-five including the Secretary General of the Party, the Supreme Leader of the Revolution, all elected in the Congress.

Within the Central Committee, there is an Executive of seven members including the Supreme Leader of the Revolution. This Executive is called the National Political Bureau (BPN). . . .

The Central Committee (CC) is the organ charged with responsibility for conception and orientation. It ensures the correct application of all the decisions taken at the sessions of the National Congress and the CNR. It co-ordinates the activities of the Federation and the Special National bodies. It directs and controls the life of the Nation in all aspects — political, economic, social, cultural and administrative.

It meets at least once every month. The CC functions according to the rule of collective responsibility. For this reason, every member is responsible not only for the particular sector which is entrusted to him but for the whole of the other sectors of activity of the Nation.

Besides their habitual functions the members of the CC are each charged with the organization, stimulation and co-ordination as well as the control of the diverse political, economic, social, cultural and administrative activities of one or several regions.

---

[1] This section and the next constitute a substantial modification of the provisions in the 1967 statute. Source: *Horoya*, 27 May 1972.

Appendix C   233

Every two years, there will be a rotation among the members of the CC with regard to their responsibilities in the regions.

Membership of the CC is and shall remain incompatible with the elective membership of all the other political executive bodies of the party and of the mass organizations (youth, women and workers).

However, for reasons of harmony and of efficiency, the Secretaries of State for Youth, Social Affairs as well as the Governors of Regions who are members of the CC must participate in the directing activities of the National Committee of the JRDA, the National Committee of Women and the relevant Federal Bureaux respectively.

Within the CC, four Commissions are created among which the members of the National Executive of the party are distributed.

The Commissions are as follows:

1 — an Economic Commission
2 — a Social Commission
3 — a Commission of Education and of Culture
4 — a Commission of Organization.

Each Commission is presided over by a member of the National Political Bureau.

The cadres of the party and of the state who are not members of the Central Committee, could, on the ground of their competence, their efficiency and their political and ideological commitment, belong to one or the other of the four Commissions.

The Commissions are charged with the duty of studying, with a view to advancing concrete proposals for their solution, all the questions that relate to the life of the party and the state.

The reports of the Commissions are sent directly to the Secretary General of the PDG, Supreme Leader of the Revolution, who brings them before the Central Committee for decision.

The National Political Bureau (BPN)

The National Political Bureau (BPN) is the executive of the Central Committee.

It is composed of seven members. It meets at least twice a month on the convocation of the Secretary General of the Party, the Supreme Leader of the Revolution.

The General Treasurer, the Permanent Secretary and the Deputy Permanent Secretary participate in the meetings of the BPN.

Between the sessions of the Central Committee, the National Political Bureau could take all decisions judged useful on the condition that it reports to the Central Committee.

The BPN watches over the application of the decisions of the CC.

Title VIII

Special Bodies of the Party

Bureau of the Special Committee of Youth
Article 47 – The Bureau of the Special Committee of Youth is composed of thirteen members of whom at least four are female.

Article 48 – The members of this Bureau are elected in the General Assembly for two years by all the young people of both sexes of a Base Committee registered with the PDG.

They must be at least seven years old and at most twenty-one.

Bureau of the Special Committee of Women
Article 49 – The Bureau of the Special Committee of Women is composed of thirteen members elected in a General Assembly for two years by all the female militants registered with the Base Committee.

Bureau of the JRDA Committee of Section
Article 50 – The Bureau of the JRDA Committee of Section composed of thirteen members is elected in Congress for two years.

It must include at least three female members. These members are chosen from among the leaders of the Special Committees of Youth in the Section.

Female Committee of Section
Article 51 – At the level of each of the Sections of the PDG there is a Female Committee of Section composed of thirteen

members elected for two years by the entire bureaux of the Special Committees of Women in the Section.

Regional Committee of the JRDA
Article 52 – At the level of each Federation, there is a Regional Committee of the JRDA composed of thirteen members of whom at least three are female members, elected for two years by the entire bureaux of the JRDA Committees of the Sections of the Federation.

Regional Committee of Women
Article 53 – At the level of each Federation of the PDG, there is a Regional Committee of Women composed of thirteen members elected for two years by all the bureaux of the Female Committees of the Sections of the Federation.

Regional Committee of Workers
Article 54 – At the level of each Federation of the PDG, there is a Regional Committee of Workers composed of thirteen members elected for two years by all the Committees of Production Units in the Federation.

National Commitee of the JRDA
Article 55 – At national level, a National Committee of the JRDA is elected for three years by all the Regional Committees of the JRDA assembled in a National Congress. It consists of thirteen members including at least three female members. It co-ordinates the work of the Regional Committees of the JRDA.

National Committee of Women
Article 56 – At national level, a National Committee of Women is elected for three years by all the Regional Committees of Women assembled in a National Congress. It consists of thirteen members. It co-ordinates the activities of the Regional Committees of Women.

National Committee of Workers
Article 57 – At national level, a National Committee of Workers is elected for three years by all the Regional Committees of Workers and the Bureaux of the National Unions of Workers. It consists of thirteen members. It

co-ordinates the activities of the Regional Committees and the National Unions of Workers. (Like the parent body – the PDG – the youth, women's and workers' bodies also meet in General Assemblies, Conferences and Congresses. Each organization also has a National Council modelled on the National Council of the Revolution of the parent body.)

Discipline
Article 84 – Every breach of the provisions of the statutes and every act of indiscipline on the part of a militant or a body of the party is liable to sanctions as follows:

(a) in regard to a member: warning, simple blame, public blame, suspension, removal from office, exclusion.

(b) in regard to a directing body: warning, blame, suspension, dismissal and replacement by a higher level body while awaiting the time that the competent elective body will conduct fresh elections.

(c) in regard to an entire Base Committee, a whole Section or a whole Federation: warning, blame, suspension.

Removal from office and exclusion from the party must be ratified by the corresponding instance and notified to the next higher level body.

Finances of the Party
Article 86 – The resources of the party are derived from:
(a) the membership dues whose sum is fixed by the Congress or the CNR.
(b) subscriptions.
(c) gifts and legacies.
(d) the receipts of feasts and all other manifestations [organized by the party].

Article 88 – The dues are shared among the different bodies according to a procedure determined by the National Political Bureau.

At each level, the resources are managed by a treasurer under the collective responsibility of the bureau of the directing body.

Changes in the Statutes
Article 91 – The present statutes can only be modified by the Congress of the party or the National Council of the Revolution.

Sources and Select Bibliography

Sources

The writer's study visits to Guinea enabled him to benefit from two important sources which deserve special mention. First, a number of documentary sources which are only available inside Guinea were consulted. These consist of published and unpublished government and party documents and unpublished students' *mémoires*. Among the published documentary sources, special mention should be made of the works of President Sékou Touré which now run into eighteen volumes. The abundant references to these volumes in the book show the extent to which they have been used.

Second, during the study visits, the writer was able to carry out some forms of interview and observation both in Conakry and in some cities and towns in the interior. The interviews which were sometimes structured and sometimes unstructured were used to elicit the opinions of some prominent Guineans on certain aspects of life in post-independence Guinea. The personal observations revealed some facts that were either concrete in themselves for use or were useful for interpreting other information obtained from either the documentary sources or the interviews.

In pursuing the sources enumerated above, we were aware of their limitations. For example, while the volumes of President Touré and the PDG's publications contain a considerable amount of useful factual material, especially those published in connection with the party policy of 'self-criticism', there is also some material for propaganda in them. The task of separating one from the other is clearly a delicate one. Also, the interview method is subject to what the interviewee is willing to let out and what the interviewer succeeds in eliciting from him as well as the latter's interpretation which can be either objective or subjective. We have tried to use all these sources as objectively and as impartially as possible.

General Books and Articles

Adamolekun, L., 'Politics and Administration in West Africa: The Guinean Model,' *Journal of Administration Overseas*, VIII, 3 (October 1969), 235–42.

────── 'Administrative Training in the Republic of Guinea, 1957–1970', *Journal of Administration Overseas*, XI, 4 (October 1972), 233–51.

────── 'Some Reflections on Sékou Touré's Guinea', *West Africa* (London), 19th March, 26th March, 2nd April and 9th April 1973.

Ameillon, B., *La Guinée, bilan d'une indépendance*, (Paris, François Maspéro, 1964).

Amin, S., *Le Mali, La Guinée et le Ghana: trois expériences africaines de développement* (Paris, Presses Universitaires de France, 1965).

Andrain, C., 'Guinea and Senegal: contrasting types of African socialism', in W. Friedland and C. Rosberg (eds.), *African Socialism* (Stanford, Stanford University Press, 1964).

────── 'The Political Thought of Sékou Touré', in? Skurnik (ed.), *African Political Thought: Lumumba, Nkruma, and Touré* (Denver, Denver University Publication, 1968), 101–47.

Arcin, A., *Histoire de la Guinée française* (Paris, Challamel, 1907).

Attwood, W., *The Red and the Blacks: A Personal Adventure* (London, Hutchinson, 1967).

Benot, Y., 'L'Afrique en mouvement: la Guinée à l'heure de plan', *La Pensée*, No. 94 (November–December 1960), 3–36.

Berg, E., 'Education and Manpower in Senegal, Guinea, and the Ivory Coast', in F. Harbinson and C. Myers (eds.), *Manpower and Education: Country Studies in Economic Development* (New York, McGraw-Hill, 1965), 232–67.

────── 'The Economic Basis of Political Choice in French West Africa', *American Political Science Review*, LIV, 2 (June 1960), 391–405.

────── 'Socialism and Economic Development in Tropical Africa', *Quarterly Journal of Economics*, LXXVIII (1964), 549–73.

Charles, B., 'Un Parti politique africain: le Parti démocratique

de Guinée', *Revue française de sciences politiques*, XII, 2 (June 1962), 312–59.
Chaleur, P., 'La Guinée après trois ans d'indépendance', *Etudes* (November 1961), 202–15.
De Decker, H., *Nation et développement en Guinée et au Sénégal* (The Hague, Mouton, 1967).
Demougeot, A., *Notes sur l'organisation politique et administrative du Labé avant et depuis l'occupation française* (Paris, Larousse, 1944).
Diawara A., *Guinée, la marche du peuple* (Dakar, Edition Cerda, 1968).
Du Bois, V. D., 'The Decline of the Guinean Revolution' in *American Universities Field Staff Reports Service, West Africa Series*, VIII, 7, 8, and 9 (n.d.).
Dumont, R., *Afrique noire: développement agricole: réconversion de l'économie agricole: Guinée, Côte d'Ivoire, Mali* (Paris, Presses Universitaires de France, 1962).
Fisher, G., 'Quelques aspects de la doctrine politique guinéenne', *Civilisations*, 9, 4 (1959), 457–76.
Gignon, F., *Guinée: Etat-pilote* (Paris, Plon, 1959).
Guinée, prélude à l'indépendance (Paris, Présence africaine, 1959).
Houis, M., *La Guinée française* (Paris, Editions géographiques, maritimes et coloniales, 1953).
'Independent Guinea', *Présence africaine*, Special No. (1960).
Johnson H., (ed.), *Economic Nationalism in Old and New States* (Chicago, The University of Chicago Press, 1967).
Johnson, R. W., 'Sékou Touré and the Guinean Revolution', *African Affairs*, 69 (October 1970), 350–65.
Lacouture, J., *Cinq Hommes et la France* (Paris, Editions de Seuil, 1961).
Leunda, X., 'La Réforme de l'enseignement et son incidence sur l'évolution rurale en Guinée', *Civilisations*, XXII, 2 (1972), 232–59.
Miandre, J., 'L'Expérience guinéenne', *Esprit*, 10 (October 1963), 514–31.
'Quelques aspects du problème des cadres en Republique de Guinée', *Recherches africaines*, 4 (October–December 1960), 40–7.
Rivière, C., 'Théorie de la dynamique conflictuelle dans les nouveaux etats. Réflexions à propos du cas guinéen',

cultures et développement, II, 3–4 (1969–1970), 657–78.

——— 'Les Coopératives agricoles en Guinée', *Revue française d'études politiques africaines*, 59 (November 1970), 55–64.

——— 'Les Mécanismes de constitution d'une bourgeoisie commerçante en République de Guinée', *Cahiers d'études africaines*, XI, 43 (1971), 378–99.

——— 'Les Conséquences de la réorganisation des circuits commerciaux en Guinée', *Revue française d'études politiques africaines*, 66 (June 1971), 74–96.

——— *Mutations sociales en Guinée* (Paris, Editions Marcel Rivière, 1971).

Suret-Canale, J., *La République de Guinée* (Paris, Editions sociales, 1970).

——— 'Notes sur l'économie guinéenne', *Recherches africaines*, 1, 2, 3, 4, (January–December 1964), 43–68.

Sy, S., *Recherches sur l'exercice du pouvoir politique en Afrique Côte d'Ivoire, Guinée, Mali* (Paris, Editions A. Pedonne, 1964).

Touré, A. S., *Expérience guinéenne et unité africaine* (re-edition of *L'Action politique du Parti démocratique de Guinée pour l'émancipation africaine*), Vols I & II (Paris, Présence africaine, 1962).

——— *L'Action politique du Parti démocratique de Guinée pour l'émancipation africaine*, Vol. III (Conakry, Imprimerie nationale, 1959).

——— *La Lutte du Parti démocratique de Guinée pour l'émancipation africaine*, Vol. IV (Conakry, 1959).

——— *L'Action politique du Parti démocratique de Guinée: La Planification économique*, Vol. V (Conakry, 1960).

——— *La Lutte du Parti démocratique de Guinée pour l'émancipation africaine*, Vol. VI (Conakry, 1961).

——— *La Politique internationale du Parti démocratique de Guinée*, Vol. VII (Conakry, 1962).

——— *L'Action politique du Parti démocratique de Guinée pour l'émancipation de la jeunesse guinéenne*, Vol. VIII (Conakry, 1962).

——— *Au Nom de la révolution: Conférences hebdomadaires*, Vol. IX (Conakry, 1962).

——— *La Révolution guinéenne et le progrès social*, Vol. X, (Conakry, 4th edition, 1967).

―――― *Apprendre, savoir . . . pouvoir*, Vol. XI (Conakry, 1965).
―――― *Concevoir, analyser, réaliser*, Vol. XII (Conakry, 1966).
―――― *L'Afrique et la Révolution*, Vol. XIII (Switzerland, 1966).
―――― *Plan Septennal, 1964–71*, Vol. XIV (Conakry, 1967).
―――― *Défendre la Révolution*, Vol. XV (Conakry, 2nd ed., 1969).
―――― *Le Pouvoir populaire*, Vol. XVI (Conakry, 1968).
―――― *La Révolution culturelle*, Vol. XVII (Conakry, 1969).
―――― *La Technique de la Révolution*, Vol. XVIII (Conakry, 1972).
Wallerstein, I., 'The Political Ideology of the PDG', *Présence africaine*, XL, 1 (1962), 30–41.
Weinstein, B., 'Guinea's School of Public Administration', *Journal of Local Administration Overseas*, IV, 4 (October 1965), 239–43.
Zolberg, A., *Creating Political Order, The Party-States of West Africa* (Chicago, 1966).

Official Documents

Government of French Guinea
Journal officiel de la Guinée française, weekly 1899–1958 (selected numbers).
Ministère de l'Intérieur, Territoire de la Guinée, *Nouvelle Structure Administrative* (Conakry, Imprimerie du gouvernment, 1958).

Government of the Republic of Guinea
Agence guinéenne de presse, *Guinée actualités* (1967– irregular).
Assemblée nationale, *Exposé fait le 25 octobre 1963 par le Ministre de la Fonction Publique et du Travail* (Conakry, mimeo).
Journal officiel de la République de Guinée (Conakry, fortnightly, 1958–   ).
Ministère du Domain Economique (formerly Ministère du Développement Économique), *Revue du développement économique* (Conakry, 1964–   irregular).
Ministère d'Etat chargé des Finances et du Plan, *Instructions aux payeurs, aux chefs des services financiers, aux inspecteurs et contrôleurs des contributions diverses*

Conakry, Imprimerie national Patrice Lumumba, n.d.).

Ministère de la Fonction Publique et du Travail, *Etat des fonctionaires guinéens en service avant l'indépendance* (Conakry, August 1964, mimeo).

────── *Statut particulier des divers cadres uniques* (Conakry, Imprimerie nationale Patrice Lumumba, n.d.).

Secrétariat d'Etat à l'Idéologie, au Télé-Enseignement et à l'Alphabétisation, *Les Budgets. Séminaires de formation professionnelle* (Conakry, Centre de diffusion Télé-Enseignement, 1 er trimestre, 1970, mimeo, Cours Nos. 1 and 2).

────── *Gestion de l'entreprise. Responsabilité du comptable* (Conakry, Centre de diffusion Télé-Enseignement, 2eme trimestre, 1970, mimeo, Cours Nos. 11 et 12).

────── *Le Phénomène de l'échange* (Conakry, Centre de diffusion Télé-Enseignement, 2 eme trimestre, 1970, mimeo).

────── *Problèmes monétaires et cours des comptes* (Conakry, Centre de diffusion Télé-Enseignement, 1er trimestre, 1970, mimeo).

République de Guinée. *Huitième congrès du Parti démocratique de Guinée (RDA), tenu à Conakry du 25 septembre au 20 octobre 1967* (Conakry, Imprimerie nationale Patrice Lumumba, n.d.).

────── *Statistique du travail au 15−12−67* (Conakry, mimeo).

────── *Textes des interviews accordées par le Président Sékou Touré*, Avril 1959 (Conakry, mimeo).

The Democratic Party of Guinea

Parti démocratique de Guinée-RDA, *Bulletin d'information du BPN* (formerly *Bulletin du compte-rendu des activités du BPN)* (Conakry, irregular, 1962−   ).

────── *Horoya*, official organ of the party (Conakry, daily, April 1961−January 1969, occasional appearance since 1969).

────── *Horoya-hebdo*, official organ of the party (Conakry, weekly, 1969−   ).

────── *La RDA−PDG*, occasional publication of the party (1966−   ).

────── *Rapport annexes diffusés au cours de la 4ème*

conférence national réunie à Labé, du 25 au 29 décembre 1961 (Conakry, n.d., mimeo).
——— *La Guinée Nouvelle*, official organ of the party (Conakry, iregular, 1958 issues only).
——— *Statut du PDG*, Edition 1969– Permanence nationale (Conakry, Imprimerie nationale Patrice Lumumba, 1969).
——— *20ème anniversaire du Parti démocratique de Guinée 14 mai 1967, points de repère* (Conakry, 1967, mimeo).

Unpublished Materials

Adamolekun, O. O., 'Central Government Administration in Guinea and Senegal Since Independence: A Comparative Study', D.Phil (Politics) Thesis (University of Oxford, 1972).

Baldé, O. D., 'La Portée de la loi-cadre du 8 novembre 1964 dans le développement économique de la Guinée', Mémoire de fin d'études supérieures (IPC (ESA), 1966–67).

Bah, T. O., 'Étude du système du budgets locaux et d'arrondissements appliqué aux régions administratives de Conakry et Forécariah', Mémoire de fin d'études supérieures (IPC (ESA), 1969–70).

Barry, M. A. S., 'Contribution à l'étude des techniques et des méthodes de planification de l'économie guinéenne', Mémoire de fin d'études supérieures (IPC, Faculté des sciences sociales, 1969–70).

Bokoum, B., 'Importance des entreprises d'État dans l'économie guinéenne', Mémoire de fin d'études supérieures (IPC (ESA), 1969–70).

Camara, L. P., 'Les Structures de l'administration de la Guinée sous la colonisation française (1890–1958), Etude analytique et critique', Mémoire de fin d'études supérieures (IPC (ESA), 1967–68).

Charles, B., 'Cadres guinéens et appartenance ethnique', Thesis for the *doctorat de recherche 'Etudes politiques'* (Paris, Fondation nationale des sciences politiques, Cycle supérieur d'études politiques, 1968).

Dequecker, M., *La Guinée de la loi-cadre à l'indépendence* (Paris Centre militaire d'information et de spécialisation pour l'Outre-mer, 1960, mimeo).

Diallo, A. L., 'L'Évolution des institutions administrative de la République de Guinée de 1958 à 1968', Mémoire de fin d'études supérieures (IPC (ESA), 1967–68).

Dioubaté, M. L., 'Les Institutions politiques de la République de Guinée', Mémoire de fin d'études supérieures (IPC (ESA), 1966–67).

Douno, M., 'Le Rapport du parti avec l'Etat guinéen', Mémoire de fin d'études supérieures (IPC (ESA), 1969–70).

Du Bois, V., 'The Independence Movement in Guinea: A Study in African Nationalism' (A Dissertation at the Princeton University, March 1962).

Kéita, S. K., *L'État de domination française en Guinée de 1945 à 1958*, Cours de l'Institut polytechnique Gamal Abdel Nasser (Conakry, October 1970, mimeo).

Kourouma, K. R., 'L'Évolution des institutions judiciares en Guinée', Mémoire de fin d'études supérieures (IPC (ESA), 1967–68).

Olémou, M. P., 'Organisation et évolution des institutions du travail, République de Guinée', Mémoire de fin d'études superieures (IPC (ESA), 1967–68).

Index

Abbatoir, 78
Abidjan, 168
Accra, 59
Administrative divisions, 16-17, 21-3, 87
Administrative structure, 37, 69, 155
Adult literacy campaign, 68, 90
Agence Guinéen de spectacles, 109
Aggression, 157, 163, 168, 169
Agricultural development, 44, 65, 91
   production, 62, 66, 67
   services, 42
   techniques, 68
Air Guinea, 94
Algeria, 76
Allende, 166
Alumina, 92, 204
Alusuisse, 132
Ameillon, B., 2, 5
America, *see* United States
American Peace Corps, 120
Arrondissements, 21, 31-2

Ballet National Guinéen, 108
Barnes, L., 112
Base committee, 8, 16, 20, 21, 24, 30
Bauxite, 44, 60, 76, 79, 92, 158, 161
Béavogui Lansana, 148, 172
Benot, 50
Benty, 45, 47
Berg, E. 42, 200

Bettelheim, Professor, 49
Black marketing system, 66, 72-3, 85-6, 89
Bofossou, 138
Boiro, 141
Boké, 60, 76, 92-3, 96, 132, 158
Bourgeois, 66, 151-2, 163-9, 174, 189, 191
Bourgeois minority, 161, 183
Bourgeoisie, 66, 85-6, 89, 207
British, 78, 112

Camara M'Baila, 208
Cabral Amilcar, 168-9
Canada, 54
Cement, 132
Central committee, 16-17, 34, 137, 142, 148, 174, 195-6
Centres of Female Progress, 143
Centres of Rural Modernisation (CMR), 63
Chaffard, G., 121, 199
Chamber of Commerce, 46
Charisma, 11-12, 15, 134, 149, 151, 185-6, 188, 190
Charles, B., 2, 130-1
Chavanel, 80
Chile, 166
China, 54, 92, 95, 108-9, 110, 120, 140, 157; *see also* Eastern bloc countries
Cinema, 61, 205
Civic brigade, 66-7, 140
Class struggle, 60, 146, 151, 163-5, 182, 185, 189, 191
Cold war, 57

Collectivist organization, 71
College of Rural Education (CER), 68, 196
Committees of production, 35
Communism, 57, 119
Compagnie de bauxites de Guinée, 60, 76
Compagnie française de l'Afrique occidentale (CFAO), 79
Comptoir guinéen du commerce extérieur (CGCE), 80-183
Comptoir guinéen du commerce intérieur (CGCI), 80-183
Conakry, 8, 20, 24, 42, 44, 46, 49-50, 56, 58, 91, 95, 101-2, 106, 113, 120, 124, 133, 166
Congress, 17, 19, 23, 34, 59, 127, 194
Consumer goods (movement of), 65, 66, 81
Conté, Dr Saidou, 166
Cooperatives, 9, 13, 62-3, 64, 68, 72, 87, 89-90, 143
coups d'état, 67
Coyah–Forécariah, 45
Cuba, 166, 167
Cultural activities, 106-8, 113, 139
Currency, 49

Dabola, 76
Dakar, 117, 166, 168
Dalaba, 49-50
de Gaulle, General Charles, 116-17, 153, 193
Democratic African Revolution, 134
democratic centralism, 8, 17, 27-8, 39
Democratic Party of Guinea (PDG) (main references only), 2, 4, 7, 115, 147, 152, 158, 167, 170, 182-3, 188-90
Diakhité Moussa, 172
Diallo Alfa Yaya, 124, 135, 148

Diawara, A., 2, 134
Dien Bien Phu, *see* Vietnam
dioulas, 85
doctrine of supremacy of politics, 48, 51

East Africa, *see* Kenya, Tanzania, Uganda, etc.
Eastern bloc countries, 55-9, 73, 79-81, 107, 109, 118-20
Eastern European countries, 54, 198; *see also* Eastern bloc countries
Economy, 9, 48, 58, 66, 77, 80, 162, 163
Economic development, 6, 9, 41, 48, 50, 62, 71, 108, 114, 120, 158-60, 178, 184-5, 190-1
Educational expansion, 54, 97, 98, 101, 155, 157
Educational facilities, 45, 55, 61, 104-5, 113, 149
Educational institutions, 67, 100-2, 132, 204
Egypt, 118
Élite-mass gap, 8, 16, 24-6, 38, 145, 156-7, 164, 177, 184, 189
Émigré, 166-8
English, *see* languages
Enterpreneurs, 61, 76
Ethiopia, 118
Ethnic arithmetic, 130-1, 148, 156, 174
Ethnic associations, 182
Ethnic conflicts, 133, 138, 156, 179, 185
Ethnic diversity, 14
Ethnic integration, 125-30, 132, 147, 177-9, 207
Ethnic particularism, 130, 148, 156, 191
Exploiters, 60

Federal bureau, 17, 32-3
Federation, 17

Fidelity, medal of, 148
FIDES, see investment fund
Financial institutions, 96
Five-Year Plan, 51, 161
Foccard, M. Jacques, 167, 211
Foreign policy, 54, 59, 157
Forest people, see ethnic integration
Foulah, 122, 132, 138
Founding Fathers, 188
Fouta Djallon, 95
France, French, 18-19, 41, 45-7, 49, 80, 94-5, 126, 153, 166-7, 169, 184
Franco-African Community, 1, 116-17, 193
French ambassador, 206
French West Africa (FWA), 117, 150, 195, 198
Fria (consortium), 44-7, 60, 74-5, 77, 79, 92, 132, 158, 161
Fula, 105; see also languages

Gabon, 124
Gambia, 109, 166
General Stores, 64-5, 81-2
Ghana, 59, 118
Guinea-Bissau, 118
Guinean experiment, 15, 152, 153-4, 176, 182, 186-7, 190
Guinean franc, 49, 199
Guinean popular army, 67
Guinexport, 64-5, 82
Governmental structure, 16-17, 21-2, 23, 28

Health facilities, etc., see medical
Historic anniversaries, 159
Horoya, 57, 121, 164, 196
Horoya-Hebdo, 196, 197, etc.
Hospitals, 45; see also medical
Human investment, 70

Ideology, 2, 4, 7, 9, 12-13, 26, 37-40, 72, 103, 108, 110, 122, 134, 148-9, 158, 160, 162, 163, 171, 174, 185, 188, 190
Illuyshin, 93
Independence Party of Guinea and Cape Verde (PAIGC), 123, 168
Industrial enterprises, 73, 75-6, 77-8
Institute of Traditional Medicine, 98
Integration (territorial, political, ethnic), 177-8
Invasion, 1, 123, 168-9, 173
Investment code, 63
Investment fund (FIDES), 41-2, 44-7
Iron ore, 76
Irrigation schemes, 90
Islam, 133, 139
Italy, 95
Ivory Coast, 163, 166, 169, 184

Japan, 76
Jeunesse de la révolution démocratique Africaine (JRDA), 10, 23, 100, 127, 139-42
Judicial administration, 29, 31, 36
Judiciary, the, 13

Kamsar, 92-3
Kankan, 45, 91, 95, 101-2
Kéita Mamadi, 172
Kéita Modibo, 141
Kéita N'Famara, 173
Kennedy, John F., 188
Kenya, 184, 187
Kindia, 45, 76, 158
Kisie, see languages
Konkouré, 95, 204
Kpélé, see languages

Labé, 93, 95
Lambrakis Medal for Peace, 211
Languages, 105-6, 128, 132, 147, 210

Index

Lenin, 54, 190, 211 (Lenin Peace Prize)
Liberia, 109, 118, 166
Libya, 118
Lipset, Professor S., 134, 187, 208
Local revolutionary authorities (PRL), 16, 19-21, 135-6
Loi-cadre, 19-21, 117, 126, 195
Loma, see languages
Lusignan, Guy de, 2

Mali (Republic of), 132, 203
Malinké, 85, 122, 130, 133, 138; *see also* dioulas
Mamou, 93, 106
Mandika, see languages
Marabouts, *see* religious differences
Marketing system, 66
Martin, M., 46
Marxist–Leninist, 5, 196
Mass-line (doctrine of), 7-8, 24, 39, 59, 61, 71, 110, 121, 123-4, 130
Mauritania, 124
Mazrui, Professor Ali, 186-7
Medical facilities, 55, 61, 97, 113, 132, 149
MIFERGUI, 76, 92, 158
Military plot, *see* plot of the military, 145, 151
Military power, 46
Mineral deposits, 44, 60, 76
Mining industry, 59, 76, 121
Minister of State for Justice and Administration and Financial Control, 78
Ministry of Justice, 35
Ministry of Planning and Statistics 52
Ministry of Youth, Arts and Sports, 109
Mobilization (political), 15, 45, 62, 159-60, 175, 178, 184-5, 188
Monde, le, 123, 198

Morocco, 118
Musical instruments, 110
Mutual Society for Rural Development (SMDR), 62

Nafaya, 82
Nation building, 6-7, 9, 11-12, 14-15, 34, 40, 72, 111-12, 155, 158, 176-7, 179-81, 183, 187, 191
National Academy of Languages, 105
Nationalism, 116, 121, 188
Nationalization, 61, 95
National Assembly, 28, 33-5, 109, 173, 189, 191
National Centres of Agricultural Production (CNPA), 63-4, 87
National Conference, 48-9
National Council of the Revolution (CNR), 17, 35, 50, 109
National enterprise, 65; *see* Guinexport
National Political Bureau, 7, 17, 34, 50, 52, 121, 139, 144, 171, 194, 196
Neutrality, 56, 119, 120, 121, 123, 157, 188
Nigeria, 76, 94
Nimba-Simandou, 76, 92, 132
Non-alignment, 56, 119
North Africa, 121
Nkrumah, President, 140, 186, 201
Nyerere, President, 186-7
N'zérékoré, 92

Office de Commercilisation agricole (OCA), 64, 82
Office national des chemins de fer, 91-2
Ouassoulou Empire, 124
Oneyann, see languages
Operation self sufficiency, 88

Opposition, 163
Oumar, Dr Barry, 173

Palace of the people, 109
Pan-Africanism, 220, 224
Pan-American Airways, 59, 120
Paris, 49, 167
Party Committee of Production (CUP), 11, 24, 134
Party congress, 17, 23, 34, 109
Party nation, 134-8, 171
Party structure, 16-17, 21-3, 28, 30-1, 38
Party supremacy (doctrine of), 2, 10, 12-13, 16, 18-19, 39, 48, 53, 71
Paterson-Zochonis, 12, 80
PDG, *see* Democratic party of Guinea
People's class, 164
People's Republic of China, 85, 200; *see also* Eastern bloc countries
Permanent plot, 121
Peyrissac, 80
Plot of the military, 123, 141
Political consciousness, 175
Political mobilization, *see* mobilization
Polygamy, 143
Populaire de Guinée, le, 167
Popular Stores, 64-5
Popular tribunal, 29-33, 35-6
Portuguese, 1, 123, 151, 161, 202
Positive neutrality, 119
Pré, Mr Roland, 42
Preparatory Economic Conference, 49
Price control, 66, 84
Private enterprise, 44, 54, 58-60, 66, 71, 77, 81-2
PRL, see Local Revolutionary Authorities
'Progressive' society, 5
Public enterprise, 35, 94
Public utilities, 94
Pye, Lucian, 176

Qualities of leadership, 150
Quinzaine artistique, 108

Railway, *see* transport
Recreational facilities, *see* sport
Regional assembly, 32
Religious associations, 182, 185
Religious differences, 133, 136, 138-9, 147, 156, 179
Revolutionary camps, 140
Rivière, C., 2, 5-6, 129-30
Rural development, 196; *see also* College of Rural Education
Russia, *see* Soviet Union

Sabouya, 82
Sangaredi, 92
Scientific socialism, 2
Second World War, 41
Secretary-General for African and Malagasy Affairs, 167
Senegal, 117, 163, 166, 169
Seven-Year Plan, 50, 71, 75, 87, 91, 93, 96-8, 199
Sierra Leone, 166
Sily-phone, 109-10
Smelser, Professor, 12, 40, 161, 194
Smuggling, 84-5
Socialism, 5
Socialist communities, 9, 13, 203; *see also* cooperatives
Société africaine d'expansion, 80
Société commerciale de l'ouest africain (SCOA), 79-80
Société industrielle et automobile de Guinée (SIAG), 80
Sociétés indigènes de prévoyance (SIP), 62
Solod, Daniel (Soviet ambassador), 37, 120
Soso, *see* languages
Soumah, David, 166
Soussou, *see* languages
Soviet Union, 56-57, 59, 73, 76, 78, 93, 95, 101, 110, 120, 161, 167, 172, 200

Index

Spain, 76
Sporting facilities, 106-7, 113, 132, 139-40, 149, 205
Stalin, 172, 189
State farms, 63, 68
State marketing system, 66
State trade, 58, 81, 83, 89
Steering committees, 7, 16, 21, 31-3
Sudan, 118
Suret–Canale, Jean, 2, 75, 89, 198-9
Switzerland, 76
'Syli', 150
Syliart, 109
Syli–cinema, 110
Syro–Lebanese, 80, 82

Tanzania, 184, 186-7, 189
Teachers' Plot, 122, 151, 189, 200
Teachers' Union, 122, 200
Telecommunications, 94
Territorial Assembly, 19, 126
Thierno Diallo, 166
Three-Year Plan, 48-9, 67, 70, 73-5, 81, 87-8, 91, 96, 97, 107, 109, 132
Tomas, 138
Tougué, 76, 132
Touré, Ismael, 172, 194
Touré, Samory, 124
Touré, Sékou (main references only), 2, 5, 6, 11, 27-9, 126, 147-51, 156, 169-70, 172, 196, 202, 211, 237
Tractor bourgeoisie, 89
Tracheomycosis, 42
Traders' Plot, 58, 123, 140, 151, 189, 201

Traditional chieftaincy, 126
Trans-Guinea railway, 92
Transport, 44-6, 55, 58, 91
Tunisia, 118

Uganda, 187
Unesco, 105
United Nations Organisation, 56, 118, 122
United States, 54, 58, 73, 120, 188, 190

Vietnam, 121

Wallerstein, 2
Wammey, see languages
Western bloc countries, 55, 57, 59, 73, 81, 102, 119-20
Western European countries, 54, 95
Women's organizations, 10, 18, 23-4, 32, 142, 174, 182
Workers' organizations, 10, 23-4, 32, 174, 182

Yeye (music) ban, 142
Youlah Naby, 166
Youth camps, 140
Youth of the African Democratic Revolution (JRDA), 10, 23, 106, 108, 120, 127, 139-42
Youth organizations, 10, 18, 23-4, 32, 174, 182
Yugoslavia, 76, 82, 95

Zaire, 76, 109